1990

Velma Cummins

THE PIONEER LADY'S

COUNTRY KITCHEN

The Pioneer Lady's Country Kitchen

A SEASONAL TREASURY OF TIME-HONORED AMERICAN RECIPES

by

Jane Watson Hopping

VILLARD BOOKS
New York 1988

*Grateful acknowledgment is made to the following for
permission to reprint previously published material:*

CONTEMPORY BOOKS: "A Christmas Carol" and "Old Years and
New" from *Collected Verse* by Edgar A. Guest. Copyright
1934 by Contemporary Books. Reprinted by permission of
Contemporary Books.

THE NATIONAL GRANGE: Excerpts from the lyrics to "Harvest
Song" by Jas. L. Orr and E. R. Latta and "The Quilting
Party" from *The Patron*. Used by permission granted by The
National Grange, Washington, D.C.

CHARLES E. TUTTLE COMPANY: Excerpts from the following
poems by Daniel L. Cady: "Setting the Table in Vermont,"
"May in Vermont," and "An Old Vermont Cellar Home" from
Rhymes of Rural Life. Reprinted with the permission of the
Charles E. Tuttle Company, Tokyo, Japan.

Library of Congress Cataloging-in-Publication Data

Hopping, Jane Watson.
  The pioneer lady's country kitchen/by Jane Watson Hopping.
    p. cm.
  Includes index.
  ISBN 0-394-57197-5
  1. Cookery, American.   I. Title.
TX715.H7865   1988
641.5973—dc19   88-11692

Manufactured in the United States of America
9 8 7 6 5 4 3

Book design Staub/Del Valle

For Mama, Daddy, and Grandpa

And lo! through mists that may not be dispelled,
I see an old farm homestead, as in dreams,
Where, like a gem in costly setting held,
The old log cabin gleams.

ACKNOWLEDGMENTS

This cookbook has been enriched by the talent, enthusiasm, and hard work of many good people and graced with recipes and stories from others. It is, therefore, my pleasure to recognize all who have had a hand in bringing it into being, and to offer my warmest thanks.

Especially, I would like to acknowledge the lovely decorative art that my sister, Sheila Christman, has contributed to this work. Vera Kamping, thank you for old-time recipes that have spiced these pages. My sincere appreciation to Ben and Sheila Tarahteeff for the use of one very special personal story.

I would also like to express here my gratitude and affection for writing friends who have shared, encouraged, and at times suffered with me as I've learned my craft: Arlene Fitzgerald, Lee Arlandson, Peggy Ede, Reg Bretnor, Gene Olson, and not least Con Sellers whose introduction to Meg Ruley of the Jane Rotrosen Agency has changed my life. Meg: Many thanks for guidance, astute editorial comment, time and effort on my behalf.

All of us who have worked on this book are impressed by the vitality and professionalism of Alison Acker, the talented editor who has carried the book on a wave of enthusiasm from the start and brought it to fruition with the help of the skilled staff at Villard: Wendy Bass, Sally Ann Berk, Janis Donnaud, and Naomi Osnos. I offer my sincere appreciation for all the hard work you contributed to this book.

And now a bit of praise for Paulette Rittenberg, a free-lance copy editor who deserves considerable recognition for the enthusiasm and skill that she brought to the book. Well done, Paulette!

Finally, as you will notice, this cookbook has been made lovely by poets and illustrators of the past. I would like to express appreciation for their work and recognize their valuable contribution.

I am also very pleased to take this opportunity to praise the work of James Whitcomb Riley. Called the "Hoosier Poet," Riley's poems were songs of beauty, touching chiefly on the sadness and humor of everyday life. Much of what he wrote was in pure English, but his most loved works were those written in the dialect of his native Indiana. When illustrated with the fine hand of Will Vawter or Howard Chandler Christy, Riley's poems evoke a simpler rural life-style that warmed hearts as readily then as they do today.

ACKNOWLEDGMENTS

CONTENTS

INTRODUCTION:
*About a Country
Cooking Heritage xvii*

APRIL *Wild Salad Greens and the Scent of Lilacs* 37

MAY *Fresh Herbs and Candied Violets* 65

JUNE *Strawberries, Whipped Cream, and the Taste of Golden Butter* 87

NOVEMBER *God's Gift, a Time of Plenty* 203

INTRODUCTION

About a Country Cooking Heritage

During the Depression my family lived on the old Hubbard farm, which had its heyday before the turn of the century. We had a plum, peach, and pear orchards, a large garden, several great fig and mulberry trees, a barn in which harness for work horses hung, and pigpens. Behind the fruit shed was an ancient apple tree that bore yellow- and red-striped fruits so huge we called them "horse apples." From that one tree, Mother was supplied with enough apples to can all of our applesauce, and there were still bushel basketsful for the livestock.

As a child, I loved the fields, creeks, and ponds; animals both domesticated and wild; hedgerows of thorny blackberry vines, white with blossom in late spring and hanging thick with huge berries in midsummer; and most of all the great old white farmhouse with its cheery kitchen.

That farm kitchen was the center of all family activity. Cooking was done there while neighbors sat at the table sipping boiling hot coffee and eating handfuls of cookies or big hunks of cake. Games such as pitch and cribbage were played on the table. And on rainy or cold nights, tools were sharpened or harness mended near the warmth of the big, black wood-burning cookstove.

Winter and summer, pots and kettles bubbled on the top of our old stove, while the water tank, heated by the same stove, gurgled, growled, and occasionally belched steam. From our oven came loaves of golden-crusted bread, huge beef roasts, plump well-browned chickens, apple and mulberry pies, all of which perfumed the house with their fragrance.

Mother, like other women of the day, cooked not only breakfast, dinner, and supper, but cooked for her pantry as well. There were no "fast foods." In summer we ate fresh fruits and vegetables, cold roasted meats, and flavored homemade breads for quick meals. In winter we added thick meat stews and hot kettles of soup, topped off with some bit of home-canned or preserved fruits or vegetables.

Life was simpler then. We were poorer in things, but richer in family. Those were the days of "aunts and uncles and cousins by the dozens," all dearly loved and often seen. At the drop of a hat, we would have a get-together, which always meant fun and food.

Cousins cuddling all in one bed, we children often went to sleep to the sound of adults laughing as they sat around the kitchen table playing cards. In the early hours of the morning there was sometimes the fragrance of impromptu cookie baking and the scent of freshly perked coffee. If a child woke up and wandered into the kitchen, she was kissed, handed a cookie, and told to go back to bed.

Ours was a life spiced with melon feasts, Easter picnics, family dances, and potlucks. Birthdays, Valentine's Day, St. Patrick's Day —all holidays were celebrated. Every occasion was a chance for the women and girls to demonstrate new or old cooking skills, and show off they did, whipping up thick lemon pies piled high with cloud-light meringues, lightly browned and sparkling with little drops of sweetness; meat pies filled with chunks of pork and flavored with home-grown onions; and many other dishes reflecting the bounty of the land and the ability of the cook.

Out of this very traditional farm family life, my sister, cousins, and I learned the lessons of solidarity, home, and roots. We grew up expecting to work, have values, and show creativity. I don't believe, though, that any of us ever realized until we were grown that the excellent meals we ate and the wonderful parties we enjoyed were not only the heart of our own family life, but of a national down-home cooking heritage as well.

This book, which has grown out of those enduring childhood memories, is about rural people, their wit and wisdom; the countryside in all its beauty, and its desolation in the face of natural calamities; the animals, wild and domesticated; the seasons—the times of plenty and the times of want—and the crops.

The chapters begin with blustery March, the age-old first month of the farm year, and end the next February. As the seasons flow, the reader is initiated into the movement of farm life and the events that color it—an old-time kitchen dance . . . a Mother's Day trip to the marshes to see wild goslings waddle about before they are big enough to fly away . . . a country wedding . . . a trip to the county fair . . . a frolicking cakewalk . . . a pie social . . . Easter sunrise service high on a hill . . . Thanksgiving and Christmas on the farm.

But most of all, this book is about the very traditional, good old-fashioned country cooking I learned to love. The recipes that belonged to old-time women like Mother, Grandma White, Grandma Hopping, Emma, and Vera were passed on to little girls when they learned to cook at their mothers' elbows. Boxty, Country Lass with a Veil, Bachelor's Buttons, Calico Slaw, Stuffed Veal Leg Roast with Sour Cream Sauce, Fried Squash Blossoms, Mock Candied Ginger, Nun's Sighs—all these were the flavors of the rural America in which I was raised.

Some of the recipes in my *Country Kitchen* cookbook are generations old, handed down to me by family and friends from their personal recipe collections. None of the ones I've included here are very difficult or are extremely time consuming. After all, old-time cooks were usually experts in their kitchens, but they had plenty of other work to do, too! So, whether or not you learned to cook at an early age as I did, you'll be able to prepare and enjoy these wholesome, delicious foods. If you need a little extra help with the basics—if making pastry or bread from scratch is new to you—make sure you read my "And a Little Bit More" at the end of the book for some easy, country-style hints. You'll also find there the basics of candy making and storing your homemade baked goods.

While the ebb and flow of this book has followed the seasons, one can use these recipes at any time of the year. For me it has always been pleasurable, though, to cook my way from spring through winter, using ingredients as they come into season. In the old days they would cut down on red meat and pork in summer (thinking it made them too warm to work in hot weather) and instead use chicken and fish in modest amounts. From early spring through late fall they would harvest abundance from the gardens, fields, and orchards. True, in markets today, produce especially is found both in and out of season—but one can pretend a little. So, use the recipes that are in season, or just pick the ones that look best to you.

Quite without intent or purpose, I have become in my own time one who shares skills and lore with the young, by teaching girls to cook and can, teaching youngsters in schools about our heritage, sharing with them my own family stories and treasures. What fun it has been to teach them an old "churning chant": *Come butter come! Come butter come! Peter's at the garden gate waiting for a butter cake. Come butter come!* And it has been delightful to watch their faces as the cream suddenly turns into a solid golden ball of butter, which we immediately spread on my old-fashioned whole-wheat bread to a chorus of *Umms!* and *Yums!*

As the years have passed, I've been aptly named the "Pioneer Lady" by the little ones who can't remember my name. Perhaps they perceive in me something that lies close to the earth, an intense feeling of oneness with it. Indeed, I'm bound to it and to those rural people who were so much a part of our past. My life has been enriched by Mama, Grandma, and others who flitted about their kitchens, throwing a pinch of herbs into a pot, tasting for flavor, or pulling pans of freshly baked bread out of the oven. For me, the memories of old-time kitchens and cooks I've known have yielded up not only physical sustenance, but emotional and spiritual filling as well. And when I talk with young and old alike, and listen with the heart, I know I'm not alone.

Could it be that my tugging at the heart strings plays upon a universal need to touch base with our past, to feel our continuity with those who have gone before, to be reminded of our roots, of home, family, and the simplicity of a not-too-distant time?

If so, I do hope that the fruit of this book will bring warmth and pleasure into your life, good food, and a sense of strength and comfort.

OUT TO OLD AUNT MARY'S

Wasn't it pleasant, O brother mine,
  In those old days of the lost sunshine
Of youth—when the Saturday's chores were through
And the "Sunday's wood" in the kitchen, too,
And we went visiting, "me and you,"
    Out to Old Aunt Mary's?

James Whitcomb Riley

THE PIONEER LADY'S

COUNTRY KITCHEN

WHEN THE GREEN GITS BACK IN THE TREES

In spring, when the green gits back in the trees,
   And the sun comes out and *stays*,
And yer boots pulls on with a good tight squeeze,
   And you think of yer bare-foot days;
When you *ort* to work and you want to *not*,
   And you and yer wife agrees
It's time to spade up the garden-lot,
    When the green gits back in the trees
     Well! work is the least o' *my* idees
     When the green, you know, gits back in the trees!

                  —*James Whitcomb Riley*

MARCH

Daffodils and Fresh Asparagus

About our farm, March, age-old first month of the seasonal year, comes roaring in like a lion, bringing with it an excitement in the whistling wind. Shortly, asparagus will grace our tables. Down by the creek, pussy willows are already greeting the new season with bursting catkins, and in the woods wild flowers gently bloom, changing the dull winter landscape. To the east of the house, nearly wild daffodils herald the coming of spring on small golden trumpets.

Hidden in pockets of brush, cows on high pastures stand guard over steaming newborn calves. And hens snuggle out nests in barns and sheds, and lay a dozen or more eggs before settling down to hatch off bits of fluff.

We too feel the surge of seasonal rhythm: March is the time to get going! But as the wind blows about the corners of the farm buildings and rain pelts on the roof, tapping not yet . . . not yet . . . I, like Mother and Grandma before me, am not ready yet to give up the winter's welcome rest, and so knit or do a little cooking.

As I listen to the blowing, gusting rain, long-remembered tales of the old days and family farms of yesteryear come to mind. Memories of childhood drift in and out of my thoughts and I can almost see and hear again aunts and uncles, cousins, Grandpa, all gathered in the kitchen on stormy evenings.

JANE WATSON HOPPING

🌿 LITTLE SWEETS

On old-time farms, families gathered in the warm kitchen during cold winter evenings, huddling around the coal-oil lamps to work or talk. Women often stirred up quick-to-bake cookies and tea cakes from memory while children played at their feet, begging for nibbles of the raw dough. Such cookies and cakes were very lightly sweetened and contained little fat. Nicknamed "little sweets," they were made to be eaten by the handful with hot coffee or icy-cold milk right out of the cool room or springhouse.

Best Jumbles

These are small, delicious cookies my mother called "good keepers." When sealed in a tight container, they will stay fresh for two weeks, or if the milk is left out of the recipe, for up to one month.

2 cups sugar	1 teaspoon rose extract
1 cup butter or margarine	4 cups all-purpose flour, plus
4 eggs, well beaten	flour for rolling out dough
3 tablespoons milk	1 tablespoon baking powder
1 teaspoon almond extract	1 teaspoon salt

Note: Rose extract purchased at health food stores is used in cooking; on the other hand, rose oil is purchased for cosmetic uses or for sachets and potpourris and may be obtained at hobby shops. (Rose blossoms may be eaten in desserts or used for herb teas.)

Preheat oven to 350°F. Combine the sugar and butter in a large bowl and cream until light. Gradually add the eggs, stirring until well blended. In a small bowl, combine the milk and extracts. Into a separate bowl, sift together the flour, baking powder, and salt. To the sugar mixture, alternately stir in the milk and flour mixtures. Turn dough lightly onto a floured surface. Roll out the dough (it will be soft) to a thickness of ¼ to ½ inch. Cut dough into circles with a medium-size doughnut cutter and place one inch apart on greased cookie sheets. Bake until light brown, about 7 to 10 minutes. Immediately remove from pans with spatula and cool on a wire rack or on kraft paper—an opened brown grocery bag will do nicely. *Makes 5 to 6 dozen cookies.*

Honey Cookies

This honey cookie, a favorite of mine, tastes even better after standing in a crock for three to four months. It will remain soft, moist, and delicate in flavor for up to three years in a tight container! (The honey acts as a preservative.) Some old-time cooks called it manna.

2 cups honey
3 tablespoons baking soda
1 cup shortening or margarine
¼ cup hot water
2 teaspoons ground ginger
½ teaspoon salt
3 to 4 cups all-purpose flour,

plus flour for rolling out dough
Cinnamon, nutmeg, and ginger, optional, for sprinkling on baked cookies
Powdered sugar, optional, for sprinkling on baked cookies

Preheat oven to 375°F. In a large saucepan, warm the honey over low heat, then stir in the baking soda. Add the shortening, water, ginger, and salt and continue warming gently until the shortening melts. Remove from heat and stir in enough flour to make a stiff dough (start with 3 cups flour, then add more if needed). Turn onto a floured surface; roll ⅛ to ¼ inch thick. Using a small glass dipped in flour (or a cookie cutter) cut into small circles and place on a greased cookie sheet. Bake until cookies are lightly browned on the bottoms, about 8 minutes. (Honey browns cookies faster than sugar would, so be careful they don't overbrown.) Immediately remove from pan with a spatula and cool on a wire rack or on kraft paper—an opened grocery bag. Store in an airtight container in a cool, dry place. *Note:* If desired, you may dust the cookies lightly with mixed spices and powdered sugar as you layer them in the container. Remember that cinnamon may be used generously and that nutmeg and ginger should be used sparingly. *Makes 5 dozen cookies.*

Mincemeat Drops

At butchering time, when beef was being cut up and put down for winter storage, Grandma made mincemeat out of the lean scraps, then canned it for winter pies, cookies, and tarts. When making pies, she often added brandy, and perhaps a few freshly sliced apples just before baking. Cookies were made from mincemeat taken right out of the jar with nothing added.

1½ cups sugar
⅔ cup butter or margarine

3 eggs, well beaten
1½ cups Old-fashioned

Mincemeat (preferred)
(page 205) or store-bought
mincemeat
3 cups all-purpose flour

1 teaspoon baking soda
¼ teaspoon salt
1 cup walnuts, chopped,
optional

Preheat oven to 375°F. In a large bowl, cream the sugar and butter until light. Add the eggs and mincemeat; stir to blend. Sift together the flour, baking soda, and salt and add it to the mincemeat mixture. Add the walnuts, if desired. Stir to form a soft dough. Drop by heaping teaspoonfuls onto a lightly greased cookie sheet. Bake about 10 to 12 minutes until lightly browned and done. Immediately remove from the baking sheet with a spatula. Cool on a wire rack or on kraft paper —a grocery bag will do. *Makes 3 to 4 dozen cookies.*

Ginger Crisps

A traditional favorite, this cookie was baked for storage, to be brought out when company came unexpectedly.

½ cup butter or margarine
½ cup sugar
1 cup light or dark molasses
2 cups all-purpose flour, plus
flour for rolling out dough

1 teaspoon each cinnamon,
nutmeg, and ginger
2 teaspoons baking powder
1 teaspoon salt

Preheat oven to 400°F. In a large bowl, cream the butter and sugar until light; add the molasses and stir until well blended. Sift together the flour, cinnamon, nutmeg, ginger, baking powder, and salt. Add the dry ingredients to the butter mixture and stir into a stiff dough. Turn onto a floured surface and roll ¼ inch thick; cut into small cookies and bake on a lightly greased cookie sheet until lightly browned, about 8 to 10 minutes. (Molasses browns a baked product much faster than plain sugar; take care not to overbrown.) Remove from oven; transfer to wire rack. When thoroughly cooled, store in airtight container. *Makes 2 to 3 dozen cookies.*

❧ A KITCHEN DANCE

Early in March, Uncle Ben, as a young man bent on sowing a few wild oats before settling down along with the seed oats—"Dakotas" —he was planting in Grandpa's fields, often rode miles into the hill

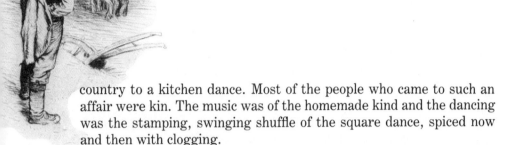

country to a kitchen dance. Most of the people who came to such an affair were kin. The music was of the homemade kind and the dancing was the stamping, swinging shuffle of the square dance, spiced now and then with clogging.

The dancing took place in the kitchen of a farmhouse, on floors made of rough-sawn native hardwood. The door stood open because the room would be crowded. From a lean-to porch, couples came in to take their turn on the dance floor. In one corner of the room, one man with a fiddle, another with a mouth organ, and perhaps another with a mandolin played for the dancers under a coal-oil lamp set on a high shelf. One of the musicians called the dance in a high-pitched voice, his accent in cadence with the music.

> Swing your partners, dos-a-dos,
> Chicken in a breadpan scratchin' out dough.

Young girls stayed in sight of aunts, mothers, and grandmothers, all of whom kept a steady eye on them. Young men slipped out to take swigs of corn whiskey until some young girl whispered to one of them, "Don't go out there no more," and love was born.

At midnight, tired and happy farm folk stopped clapping and dancing, awakened the children, and set out a great potluck supper. The table, draped with a clean white cloth, groaned under platters of meat, stew, pies, cakes, and bread of every variety. Young girls circled the table with newly won beaus and showed off their contributions to the feast.

When the midnight supper was over, the musicians picked up their instruments to "play the folks home." Couples gathered on the floor: husbands and wives, boys and girls in love at first sight, young men reluctant to give up their sweethearts and take up the task of earning enough to be able to afford wives. The music, often a tenderly played version of "Home Sweet Home," eased people into their wraps and helped women collect worn-out children and get them ready for the long journey home.

The table was cleared, dishes were claimed and packed away, and for the trip home, children were tucked under piles of quilts in wagon beds. Parents, huddling together on the wagon seat with robes about them, set off down the road, sleepily visiting about the evening festivities. Young men hunched in great coats, hats pulled low, settled their horses into steady walks toward home. By dawn they might see small lights in distant kitchen windows and know that their mothers were already up making breakfast.

Sitha Jane's Veal Stew with Celeriac and Dried Morels

Morels, picked in spring, can be dried easily for later use, the best ones being those just poking their heads through the mulchy earth. Today, dried morels can be found in special produce sections.

1½ pounds boneless veal, cut into 2-inch square bite-size pieces
About ½ teaspoon salt
About ½ teaspoon black pepper
½ cup all-purpose flour
About 3 tablespoons butter
½ cup chopped red onions
1 clove garlic, peeled
4 cups Homemade Chicken Broth (recipe follows) and boiling water as needed

1½ cups peeled and cubed potatoes
1 cup peeled and cubed carrots
½ cup peeled and cubed celeriac (root celery)
About ¼ teaspoon marjoram
About ½ teaspoon thyme
About ¼ teaspoon savory
1 cup dried morels, or 1 pound fresh store-bought mushrooms

Remove excess fat from the veal and discard, season with *½ teaspoon* salt and *¼ teaspoon* pepper. In a medium-size bowl, dredge meat lightly in flour and brown it in a minimum of fat in a large Dutch oven. Add the onions and the garlic clove; add enough boiling chicken broth to cover the meat and onions. Simmer until the meat is cooked through, but not quite tender, about 1 hour. Add the potatoes, carrots, celeriac, and, if needed, water. Adjust the salt and pepper to taste. Add a sprinkling of marjoram, thyme, and savory. Add the mushrooms (they will soften during the cooking period) and simmer until the vegetables are done, stirring the vegetables about in the gravy, but being careful not to break them up. The gravy will be fairly thick as the stew finishes; watch it carefully so it doesn't scorch. *Makes 4 to 6 servings.*

Homemade Chicken Broth
At home we butchered chickens several at a time and reserved the bony pieces—wings or wing tips, backs and necks—for making

broth that Mother canned in her pressure cooker canner for later use. We still make chicken broth for our cooking, but we cook it, chill it, remove fat, then freeze it in cup or pint containers.

Use empty, clean 1 cup yogurt, and 1 pint or quart cottage cheese cartons for containers. Fill with cold broth, set on a flat surface in freezer until frozen, then package several containers in a plastic bag.

2 quarts chicken backs, necks and wings
2 quarts cold water
4 black peppercorns
A small bay leaf
½ teaspoon crushed thyme
3 or 4 generous sprigs of parsley

Half a medium onion, peeled and chopped
2 small whole peeled carrots
3 stalks of celery, cut in 3- or 4-inch lengths

Wash chicken parts in cold water. Then put them in a large kettle; add cold water to cover, about 1½ to 2 quarts; add the rest of the ingredients. Over high heat, bring liquid to a boil; reduce heat and simmer about 2½ hours or until liquid is reduced by half. Strain broth; remove meat from chicken, return to broth if you wish to make a light soup, otherwise use only the broth (all other ingredients removed) in soups or other dishes that call for it. *Makes 1 quart.*

Aunt Nancy's Cornish Pasties

Aunt Nancy, a vigorous, robust woman of almost six feet, lived in Grass Valley, California, during the early part of this century when the Cousin Jacks, transplanted from Cornwall, England, were working there in the mines. Aunt Nancy cooked for the miners, making endless pasties for their lunches. These pasties reminded the miners of home, since in Cornwall they were carried down into the tin mines, out on the fishing boats, or into the fields. At home, each pasty was marked with the initial of the person who would eat it, so that if his work demanded, he could lay it down, and when he returned, would find his own meat pie and finish his lunch.

These little meat pies were not only popular with the Cornishmen. Aunt Nancy made great platters of them for dances, potlucks, or family holidays.

2 cups all-purpose flour
1 teaspoon salt
¾ cup lard

Ice water, to mix the dough, ⅓ cup or slightly more if needed

1 cup finely chopped potatoes	Black pepper
½ cup finely chopped onions	1 teaspoon fresh parsley,
1½ cups boneless lean red meat,	chopped, or 1 tablespoon
cut into 1-inch cubes	coarsely chopped celery
Salt	Butter

Preheat oven to 400°F. In a medium-size bowl, combine the flour and salt. With your fingers, work the lard in until the mixture looks grainy. Add enough water to form a dough that will barely stick together. Knead the dough on a floured surface 4 or 5 times, roll it about ¼ inch thick and using a saucer, cut into 6-inch circles. Reserve dough scraps. In the center of each circle, place about 1 tablespoon potatoes, about ½ tablespoon onions, and about 1½ to 2 tablespoons meat to fill. Sprinkle salt and pepper to taste over the filling and perhaps a little parsley or celery; dot with butter. Moisten the edges of the circle of dough with water. Fold the circle in half over the filling (filling should come within about 1 inch from the edge), press the edges together to seal and crimp edges. Score top of each pie once to let steam escape while baking. Cut an initial from the leftover dough and, using a little water for glue, "glue" the initial to the top of the pasty. Place on ungreased cookie sheet. Bake at 400°F for 15 minutes, then reduce heat to 350°F and continue baking for about 30 minutes or until pasty tops are browned. Serve piping hot. *Makes 5 or 6 individual pies, one or two to a serving.*

Old-Time Light Bread or Rolls Made from a Potato Ball

In the old days, light bread meant yeast-bread—as opposed to breads made with other leavening agents such as baking powder. This traditional "potato-ball yeast starter" is said to have remained strong and good-flavored for a month. Women made the potato ball at noon, let it rise until night, then made a sponge (starter) and let that rise overnight. The following morning they mixed it with more flour before breakfast, let it rise for one to two hours, and then baked it while the woodstove was still hot.

Potato Ball
4 to 5 medium-size potatoes,	1 tablespoon salt
peeled	2 packages dry or granulated
2 tablespoons sugar	yeast

Note: The yeast most commonly available to old-time cooks was cake yeast, but nowadays dry and granulated yeasts are more often used. A yeast cake, usually ⅔ ounce in size, is interchangeable with dry or granulated yeast by substituting 1 package (which equals 1 tablespoon) of dry or granulated yeast for each yeast cake. If you use a yeast cake, use about 2 tablespoons of hot water to moisten, keeping the maximum temperature at 80°F.

Sponge

1 quart milk	1 rounded tablespoon salt
½ cup sugar	4 cups all-purpose flour
½ cup butter	

Bread

About 6 cups all-purpose flour
About ⅓ cup melted butter or
  margarine, to brush on loaves
  or rolls

Make the potato ball: Boil the potatoes until tender; drain well and mash. Let cool in the pan until lukewarm. Add sugar, salt, and yeast and knead on a lightly floured surface, just enough to make a ball. Turn into a medium-size bowl, cover, and let rise in a warm place until light and spongy. Once the potato ball has risen, the sponge may be made, covered with a towel, and set in a warm spot to rise.

Make the sponge: Heat the milk to scalding; add the sugar, butter, and salt. Remove from heat. Allow the butter to melt and the mixture to cool until lukewarm. In a large bowl, combine the milk mixture with about half of the potato ball and the flour; stir well to blend. Cover with a dry towel and set the sponge aside in a moderately warm place to rise slowly until bubbly, about 2 hours.

The sponge will be about as thick as pancake batter. Put the remaining half of the potato ball in a cup or small bowl, cover, and reserve for another baking. Before baking set the ball out in a warm spot and let the yeast begin to work again. Use within a month for lively action.

Make the bread: Preheat oven to 425°F. Stir in enough flour (about 6 cups) to the sponge to make a soft dough, one that is not sticky to handle, yet yields easily when kneaded. Turn out onto a floured surface and add only enough flour to keep dough from sticking to your hands; knead dough until firm and elastic, but not stiff. Divide dough into two equal portions and shape into loaves. After shaping, put dough into greased 9x5x2½-inch bread pans. Cover with a dry towel and let rise until each loaf doubles in bulk, nearly 2 hours. Bake at 425°F for 15 to 20 minutes, then reduce heat to 350°F and continue baking for another 40 minutes or until the crust is brown and the bread sounds hollow when the top is tapped with the knuckles. Remove from oven, let set 10 minutes, then turn out onto a wire rack to cool. While still hot, brush tops of loaves with a bit of butter or margarine. *Makes 2 loaves.*

Make the rolls: Knead the bread dough lightly on a floured surface. Pinch off pieces about the size of a large egg. Tuck into a 13x9x2-inch baking pan, fitting snugly against each other and the sides of the pan. Cover and let rise until rolls are double in bulk and very light. Bake at 425°F for 30 to 35 minutes or until they are golden brown and feel firm to the touch. Remove from oven, let set 10 to 15 minutes, turn out of pans onto a wire rack and while still hot brush tops with melted butter or margarine. *Makes about 3 dozen rolls.*

Old-Time Carrot Pie

Because both stored carrots and those left in the field over the winter would not keep much longer than late March, women and girls devised as many ways as they could to use them. Besides making the usual salads and soups, they made carrot pies, cakes, cookies, jams, and pickles.

Hot Water Pastry
(recipe follows)
1 pound carrots, peeled,
cooked tender, and run
through a food grinder or
food processor enough to
yield 1½ cups pulp
1½ cups light cream
2 large eggs (preferably
brown), well beaten
½ cup, packed, maple sugar (or
light brown sugar)

½ cup chopped walnuts
1 teaspoon ground cinnamon
½ teaspoon salt
Dash of freshly grated
nutmeg
Whipped cream, optional
Freshly grated nutmeg or
finely chopped walnuts for
garnish, optional

Preheat oven to 450°F. Make the pie shell and refrigerate until ready to fill. In a medium-size bowl, combine the carrots, cream, eggs, and sugar; stir to blend. Stir in the walnuts, cinnamon, salt, and nutmeg. Pour the filling into the prepared pie shell. Bake at 450°F for 15 minutes, then reduce heat to 350°F and bake until a knife inserted into the filling comes out clean, about 30 minutes more. Serve warm or cold, plain or with whipped cream. (If you use whipped cream, you may wish to grate a bit of nutmeg over it or sprinkle a few walnuts on top.) *Makes one 9-inch pie.*

Hot Water Pastry
You will notice that this is a very plain dough, not as rich (not as much fat in proportion to flour) as most, and that it is a good compliment to the rich carrot custard in the above pie recipe.

⅓ cup shortening or margarine
3 tablespoons hot water
1 cup all-purpose flour, plus
    flour for rolling out dough

½ teaspoon salt
¼ teaspoon baking bowder

Place the shortening in a medium-size bowl and pour the hot water over it; mix until creamy. Sift together the flour, salt, and baking powder. Add to the shortening; mix to form a dough. Cover and refrigerate until thoroughly chilled. Turn the dough onto a floured surface; shape into a ball and roll out to fit a 9-inch pie pan with about a 1½-inch border. Line the bottom and sides of the pan with the dough, taking care not to stretch the pastry. Trim edges, leaving about 1 inch of dough hanging over the edge of the pan. Fill and bake as directed in the above recipe. Fold the extra dough under itself and flute edges. *Makes one 9-inch pie shell.*

Feather Cake

Old-time cooks often frosted cakes like this one with whipped cream.

½ cup butter
1 cup sugar
¼ teaspoon salt
2 eggs
1 teaspoon lemon extract
1 cup milk
2½ teaspoons baking powder
2½ cups all-purpose flour
    Whipped cream (see recipe
    page 61)

Preheat oven to 350°F. In a large bowl, cream together the butter and ½ *cup* of the sugar; set aside. In a separate bowl, combine the

JANE WATSON HOPPING

salt and eggs and beat with a spoon or an electric beater until frothy; gradually add the *remaining ½ cup* sugar, beating constantly until the eggs are light and lemon-colored. Add the lemon extract to the milk. Add the baking powder to the flour, which has been sifted once and measured (run a knife blade both ways through the measuring cup to settle the flour), then sift again. Fold the eggs into the creamed butter mixture, then alternately mix in the milk and flour. Beat for 2 minutes more. Turn into a greased and floured 10-inch angel cake pan or into a 13x9x2-inch cake pan. Bake until lightly browned and firm to the touch, about 45 minutes. Cool cake thoroughly. Just before serving, beat the cream just until thick enough to spread and ice the cake on the top and sides with it. *Makes 1 tube cake.*

WHEN GRANDMA COOKED FOR A VISITING PREACHER

At the turn of the century, social activity centered in the home, the church, the grange, school, or in the saloons. Women were classified by society as either "good women" or the other kind. Good women felt it was their duty to exert a civilizing influence on the community, and as such were the shapers of the era. Plaques and samplers were inscribed with bits of homey wisdom such as THE HAND THAT ROCKS THE CRADLE IS THE HAND THAT RULES THE WORLD. Motherhood was a calling and women took the job seriously.

Men raised by old-fashioned women in such homes spoke of mothers who not only loved and cared for them, but who directed the growth of their characters with firm hands.

For such ladies, the arrival of a visiting preacher was an occasion to set steady hearts aflutter. Such a gentleman, welcome wherever he chose to preach, tended to be of an evangelical bent. Sometimes he was paid for his services with only "love offerings"—whatever the congregation dropped in the collection plate. Congregations of the day tended to pay more for a good "hellfire and damnation" service than for a tamer one.

When a Christian lady was able to capture the preacher, the man who was causing such a stir in town, for an after-church dinner or tea with her family, it was a social coup not soon forgotten, often talked about for years. Any woman so privileged dug deep into her stores— nothing was too good for the preacher.

Out came the best china. Silver was polished and the house was scrubbed. Clothes were washed and ironed with starch so stiff that children could hardly sit down. Husbands found emergency work to

do in the fields and younger children snuck off to fish as all conversation seemed to begin with ". . . The pastor this . . . and the pastor that. . . ." Neighbor girls were called in to help with pie baking and other lavish preparations. And tension could rise to a high pitch if specialty items like oysters were a bit late in arriving.

But finally the day arrived. Children were warned repeatedly to be seen but not heard. Then the family departed for church, leaving behind a home in perfect order ready for a "delightful dinner and an uplifting afternoon."

If all went well, and Brother So-and-so was not too straitlaced, there might be first an enjoyable dinner with conversation that tended to be biblical, and then a rest, followed by croquet or horseshoes in the afternoon. Later, of course, there was the evening service.

JANE WATSON HOPPING

At that point, the woman whose whole life was devoted to God, family, home, and what was constructive and right could lean back, tired but happy, and let the words from the pulpit wash over her. Should the preacher compliment her cooking and praise the afternoon spent at her home before friends and a Higher Power, the day could be termed a smashing success.

Cream of Asparagus Soup

If a visiting preacher came in March, women were hard pressed to find any fresh vegetables for the after-church dinner. Asparagus, greens, or other early spring edibles were just popping out of the ground and not always ready to eat. But if enough asparagus tips could be found, this delicious spring soup greeted the pastor.

40 medium fresh asparagus spears
1 medium-size onion, peeled
3 tablespoons butter or margarine
4 sprigs fresh parsley
One 2-inch snippet fresh thyme
6 leaves fresh oregano
1 whole bay leaf

3 tablespoons all-purpose flour
4 cups chicken broth (Homemade Chicken Broth recipe page 11)
½ cup heavy cream
3 egg yolks, lightly beaten
Salt
White pepper (if you have it) or black pepper

Cut tips from the asparagus spears and set tips aside. Cut the stalks and the onion into thin slices and place them in a saucepan with the butter, parsley, thyme, oregano, and bay leaf; cook gently for 15 minutes. Remove bay leaf. Stir in the flour, then add *3½ cups* of the broth and simmer over low heat until the flavors marry and the vegetables are tender. Meanwhile, steam the asparagus tips over the *remaining ½ cup* broth until they are tender and set them aside. When the stalk-and-onion mixture is done, strain through a sieve, forcing mixture through with the back of a spoon to make a puree. Add the cream and egg yolks and season with salt and pepper to taste. When ready to serve, reheat, but take care not to boil soup. Just before serving, gently stir in the asparagus tips and the broth over which they were steamed. *Makes 6 to 8 main course servings.*

Grandma's Creamed Oyster Shortcakes

In the late 1800s, railroads began to cross the country, making it possible to ship highly perishable food on ice. Coastal delicacies—like oysters—became popular wherever the tracks ran and were considered the epitome of elegant eating.

Shortcakes

2 cups all-purpose flour, plus
   flour for rolling out dough
2 teaspoons baking powder
½ teaspoon baking soda

½ teaspoon salt
½ cup butter or margarine
1 cup buttermilk

Creamed Oysters

4 cups small to medium-size
   shucked oysters
¼ cup butter
¼ cup all-purpose flour
2 cups light cream
   Salt

Black pepper
2 tablespoons minced fresh
   parsley
   Dusting of sweet paprika,
   optional

Preheat oven to 425°F.

Make the shortcakes: Combine the flour, baking powder, baking soda, and salt; sift twice and place in a large bowl. Work the butter in with your fingertips until the mixture feels granular. Gradually, without beating, stir in the milk. The dough at this point should be soft, just firm enough to handle. Turn onto a floured surface and knead into a cohesive mass. Roll out dough ½ to ⅔ inch thick and cut into portions for individual servings. If oysters are tiny, make two small 2½-inch shortcakes; if medium make one large 3- to 4-inch shortcake per serving. When *cut out*, put the shortcakes on a greased baking sheet and bake until nicely browned, about 15 minutes.

Prepare the creamed oysters: Drain the oysters and rinse if gritty with cool water; drain again. Melt the butter; add the flour and stir until combined. Add the cream, stirring until a smooth sauce forms. Add the drained oysters, then salt and pepper to taste. Cook just until oysters are plump and edges curl; do not overcook.

When the shortcakes are done, remove from the oven and place on serving plates. If shortcakes are small or flat, do not split them; instead, spoon oysters only over the tops. If shortcakes are large or thick, split each in half with a knife and spoon creamed oysters over the bottom half; then place top half back on the bottom and spoon more creamed oysters over the top. (If necessary, gently reheat oysters to serving temperature, taking care not to overheat.) Sprinkle tops with parsley and, if desired, a little paprika. Serve immediately. *Makes 6 to 8 servings.*

Old-fashioned Carrot Salad with Creamy Dressing

2 cups, well packed, peeled, grated carrots
1 large sweet apple, peeled and chopped (Golden Delicious preferred)
½ cup minced pitted prunes

½ cup Creamy Dressing (recipe follows)
¼ teaspoon salt
Black pepper to dust on salad very lightly

Combine the carrots, apple, and prunes. Dress with Creamy Dressing. Adjust salt and pepper, if needed. Chill well before serving. *Makes 4 to 6 servings.*

Creamy Dressing
½ cup heavy cream
2 tablespoons cider vinegar
1 to 2 tablespoons sugar

Salt
Black pepper

In a small bowl, stir together the cream and vinegar. Sweeten to taste with sugar and pour over carrot, apple, and prune mixture using just enough to moisten. Season with salt and pepper to taste. *Makes ½ cup dressing.*

Honey Daffodil Meringues

2 cups water
¼ cup cold water
2 tablespoons cornstarch
½ cup plus 1 tablespoon light honey

2 tablespoons lemon juice
1 tablespoon butter
3 eggs, separated
Small pinch of salt

Preheat oven to 325°F. In a saucepan, bring the 2 cups water to a boil. Meanwhile, measure the ¼ cup cold water into a teacup and stir in the cornstarch. When blended, stir the cornstarch mixture into the boiling water; cook until clear, stirring constantly. Remove pan from

Lemon

heat and add ½ *cup* of the honey, the lemon juice, and the butter, stirring until the honey is dissolved and butter is melted. In a bowl, beat the egg yolks until frothy. Pour 1 tablespoon of the hot mixture into the yolks and stir to blend. Then gradually pour the yolk mixture into the saucepan with the rest of the hot mixture, stirring until well blended; return to the heat and cook for about 3 to 5 minutes to set the yolks. Pour into 4 to 6 custard cups and set aside.

Beat the egg whites by hand or with an electric mixer until stiff, adding the *remaining 1 tablespoon* honey and the salt once the whites begin to firm up. Spoon egg whites over the filling in the cups, covering filling completely; bake until the meringue is lightly browned, about 25 minutes. Refrigerate until well chilled before serving. *Makes 4 to 6 servings.*

THE HAT MY FATHER WORE

I'm Paddy Miles an Irish boy,
Just come across the sea;
For singing or for dancing boys,
I think that I'll please ye.
I can sing and dance with any man
As I did in days of yore
And on St. Patrick's Day
I love to wear the Hat me father wore.

It's old but it's beautiful,
The best was ever seen,
'Twas worn for more than ninety years,
In that little Isle so green.
From my father's great ancestors,
It descended times galore!
It's a relic of old Dacincy,
The Hat me father wore.

—Words by Daniel McCarthy
—Sung by Johnny Roach, 1876, Harding

ST. PATRICK'S DAY CELEBRATION

For scores of years, St. Patrick's Day has been celebrated in America by Irish immigrants as well as those not of the blood, on March 17, in honor of the missionary bishop who is said to have "found Ireland all heathen and left it Christian."

Irish Spiced Beef

In old-time Irish homes, a platter of this delicious beef sat at the center of the table, along with the potatoes and cabbage, and other old-country dishes. And after the meal, the sweet songs of home rang throughout the house, and the dancing feet proclaimed a Gaelic heritage.

To Cure Spiced Beef
Start curing the meat on the first of March for use on St. Patrick's Day, or about seventeen days (fifteen days for curing, two for cooking) before serving.

1 pound pickling salt
1 cup, packed, light brown sugar
3 crushed bay leaves
1 fresh hot red cayenne pepper
1 tablespoon mustard seed
2 heaping teaspoons saltpeter (see Note)
1 teaspoon whole cloves
1 teaspoon coriander (cracked preferred)
1 teaspoon coarsely ground black pepper
1 teaspoon whole allspice
1 teaspoon freshly grated nutmeg
1 teaspoon crushed whole dried ginger
1 (6-pound) lean boneless beef rump or topside roast

Note: Saltpeter can be purchased at drugstores.

Rub together all the dry ingredients, mixing until well blended. Place the roast in a large earthenware or glass dish with a cover, and rub the spice mixture thoroughly over the meat's surface. Once meat has been rubbed on the surface with curing ingredients it will not spoil. The salt, saltpeter, and spices destroy any bacteria.

Store the curing meat, covered, in the refrigerator. Every day for a week, turn the meat over, then take up the spice mixture from the bottom of the dish and rub it all over the meat's surface again. During the remaining eight days that the meat is curing, "overhaul" (repeat the turning over and rubbing on spice procedure given above). When the meat is done, it will be corned beef—red all the way through—and will be ready for cooking. Remove from dish, wash, and pat dry.

To Cook the Cured Spiced Beef for St. Patrick's Day
Cured spiced beef, once cooked, may be eaten hot or cold, but usually it is cut into thin slices and served cold.

1 teaspoon ground cloves
1 teaspoon ground allspice
1 teaspoon ground cinnamon
1 recipe Cured Spiced Beef
  (recipe above)

3 medium onions, sliced
3 carrots, sliced
  Warm water to cover

In a small bowl, combine the cloves, allspice, and cinnamon and rub the mixture over the meat. Place the onions and carrots in a large kettle; lay the meat on top of the vegetables and cover all with water. Place the lid on the kettle and simmer gently for nearly 3 hours or until tender. Serve, thinly sliced, while still warm with baked or boiled potatoes with their jackets on, fresh young Irish peas flavored with a bit of mint and chives. For chilled spiced beef, cook *the day before it is needed*. While warm, remove from liquid and press lightly by putting between two dishes with a light weight on top. Refrigerate until well chilled, then slice. *Makes 8 to 12 servings.*

The O'Daly Family Recipe for Boxty

When the Irish settled in America they brought with them their old sod cooking traditions. This recipe for potatoes, which the Irish call "farls," has been in the O'Daly family for generations.

3 cups peeled and grated
  potatoes
2 cups leftover mashed
  potatoes
1 teaspoon salt
1 teaspoon baking soda
¼ cup all-purpose flour, plus
  flour for rolling out dough

1 teaspoon caraway seed,
  optional
½ cup finely chopped onions,
  optional
½ cup chopped ham, optional
  About ¼ cup bacon drippings

In a large bowl, combine the raw and mashed potatoes. In a separate bowl, mix the salt and baking soda into the flour and add to the bowl with the potatoes; if you wish to add caraway seed (or onions or ham), do it now. Stir well to form a dough. Roll out dough on a floured surface and form into a circle ½ inch thick. Cut into 4 to 6 serving-size wedges. In a skillet, heat the bacon drippings until sputtering hot, then slip wedges into the hot fat and cook until brown on both sides. Drain on paper towels. Add more bacon drippings as needed. *Makes 4 to 6 servings.*

Veda's Glazed Onions

3 cups small white cooking
  onions, peeled
  About 1 cup hot chicken broth,
  store-bought or homemade
  (see recipe page 11)
2 tablespoons butter

1 tablespoon sugar
Salt
Black pepper
Toasted sesame seed or finely
  chopped fresh thyme,
  optional

Place the onions in a heavy skillet. Add enough broth to have ¼ inch of liquid (if you don't have enough broth, add water) and simmer until the liquid has reduced by half. Then reduce heat to low, add the butter and sugar, and season to taste with salt and pepper. Reduce heat to very low. Cook until the liquid becomes a glaze, turning the onions occasionally. If desired, sprinkle with sesame seed or thyme (which is just leafing out in March). Serve immediately. *Makes 4 to 6 servings.*

Arlene's Crusty Oat Bread

Because wheat is difficult to grow in Ireland's damp climate, the Irish have for centuries made bread out of oats. This crusty oat-bread recipe crossed the ocean with Gaelic immigrants and no doubt warmed many a heart with memories of the hearths of home.

3 cups unbleached all-purpose
  flour
2 cups rolled oats
3 tablespoons butter

1½ teaspoons baking soda
1 teaspoon salt
About 2 cups buttermilk

Preheat oven to 425°F. In a large mixing bowl or bread bowl, combine the flour and oats. Work in *2 tablespoons* of the butter until mealy. Stir in the baking soda, salt, and some of the buttermilk, using a little more or a little less of the buttermilk as required to make a soft, manageable dough that is not sticky. Turn onto a floured surface. Knead lightly and form into a ball; flatten dough on a lightly floured cookie sheet, making a circle 1½ inches thick. Using a floured knife, make a cross ¼ inch deep on top of the loaf. Bake at 425°F for 30 minutes, then reduce oven setting to 325°F and bake until nicely browned and cooked through, about 15 minutes more. Remove from oven and brush top with remaining butter.

To serve hot, break into chunks on cross lines and serve immediately with butter on the side. If you prefer to slice the bread, let it cool for 5 minutes at room temperature. Store in an airtight container. *Makes 1 loaf.*

Barmbrack

This old Irish recipe for sweet bread yields a loaf that is firm and of excellent flavor. Many thanks to Irish friends who shared it from their private family collection entitled Recipes of the Irish Goldrushers, *©1984, written by Shelly Machado.*

4 cups all-purpose flour
½ teaspoon salt
½ teaspoon nutmeg
¼ cup butter
¼ cup sugar
1 tablespoon dry or granulated yeast (Do not substitute cake yeast.)
1¼ cups milk
2 eggs, well beaten

1½ cups seedless raisins
1 cup chopped dried currants (or substitute dried prunes, dried apricots, or dried peaches)
¼ cup candied orange peel or lemon peel
Melted butter to brush top of bread, optional

Preheat oven to 425°F. Into a large bowl, sift together the flour, salt, and nutmeg; cut in the butter. Add the sugar and yeast. Warm the milk slightly, until lukewarm, and mix in the eggs; add to the dry ingredients and beat with a spoon until the dough is stiff but pliable. Fold in the raisins, currants, and orange or lemon peel. Shape dough into a round ball and place in a well-greased and floured 9-inch round baking pan that is at least 3 inches deep. (Dough should fill the pan halfway.) Press down as needed to spread dough evenly in the pan. Cover with a dry cloth and set in a warm place to rise until dough is double in bulk, about 1 hour. Bake at 425°F for 15 to 20 minutes, then reduce oven setting to 350°F and continue baking for the balance of 1 hour. Remove from the oven and immediately turn out onto a rack to cool, right side up. Brush with butter, if you wish. Serve at room temperature, thinly sliced. *Makes 1 loaf.*

🌿 PIN MONEY

On old-time farms, in spring, hens laid basketsful of golden-yolked eggs and hatched off dozens of fluffy baby chicks. It was the duty of women and girls to tend the flocks. Extra eggs—those not used at home—belonged to the woman of the house and she could sell them at the store for pin money. From a list my sister and I found in a purse that belonged to our grandmother, we learned that she spent her pin money on "a dress fabric for Gladys (my mother), buttons for Freddie's pants, a spool of white thread and six ropes of licorish." For women like her, the amount of pin money on hand was never great, because a good farm cook could in a trice turn her hens' bounty into edibles for her family.

Slipped Custard Pie

A sleight-of-hand cooking technique creates this mouth-watering contrast of flaky pastry and smooth custard. Women in the past gauged cooking skill by one's ability to make this pie without demolishing the custard.

4 eggs, slightly beaten
½ cup sugar
½ teaspoon vanilla extract

¼ teaspoon salt
2½ cups milk, scalded
Flaky Pastry (recipe follows)

Preheat oven to 350°F. In a bowl, blend the eggs, sugar, vanilla, and salt. Gradually stir in the milk. Place a buttered 8-inch pie pan in a shallow baking pan; fill the pie pan ¾ full of custard; pull the oven rack out just enough to be able to set the double pans in place; pour the last ⅓ of the filling into the pie pan. Pour enough cold water into the baking pan around the base of the pie pan to have ¼ inch of liquid. Bake for 35 to 40 minutes. Remove custard from oven and from baking pan; gently place on a wire rack to cool. Meanwhile, bake the pie crust. (See Flaky Pastry recipe below.) When the custard and cooked crust are cooled, carefully run a spatula around the edge of the custard to separate it from the plate. Shake the plate gently to completely loosen the custard. Hold pan containing custard just above and a little to the side of the rim of the pan containing the baked pie crust; gently slip custard into the crust being careful to keep the custard intact. Chill well before serving. *Makes one 8-inch pie.*

Flaky Pastry
1 cup all-purpose flour, plus
    flour for rolling out dough
½ teaspoon salt

½ cup cold butter
2 to 4 tablespoons cold water

Preheat oven to 450°F. Sift the flour and salt together into a large bowl. Cut the butter in, using a pastry blender or two dinner knives, or rub butter into the flour with your fingertips until all pieces of dough are the size of small peas. Gradually sprinkle just enough water to hold the pastry together, mixing lightly and quickly with a fork after each addition. (This leads to a flakier pie crust.) Turn onto a floured surface and form into a ball (it will be soft). Roll out and fit into a 9-inch pie pan; flute the edges. With a fork, prick the sides and bottom of uncooked shell, or if you wish, fill with dry beans to hold crust in place while cooking. Bake crust 15 minutes, then remove beans and continue baking until light brown, 5 or more minutes. Place on a wire rack to cool. *Makes one 9-inch pie crust.*

Meringues

Beginning in late February and early March, baskets of brown and white eggs grace our kitchens, laid by flocks with colorful names like

Rhode Island Red and Buff Orphington, Barred Plymouth Rock and Wyandotte. Some hens called Easter chickens are kept to please the children—and parents surprise their little ones by showing them the blue-and-green eggs these hens have laid.

6 egg whites	½ teaspoon cream of tartar
Pinch of salt	1½ cups sugar

Preheat oven to 250°F. Using a metal whisk, beat the egg whites in a medium-size bowl until soft peaks form; add salt and cream of tartar. Gradually add the sugar, beating constantly until stiff, moist peaks form. Cut a piece of heavy brown wrapping paper and place it on a cookie sheet. Using a large spoon, mound the egg-white mixture on the paper; take care to make the mounds of equal size. Bake for 1 hour, then turn off the oven, leaving the meringues in the oven until they are cool. *Makes about 1 dozen meringues*—which never last long enough to store!

Grandma Boardman's Floating Island Custard

Grandma Sarah Boardman made this delicious custard for special occasions, such as birthdays and family dinners after church. All the little Hoppings loved to go to her house after Sunday school.

5 egg yolks	teaspoon lemon extract if
2 egg whites (reserve the other	desired)
egg whites for the Floating	4 cups milk, scalded
Islands)	Floating Islands (recipe
⅓ cup sugar	follows)
1 teaspoon vanilla extract (or 1	

In a bowl, combine egg yolks, egg whites, sugar, and vanilla; beat lightly with a slotted spoon. In a large saucepan, scald the milk, then stir egg mixture into the milk and cook until the custard thickens. Remove from heat and cool until lukewarm (so as not to break the dish), then pour into a large glass bowl; cool thoroughly, but don't chill, and top with the floating islands. *Makes 6 to 8 servings.*

Floating Islands

3 egg whites (reserved above)	a few drops lemon extract if
3 tablespoons sugar	desired)
A few drops vanilla extract (or	

Whip the egg whites into a stiff froth. Add the sugar and vanilla to taste and beat until glossy, stiff, firm elastic peaks are formed. Fill a large shallow skillet ¼ inch deep with boiling water; return to a boil. Pour the mixture over the boiling water and let cook for about 1 or more minutes until puffed and firm to the touch. (Or drop the meringue by generous teaspoonful over the surface of the boiling water to form "floating islands"; be sure to pull up a little peak with the spoon.) When the meringue is cooked, remove from heat, put on a platter to cool, and drop it by spoonfuls over the top of the cooled custard to form little floating islands. Meringue cools almost instantly. *Makes one large meringue or 12 to 18 floating islands.*

SPRING ON THE VERMONT FARM

Shake, thrifty farmer, now your trade
　Beats anything a-going;
You can't step out unless you step
　On something up and growing;
Each stalk of corn that stands as straight
　And stylish as a feather
Upon a Scotchman's cap, proclaims
　The wonder-working weather.

—Daniel L. Cady

First Day of Spring

For those of us who live on the farm, the coming of spring has always been a turning point, a time when the sunrise and sunset are exactly twelve hours apart, and when the sun rises exactly in the east and sets exactly in the west. On March 22, the vernal equinox, rural people have always celebrated with parades, flowers, dancing, and feasting. Even Julius Caesar's changing of the calendar to make cold January the official first month of the new year did not stop the joyful celebrations in March. For centuries after, many countries continued to celebrate New Year's Day on the vernal equinox; in fact, England did not make the change until the middle of the 1700s.

Chicken and Feather-Light Dumplings

When I was growing up, all through the winter much of the meat by necessity had been salted meat, ham, or bacon. Hence, chicken was a welcome addition to spring meals and no dumplings were lighter than Mother's.

2 quarts hot water	1 teaspoon black pepper
2 cups milk	2 stalks celery
1 (3- to 5-pound) stewing chicken, cut into serving pieces	1 small onion, peeled and quartered
2 teaspoons salt	Feather-Light Dumpling Batter (recipe follows)

In a large kettle, bring the water and milk to a boil. (The milk whitens the meat.) Ease the chicken into the water; add salt and pepper, celery and onion. Simmer slowly until meat is tender, 2 to 3 hours, removing the scum which rises to the surface as the chicken begins to boil. While cooking, keep the chicken under the broth; if necessary, weight it down with a plate. Meanwhile, make the dumpling batter.

When the chicken is done, transfer it to a covered dish to keep it warm, leaving the kettle containing the broth behind. Bring the broth to a rolling boil, then drop the dumpling batter by small spoonfuls into the boiling broth. Cover kettle tightly and cook just until dumplings are cooked through, about 15 minutes. (To test for doneness, open at least one dumpling with a fork; don't overcook these light dumplings—test for doneness frequently.) Serve tender chicken and dumplings in a wide, shallow soup plate or on a dinner plate with a good lip. Spoon the broth that has thickened into a gravy during the cooking over both. *Makes 6 to 8 servings, less if the folks are hungry.*

Feather-Light Dumpling Batter

2 cups all-purpose flour	1 egg, beaten
1 tablespoon baking powder	3 tablespoons butter, melted
1 teaspoon salt	⅔ cup buttermilk
½ teaspoon baking soda	

Sift together the dry ingredients into a large bowl. Make a well in the center of the dry mixture and in the well place the egg, butter, and buttermilk. Stir just enough to form a heavy batter. Cook as directed in the above recipe. *Makes 6 to 8 servings of dumplings.*

Old-fashioned Preboiled Ham

Home-cured hams tended to be a bit too salty to eat right out of the smokehouse. This preboiling not only removed salt but excess fat, leaving a tender, sweet-flavored piece of meat that was not greasy.

1 (10-pound) old-fashioned cured
   ham
   Boiling water to cover
3 whole cloves
1 whole, firm apple, unpeeled

1 bay leaf
1 stick cinnamon
   Glaze: Honey Butter Glaze
   (recipe follows)

Place the ham in a large enamel pot and cover with boiling water. Stick the cloves into the apple and add the apple, bay leaf, and cinnamon stick to the pot. Cover and simmer 3 to 4 hours or until the meat is tender when tested with a fork. Remove pot from heat and set it in a cool place, with the lid off. When the broth has cooled, cover pot and let the meat sit in the pot overnight under refrigeration (or in a very cool place, 45°F or less).

On the following day, preheat the oven to 350°F. Lift off the layer of fat which formed on top of the broth and reserve it for other cooking or baking. (Substitute for fat in biscuit recipes, or add to green beans as a seasoning ingredient.) Place the ham in a large baking pan and trim off excess fat. Score the top and glaze. Bake until the meat is hot and glaze sets, about 30 minutes to 1 hour. Serve immediately with sweet potatoes rubbed with fat and baked in their jackets and fresh steamed asparagus. Or chill the ham and serve it cold, thinly sliced. *Makes 25 or more servings.*

Honey Butter Glaze

½ cup honey
½ cup water

1 tablespoon butter
   Sprinkling of freshly grated
   nutmeg (about ½ teaspoon)

In a small saucepan, heat honey, water, and butter together. Spoon over ham and grate fresh nutmeg over the top. *Makes about 1 cup.*

Baked Jerusalem Artichokes with Toasted Sesame Seeds

Like many root vegetables, tuberous artichokes, which grow abundantly underground, were once a popular animal food. Planted like potatoes, they were originally harvested by herds of swine in the fall that rooted them out just like truffles. Farm women also learned to cook these delicious little tubers for their families (in which case they dug them up themselves!), using their recipes for potatoes.

2 pounds Jerusalem artichokes	½ cup grated Swiss cheese
2 tablespoons all-purpose flour	¼ cup toasted sesame seed
1 teaspoon salt	Sweet paprika
¼ teaspoon black pepper	1 tablespoon minced fresh
½ cup heavy cream	parsley, optional

Preheat oven to 350°F. Scrub and peel the artichokes, using a peeler like the one used for carrots, then slice ⅛ inch thick. In a small bowl, mix together the flour, salt, and pepper. In a 1½-quart greased casserole, alternately layer the artichokes and the flour mixture; make at least 4 layers. Pour the cream over the artichokes and bake for 1 hour. Stir once, lightly. When the tubers are tender, sprinkle the cheese, sesame seed, and a dusting of paprika evenly over the top and place under the broiler for 8 to 10 minutes or long enough to melt the cheese and brown it; watch carefully so it doesn't burn. Sprinkle parsley over the top, if desired. Serve immediately. *Makes 6 servings.*

Lemon, Parsley, and Winter-Growing Chives Butter

Each year here on the farm in Oregon, an old doe brings her new fawns down to browse in the bean patch. All of us willingly share beans with her, knowing that we are getting the best of the bargain, that watching the gangling babies, who are so close to us and watching us with as much interest as we are watching them, is payment aplenty. Our family has always canned our string bean crop (we put up about 100 quarts each season!), and we love this butter served over them. Sometimes, for variation, we form the butter into pats so that everyone can help themselves to the amount they want—or put it on their bread or other foods, too.

¼ cup butter	1 teaspoon minced fresh
⅛ teaspoon grated lemon rind	winter-growing chives
1 tablespoon lemon juice	½ teaspoon minced fresh parsley

Beat the butter until soft. Add the lemon rind and juice, stirring the sauce gently but well. Stir in the chives and parsley. Shape into tablespoon-size pats or balls for serving at the table, or add it to hot string beans in the kitchen just before serving. (The butter will melt over the beans, turning into a sauce.) Once prepared, refrigerate until needed. *Makes about ⅓ cup butter, or enough to dress 1 quart of string beans.*

Rhubarb Custard Pie

While the main rhubarb harvest is in late May and early June, stalks may be picked anytime that they are large enough. Tender young stalks have the best flavor; older ones tend to be stringy and not as delicate tasting. Seasons for such spring crops vary with the climate, southern crops being ready much earlier than those in the north.

This old-time pie can be topped with a meringue or it can be served with a dollop of whipped cream on each slice.

Crisp Pastry (recipe follows)
1 cup finely chopped rhubarb
1 cup sugar
1 tablespoon all-purpose flour
2 eggs, beaten
1 cup light cream or milk

1 tablespoon butter or
  margarine, melted
¼ teaspoon ground ginger
Meringue or whipped cream,
  optional

Line the pie pan with the pastry dough and refrigerate until ready to use.

Preheat oven to 350°F. In a bowl, mix the rhubarb, sugar, and flour together. In a separate bowl, combine the eggs, milk, butter, and ginger, blending well. Spoon the rhubarb mixture into the prepared pie shell. Pour the egg mixture over the top and bake until firm, about 45 minutes to 1 hour. To test for doneness insert a knife blade into the filling; if it comes out clean the pie is done. For best flavor, serve at room temperature with freshly made whipped cream (my preference). *Makes one 8-inch pie.*

Note: All custard pies should be chilled in the refrigerator if they are not served immediately; remove from refrigerator early enough for the pie to warm up a bit; serve cool but not chilled.

When topping with meringue, have meringue (made from *2* stiffly beaten *egg whites* to which *2 tablespoons of powdered sugar* have been added) ready; remove pie from the oven when firm but lightly browned; working rapidly, spread meringue over the top, all the way to the edges, swirling it into high and low surfaces. Return to oven and bake until light brown, 15 to 20 additional minutes. Don't over-bake; it will overcook the custard. Remove from oven and cool away from drafts.

Crisp Pastry

¾ cup all-purpose flour
¼ cup cornstarch
½ teaspoon salt
½ cup cold butter, lard, or
margarine, as preferred
2 to 4 tablespoons cold milk, more if needed

Into a medium-size bowl, sift together the flour, cornstarch, and salt; cut the butter in with a knife until the texture resembles grains of wheat. Gradually add just enough milk to make a stiff paste; the mixture should be a bit dry. (Use fingertips to finish the blending, if you wish.) Shape the mixture lightly and quickly with your hands into a ball; place on a lightly floured surface and roll out about ¼ inch thick. With a light hand, roll from the center outward to form a circle large enough to fit an 8-inch pie pan. Place the dough in the pan and line the bottom and sides evenly; crimp the edges. Fill and bake as directed in the above recipe. *Makes one 8-inch pie shell.*

AN OLD VERMONT CELLAR
HOLE

To wander near a ruined home
　　Upon a Springtime morning,
Informs the mind and charms the eye,
　　But gives the heart a warning;
For, Oh! the sense of human change
　　That such a scene discloses—
The roses 'round the fallen walls,
　　And lilacs 'round the roses.

The hands that built the house were strong,
　　The builded house was stronger,
The flowers, a wifely afterthought,
　　But they are lasting longer;
We wonder in what grass-grown yard
　　The tenant here reposes,
And she, as well, for whom they grew,
　　The lilacs and the roses.

Some leaning wrecks of orchard trees
　　Declare that life was pleasant;

They lived, as we are living now,
  Concerned about the present;
However dear, another day
  The dearest day deposes,
And aftertime binds up the wounds
  With lilacs and with roses.

—*Daniel L. Cady*

APRIL

Wild Salad Greens and the Scent of Lilacs

On the farm and in the countryside, no month makes greater changes in the appearance of the land than April. Any ice or snow left on the ground disappears and, despite mingled rain and sunshine, the season of warmth has come at last. Around the farm buildings, crocus and daffodils bloom everywhere, while in the woodland, wild flowers are so thick underfoot that children playing there cannot help crushing them. Early butterflies can be seen basking in the sunshine, and bees venture out of their hives to gather the first honey of the season, and lilacs scent the air.

GREEN EDIBLES AND ACCOMPANIMENTS

About the tenth of April on farms, spring gardens are planted in newly warmed earth. Women and children sprinkle feather-light lettuce seeds and tiny round black-colored radish seeds carefully in rows and place onion sets or young plants in the fine earth so as to leave room for growth. Outside the annual summer garden, perennial rhubarb is unfurling giant leaves over ruby-red stalks, promising tart pies by the end of the month. Peas planted in February are standing aboveground and Swiss chard—a survivor of the winter cold—is sending out new green leaves to test the coming of spring. Out in the fields and hugging close to buildings, wild salad greens grow succulently, while under the trees white, blue, and magenta violets blanket the ground.

Salad of Wild Greens

In the past, when food was put away in the fall for winter, and fresh vegetables were nonexistent during the long cold months, country people eagerly anticipated the new growth of spring in April, or perhaps early in May. Since wild greens shoot up before any garden vegetables are ready for harvest, folks well versed in herbal lore began to search in the fields, as soon as ice and snow melted off, for plants that could be used for greens, salads, or in tonics. On farms today, such wild greens still grow in abundance and are delicious made into a salad.

    To make a salad of wild greens, take a large bowl out into the yard or into the fields. Pick only the tender, young leaves of wild miner's lettuce, chickweed, dandelion, and lamb's tongue, so named for the shape of its leaf. Add to them bits of Swiss chard, which survived the winter, a few violet leaves and flowers, and whips of chives or snips off the tops of winter onions. Find a few lemon mint leaves and keep these to the side to add to the salad dressing.

    Wash the greens and shake off the water. Dress the salad with Vinaigrette Sauce or with a little cream to which vinegar, sugar, and salt have been added to taste. Snip the mint leaves into small bits and mix into either dressing.

Vinaigrette Sauce

6 tablespoons olive oil (preferred) or vegetable oil	¼ teaspoon each salt, pepper, dry mustard, and paprika
3 tablespoons cider vinegar	

Measure into a small bowl, *1 tablespoon* of the olive oil, *1 tablespoon* vinegar, salt, pepper, mustard, and paprika. Beat with a wire whisk until smooth. Add *2 more* tablespoons of oil and *1 tablespoon* vinegar; beat again. Last, add remaining oil and vinegar. Beat a few strokes

to blend. Pour Vinaigrette Sauce into a jar, cover tightly. Refrigerate to chill until ready to use, then shake to blend just before serving.

Aunt Mabel's Veal Cutlets with Fried Apples

Aunt Mabel first helped with the cooking for a large farm family. Then in the thirties, during the darkest days of the Depression, when men couldn't get a job for love or money, she, like other women of the day, turned cooking skills into money by opening a small hole in the wall restaurant. Her little "counter" restaurant was absolutely clean, and everything was perfect when she cooked: The cut of meat was right and the vegetables and fruit were sliced into even, delicious pieces.

3 teaspoons melted butter
1 teaspoon salt
¼ teaspoon black pepper
2 pounds boneless veal loin
    cutlets (6 pieces)
    Flour, to dredge veal and
    apples

Butter for pan-frying
4 or 5 tart cooking apples,
    peeled and cut into ¼-inch
    slices
½ cup or more milk, for dipping
    apple slices

Combine the melted butter with the salt and pepper; rub the mixture into both sides of the veal and let sit for 20 minutes under refrigeration. Dredge veal in flour and pan-fry over medium heat (use just enough butter to keep meat from sticking) until meat is brown and tender, fried clear through but not overcooked. Remove from pan; transfer to warm platter and keep warm until the apples are ready.

Dip apple slices in milk, drain and dredge in fresh flour; pan-fry over medium heat in a clean skillet, using just enough butter, 2 or 3 tablespoons, to brown the apples; cook through, or until tender when pierced with a fork. Surround cutlets with apples, sprinkle the slices lightly with cinnamon if you like, and serve piping hot. *Makes 6 servings.*

Potato Omelet

When we bake potatoes for dinner, we cook extras for this hearty workaday breakfast or lunch. And, when the men insist, we serve this omelet with steaming hot coffee, fresh fruit, and potato biscuits and jam.

4 medium-size baked potatoes,
    hot or cold, peeled and
    cubed
3 tablespoons butter
¼ cup minced chives
1½ teaspoons salt
¼ teaspoon minced fresh
    thyme
    Dash of black pepper, to
    taste

3 eggs, well beaten
3 tablespoons milk
    Sweet paprika to sprinkle on
    top, optional
    Potato Biscuits, optional
    (page 167)
    Wild Blackberry Jam,
    optional (page 140)

In a medium-size ovenproof skillet, cook the potatoes in the butter over medium heat until well heated and slightly browned; stir in the chives, salt, thyme, and pepper. In a small bowl, combine the eggs and milk; pour over the potatoes and cook slowly (lower heat if necessary) until set around the potatoes. Sprinkle paprika on top, if desired, and put under the broiler for a minute to dry and lightly brown the top. Cut into 6 wedges and use a spatula to lift each wedge onto a serving plate. Serve immediately. *Makes 6 servings.*

Spring Beets with Greens

By mid-April, early planted beets may have a small bulb (root) on them, not much bigger than a quarter in circumference. At this stage of growth, both greens and root have a delicate flavor.

1 bunch small untrimmed and unpeeled young beets, rinsed well	Salt
	1 slice bacon
	Black pepper
Water to cook beets in	

Lay the beets, greens and all, in a large shallow skillet that has a lid. Measure out water in a measuring cup and, while keeping track of how much you use, add enough water to the skillet to have ½ inch of liquid. Salt the water in the pan, allowing 1 teaspoon salt for each cup of water. Simmer until the beets are done. Pour off the water and cut the green tops off the beets; peel and chop the beets and chop the greens. In the same skillet (rinse it out first), fry the bacon until crisp; drain on paper towels and crumble bacon. Return the beet roots, tops, and bacon to the skillet and heat to serving temperature. Salt and pepper to taste and serve immediately. *Makes 4 to 6 servings.*

(*Note:* For variety, young beets may be cooked and then served cold [omit the bacon] with French dressing, a mixture of lemon juice and butter, or with vinegar.)

Citron Buns

These old-time "good whenever you eat 'em" buns are nice with a little fresh butter, turned golden by the rich spring grass and clover on which the cows are grazing, and steaming black coffee for a pick-me-up.

3 tablespoons butter or margarine, plus butter to serve with buns	¼ cup sugar
	1 teaspoon salt
	1 cup milk, scalded and still hot

1 package dry or granulated
  yeast
¼ cup lukewarm water (105°F
  to 115°F)
4 cups all-purpose flour, plus
  flour for kneading dough

1 egg, well beaten
1 teaspoon ground cinnamon
1 teaspoon ground ginger
½ cup seedless raisins
½ cup finely chopped candied
  citron peel

Egg Wash
1 egg, well beaten
1 tablespoon milk

In a bowl, add the butter, sugar, and salt to the hot milk; stir until blended. In a separate bowl, dissolve the yeast in the warm water. When milk mixture is lukewarm, add the dissolved yeast, flour, egg, cinnamon, and ginger, mixing well, then stir in the raisins and citron peel. Cover with a dry towel and let stand in a warm place until double in bulk. Then turn onto a floured surface and knead until cohesive, until the dough is smooth and elastic to the touch. Divide into 15 to 20 equal portions and form into neat round buns; place in a well-greased 13x9x2-inch baking pan about 1 inch apart. Blend together the egg wash ingredients and brush on tops of buns. Bake in preheated 350°F oven until well browned and cooked through, about 30 to 35 minutes. Remove from oven and cool slightly, then remove from pan; turn top side up. Rub tops with 2 tablespoons butter. *Note:* When warm, not hot, such buns may be glazed with Simple Powdered-Sugar Glaze (page 208). Serve hot or cold and lightly buttered. *Makes 15 to 20 buns.*

🌿 APRIL FOOL'S DAY FROLIC

All Fool's Day . . . or April Fool's Day . . . a playful time of year! Even the weather pulls pranks on the unwary. Expect frost, snowfall, warm showers, and days that are as hot as midsummer.

For centuries April Fool's Day has been celebrated all over the world with food, drink, dancing, and frolic. Absurd jokes on friends and family date to the 1600s in England—the victim, an April Fool!

My grandfather once had the unexpected pleasure of being the perpetrator of an April Fool's joke that baffled a whole farming community: About 1901, the American public learned about raising large domesticated rabbits. For a time, speculation was rampant, and people made a fortune breeding and selling these small meat animals. In the rural parts of Missouri, folks didn't pay much attention to the

ALL FOOL'S DAY

The first of April some do say
Is set apart for All Fool's Day;
But why the people call it so
Nor I, nor they themselves, do know.

—Poet unknown

excitement. Then a relative from the city gave Grandpa a pair of Belgian hares.

Accustomed to hunting with his sons for all the rabbit meat the family would eat, Grandpa soon tired of tame rabbits that had to be penned and fed, so he turned the hares loose. Rabbits being what they are, they soon interbred with the wild ones.

The next year everyone in the area was talking about the huge rabbits they bagged out by Doc's place. But Grandpa, who had learned about the giant rabbits in his woods and fields early in the year, thought it was a great April Fool's joke on his neighbors and friends, and so he never breathed a word about the Belgian hares.

Jugged Hare

To make this dish, which is a wonderful way to cook full-grown rabbits, you will need a bean pot with a tight-fitting lid. You will also need a second, larger and deeper pot with a rack and lid; the pot must be deep enough to cover the bean pot (sitting on the rack and with the bean pot lid on). If no such equipment is available, cook the jugged hare in a bean pot, sealing the lid tightly onto the bean pot with aluminum foil; bake in a 350°F oven, instead of cooking it on top of the stove inside a second pot.

1 (2½- to 3-pound) domestic rabbit, cut in serving-size pieces (wild rabbit preferred)
Flour for dredging
About 1 cup butter or margarine
4 cups Homemade Chicken Broth (see recipe page 11) thickened with 4 to 6 tablespoons moistened cornstarch

1 whole medium-size onion, peeled and halved
2 small sprigs of thyme, left whole
1 teaspoon salt
½ teaspoon black pepper
Generous pinch sweet paprika, about ⅓ teaspoon
1 tart apple, peeled and sliced (Northern Spy preferred)
½ cup apple cider
Red currant jelly

Dredge the rabbit pieces in flour until well coated; pan-fry in butter, starting with ½ cup, adding more as needed. While the rabbit is frying, heat the chicken broth to boiling; add cornstarch moistened with ⅓ to ½ cup cold water and cook, stirring constantly, over medium heat until gravy is clear. Pour gravy into a deep, large bean pot that has a tight cover; add the pieces of rabbit, the onion and thyme, add salt, pepper, and paprika. Arrange the apple slices over the top and add the cider. Cover the bean pot tightly so no moisture can seep into the ingredients being cooked inside; set the bean pot on a rack fitted inside a larger kettle. Add enough water to the larger kettle to cover the bottom ½ or a little more of the bean pot with boiling water. This is much like steaming a pudding. Place on stove burner and heat the water until it is simmering, cover the larger kettle and let the rabbit stew until it is quite tender. (Cooking time will vary from 45 minutes to more than 1 hour, depending on the age of the rabbit.) Remove from heat and take the bean pot out of the deeper pot.

Serve the jugged hare right out of the bean pot or transfer it to a deep bowl platter, pouring the gravy over it. Serve red currant jelly on the side. *Makes 4 to 8 servings*, depending on the size of the rabbit.

Toad in a Hole

These spicy little pork link sausages hidden in a moist, puddinglike bread—served with poached or pan-fried eggs and a dish of cinnamon-flavored apples—make a delicious breakfast or Sunday night supper.

2 cups all-purpose flour
½ teaspoon salt
2 eggs, well beaten
3 cups milk

2 tablespoons butter or
  margarine, melted
1 to 1½ pounds spicy smoked
  pork link sausages

Preheat oven to 350°F. Sift together the flour and salt into a bowl. In a separate bowl, blend together the eggs, milk, and butter; gradually add to the flour, beating with a wooden spoon until batter is smooth. Pour the batter into a well-greased 13x9x2-inch baking dish and arrange the sausages evenly in the batter. Bake until well risen and lightly browned, about 45 minutes to 1 hour. Serve immediately.

To serve, cut into 12 squares and arrange squares neatly on a heated platter. *Makes about 4 servings.*

Sauerkraut and Apple Salad

This salad, almost a relish, is excellent with pork. It is a favorite with grange ladies, past and present. Organized in the 1800s, during the aftermath of the Civil War, the grange, a farm organization, has always valued the participation of its women and children. It was "farm men" who first gave women the right to vote and to hold elected offices; and it was "farm women" who, using their abundant cooking skills, coaxed the general public into paying for a good country breakfast or supper, thereby providing money for grange needs and projects.

Even today, the old-time cooks come out of their kitchens in times of need. This year, the ladies of the Enterprise Grange—many of them in their seventies—opened a twenty-four-hour free kitchen for forest firefighters. Young men, after hours on the line trying to stop or contain the raging fires, passed up good camp food to drive forty miles or more to the grange hall for "home cookin'" and little personal touches like a "thank-you" or to have their coffee poured for them and even get a grandmotherly hug and kiss and a "God be with you!"

2 cups drained Prizewinning Sauerkraut in a Jar (page 144) or store-bought sauerkraut
2 cups peeled and chopped tart apples
1 cup chopped celery
½ cup coarsely shredded carrots
½ cup sugar
½ cup cider vinegar
2 tablespoons vegetable oil
¼ cup chopped green onions, including tops
2 sprigs fresh parsley, minced
½ teaspoon salt
2 to 3 large, attractive lettuce leaves

In a large bowl, combine all ingredients except the lettuce leaves, stirring until well blended. Cover and refrigerate at least 1 hour. Serve on a platter lined with the lettuce leaves. *Makes 8 to 10 servings.*

Country Lass with a Veil

This simple old-fashioned dessert—one of the many desserts which feature day-old or stale bread—is combined here with tender, spiced apples and whipped cream. It adds sparkle to any meal.

4 or 5 peeled and sliced apples (choose an apple that will hold its shape when cooked, a Grimes Golden, Jonathan, or late McIntosh, perhaps) sweetened with honey and flavored with cinnamon and nutmeg
½ cup water for steaming apples
About 6 tablespoons honey
½ teaspoon ground cinnamon
Dash freshly grated nutmeg
⅓ cup butter or margarine
2 to 2½ cups toasted bread cubes
Whipped cream (see page 61)
¼ cup sugar
1 teaspoon vanilla extract
As garnish, freshly grated nutmeg or 1 to 1½ teaspoons brilliant red berry jelly, optional

In a saucepan, steam the apple slices in water until tender, then sweeten with 3 tablespoons of the honey and the cinnamon and the nutmeg. Drain the apples, reserving the liquid; return liquid to pan. Add honey (start with 3 tablespoons but add more, if desired) and the butter to the steaming liquid and heat until the honey dissolves and butter melts. Place the bread cubes in a bowl; pour the liquid over the cubes and fold to blend. Cubes should be slightly moist. Spoon into 4 to 6 dessert dishes. Spoon the drained apples over the bread mixture.

Whip the cream until it is fluffy and begins to mound. Gradually add the sugar, beating after each addition. Add the vanilla and continue beating until cream is glossy, then spoon generous dollops of whipped cream over the apples. Dust tops with grated nutmeg, if you like, or decorate each serving with ¼ teaspoon brilliant red berry jelly. *Makes 4 to 6 servings.*

Happiness Cake

Cake recipes like this were popular with the ladies, who wrote them carefully on bits of paper and tucked them away in a safe place.

1 cup good thoughts	2 cups sacrifice
1 cup kind deeds	2 cups faults, well beaten
1 cup consideration for others	3 cups forgiveness

Mix thoroughly, add tears of joy, sorrow, and sympathy. Fold in 4 cups faith. Blend into daily life. Bake well with warmth of human kindness and serve with a smile any time. *Makes a lifetime of joy and contentment.*

THERE WAS A CHERRY TREE

There was a cherry-tree. It's bloomy snows
    Cool even now the fevered sight that knows
No more its airy visions of pure joy—
    As when you were a boy.

There was a cherry-tree. The Bluejay set
His blue against its white—O blue as jet
He seemed there then!—But *now*—Whoever knew
    He was so pale a blue!

There was a cherry-tree—Our child-eyes saw
The miracle:—Its pure white snows did thaw
Into a crimson fruitage, far too sweet
    But for a boy to eat.

There was a cherry-tree, give thanks and joy!—
There was a bloom of snow—There was a boy—
There was a Bluejay of the realest blue—
    And fruit for both of you.

                —*James Whitcomb Riley*

❧ ARBOR DAY TRIP TO THE WOODS

By the late 1800s, one could travel for miles over the western plains without seeing a tree. The land had been denuded by settlers who cut down trees to clear land for farming, to build their homes, or simply for firewood to keep themselves warm. Distressed by the situation, J. Sterling Morton, founder and publisher of the *Nebraska City Register*, conceived the idea for Arbor Day, a day set aside for planting trees. His dream was realized on April 10, 1872, when the first Arbor Day was celebrated in his home state. With this success came others, as people throughout the country began celebrating this special day.

Through the years, this holiday has become one observed especially by schoolchildren. Even in the small rural schools of the past, programs were prepared and shared with parents and others in the community to emphasize the importance of trees as a national resource and to encourage the planting of trees on Arbor Day.

As part of the program, the children usually had a tree-planting ceremony on the school grounds. Old folks who attended the ceremony reminded everyone that "to plant a tree is to have faith in the future." Little boys dressed as acorns and small girls as blossoms recited in sing-song voices lines such as "I think that I shall never see a poem lovely as a tree . . ." or read essays about "mighty oak trees" and "swaying poplars."

Older children may have recited, with appropriate gestures, William Cullen Bryant's lines . . .

> What plant we in this apple tree?
> Fruits that shall swell in sunny June,
> And redden in the August noon,
> And drop, when gentle airs come by,
> That fan the blue September sky,
> While children come, with cries of glee,
> And seek them where the fragrant grass
> Betrays their bed to those who pass,
> At the foot of the apple tree.

After the tree-planting ceremony and the program, families often took a picnic to the woods. Women and girls walked about enjoying the beauty of the wild flowers and the fresh green buds on the trees, or if there had been a rain, picking mushrooms. Men talked farming and smoked pipes and drank coffee out of huge tin cups, coffee which got thicker as it simmered over a dying campfire. Boys whooped like wild Indians and ran and leaped like colts over fallen logs and through the woods.

JANE WATSON HOPPING

Honey-Coated Chicken with Homemade Morel Mushroom Seasoning

In this recipe, morels, heady with the fragrance of the earth, comple-ment the rich taste of honey, which is reminiscent of a clover field in June.

The chicken can be parboiled ahead of time; cool slightly, cover, and refrigerate until ready to bake.

1 large 2½- to 3-pound fryer,
    cut up in 8 pieces
  Water to cover the chicken
  Salt
  Black pepper
2 tablespoons butter
2 tablespoons honey
2 tablespoons hot water
1½ to 2 cups dry, very fine
    breadcrumbs
  Homemade Morel Seasoning
    (recipe follows)

Place the chicken pieces in a large kettle. Cover them with water, and lightly salt the water; parboil covered until the chicken is barely cooked all the way through, 20 to 30 minutes, even longer, depending on the size of the bird. As the bird cooks the excess fat should be rendered out into the water. Transfer the chicken pieces to a large plate and lightly salt and pepper them on both sides. Reserve the broth for another recipe; it will keep well if frozen.

Preheat oven to 375°F. In a small saucepan, warm the butter and honey with the hot water until the butter melts and honey dissolves. Dip each piece of chicken into the honey mixture, then coat it with a thick layer of breadcrumbs; season with the mushroom seasoning by sprinkling both sides as desired. Lay the pieces on a greased cookie sheet; do not crowd. Bake until brown, about 25 to 30 minutes. *Makes 4 to 8 servings.*

Homemade Morel Mushroom Seasoning

Prepare seasoning well in advance for Honey-Coated Chicken, and reserve balance of seasoning for other dishes.

In a warm (250°F) oven on an ungreased cookie sheet, lay out *1 pound morels* and dry until they are brittle hard, about 1 hour, perhaps slightly longer. When completely dry and cool, reduce to a powder.

Mix in *1 ounce ground mace, 1 ounce black pepper*, and *2 ounces of homemade or store-bought celery flakes (powdered). Makes about ¾ to 1 cup.*

Sweet Wisconsin Beans with Ground Beef and Salt Pork

Grandpa White devised this bean recipe when he was "batching." After he married Grandma, his Sweet Wisconsin Beans became a ready-to-eat supper, simmered right along with the never-ending line of water boilers heated for the laundry.

1 pound dry kidney beans, soaked overnight and drained
4 ounces salt pork
1 large onion, chopped
2 peeled garlic cloves, chopped
1 pound lean ground beef
Water for cooking the beans
2 cups tomato paste
¼ cup, packed, brown sugar, light or dark
¼ cup molasses
2 tablespoons vinegar

1 tablespoon chili powder (Grandma's Spanish Pepper if possible)
1 teaspoon ground cinnamon
¼ teaspoon cumin seed
¼ teaspoon ground cloves
¼ teaspoon ground ginger
Pinch of dried oregano
Pinch of dried sweet basil leaves or fresh minced basil
Salt
Black pepper

Place the beans in a large bean pot or soup kettle and set aside. Brown the salt pork in a heavy skillet until the fat renders out, leaving the bits of salt pork smaller by half and lightly browned. With a slotted spoon, transfer the salt pork to the pot containing the beans. In the rendered salt pork fat, sauté the onions and garlic until golden, then transfer them with the slotted spoon to the pot containing the beans. Form the ground meat into 4 large patties and fry in the same hot fat until about three-fourths done. (Grandpa said he cooked the beef this way so juices were not lost and the meat did not shrink and get hard.) Using a slotted spoon, crumble the meat patties and add them and any fat left in the skillet to the bean pot. Add enough water to the bean pot to stand about 4 inches above the beans. Place pot over high heat and bring to a boil; reduce heat and simmer until beans are tender, about 30 to 45 minutes.

Meanwhile, in another kettle make a sauce of the tomato paste, sugar, molasses, vinegar, chili powder, cinnamon, cumin seed, cloves, ginger, oregano, and basil. Stir in the beans. Continue cooking until the beans are well flavored and the sauce is thick around them, about

1 hour more. (Grandpa White never added tomatoes to the beans until they were tender. He believed the tomatoes would "harden" the beans and ruin the texture of this dish.) Add salt and pepper to taste. Serve in generous-size soup bowls as a main dish, along with hearty bread. *Makes 6 servings.*

Walnut Sticks

This quick and easy-to-make cookie is just right for very young cooks.

¼ cup butter or margarine
1 cup, packed, light brown
   sugar
1 egg, slightly beaten
1 teaspoon maple flavoring

1 cup all-purpose flour
1 teaspoon baking powder
¼ teaspoon salt
½ cup chopped walnuts

Preheat oven to 350°F. In a large bowl, cream the butter, then add the sugar and cream the two together. Add the egg and maple flavoring and beat well. Into a separate bowl, sift together the flour, baking powder, and salt; add to the butter and sugar mixture, mixing well. Fold in the walnuts. Grease an 8x8-inch baking pan and dust it with flour. Spoon the dough into the pan and with moistened fingertips spread dough evenly over the pan bottom. Bake until firm and light brown on top, about 25 to 30 minutes. Remove from oven and let sit about 20 minutes, still in the pan. Remove from pan and turn right side up. Slice into sticks (bars). Transfer to a wire rack; when thoroughly cooled, store in an airtight container. *Makes about sixteen 1x4-inch sticks.*

"CHRIST AROSE"

Low in the grave He lay—
Jesus my Savior
Waiting the coming day—
Jesus my Lord!

—*Robert Lowry*
  (©*1916 Mary Runyon Lowry*)

🌿 EASTER

In the countryside of my childhood, churches were small, with congregations often numbering fewer than fifty. But even in the littlest town there were usually two churches; one Catholic, the other Prot-

estant. We were of the Protestant persuasion. Among all churchgoing folk of the community, perhaps the most deeply revered holiday was Easter.

Old-time Baptist and Methodist churches often began their celebrations of the resurrection with a sunrise service. Country people from miles around, even those who hardly ever attended church, would gather before dawn on a high hill. Our minister erected a cross on Hobb's Butte as a backdrop for his sermon, placing it so that the congregation faced into the rising sun.

Warmly dressed, but still shivering a little in the predawn air, we all relived the resurrection through the minister's words. Then, just as the sun began to break over the horizon, the choir (or one solitary voice) would sing:

> . . . Up from the grave He arose,
> With a mighty triumph o'er His foes;
> He arose a Victor from the dark domain,
> And He lives forever with His saints to reign,
> He arose! He arose! Hallelujah!
> Christ arose!

With the music still hanging in the air, and the last words of the minister lost in the moment of sunrise and stillness, men, women, and children stood enraptured, then quietly one would speak to another, saying things like "God bless you" or "Praise God, He lives!" Then we made our way down the hill in the soft morning light, to return home for a hearty sunrise breakfast.

In the old days, after breakfast, churchgoing families put on their new Easter clothes. Hustled by the father into wagons or a sputtering Model T, everyone was ready for some holiday fun: first church, then an Easter-egg hunt, then a big dinner at home with aunts, uncles, cousins, grandparents, and friends. Then all-afternoon baseball, hide-and-seek, three-legged races, and horseshoes.

Whether the church was Catholic or Protestant, the sanctuary was decorated in honor of the day. Folk brought in flowers in profusion: simple woodland blooms, and daffodils and lilies, if any were to be found. Should a sanctuary lack a permanent cross as part of its fixtures, one was specially made for Easter and decorated with flowers to remind worshipers of the religious meaning of the day.

Choirs across the countryside sang "He's the Lily of the Valley, the Bright and Morning Star,/He's the fairest of ten thousand to my soul . . . "

My husband, Raymond, recalls that he, like other children, sat quietly listening to the Easter service, knowing better than to wiggle or whisper on this special day. But underneath he was on pins and needles, anticipating the egg hunt on the church grounds after service. He, like most (if not all) others, had peeked at the piles of colored eggs and slyly observed men and big boys slipping outside while the last song was sung by the whole congregation.

When the hunt began, the little ones were bubbling with excitement. Raymond recalls running back and forth with boys his own age in a treasure-hunting frenzy. Older girls and boys took little toddlers by the hand, leading them about the churchyard, teaching them to look in tall twisted clumps of grass and then to carry the brilliantly colored eggs hidden there carefully back to their mothers for safekeeping. Most of these treasures would appear on the table later in the day in dishes featuring hard-cooked eggs. Children kept out only three or four favorites from the dozen or so they found.

On farms, holiday dinners have seldom been well planned sit-down meals. When Mother was young, families boasted seven to fifteen children. In my childhood, families were smaller, but Easter dinner still was a family reunion, one that might be eaten out of doors on trestle tables under a powder-blue spring sky. To the feast each woman brought the best of what she had: freshly butchered lamb, pork, or veal; corned beef or ham from the winter curing; freshly made relishes and "sweet and sours" from the previous year's garden; pickled eggs and deviled eggs, usually decorated with fresh young parsley and a dusting of paprika; and desserts of every kind, though cakes—most of which were light and airy egg-white or egg-yolk concoctions—carried the day.

Asparagus Salad with Cream Mayonnaise

Late in April, the asparagus harvest is in full swing, and country people who have asparagus beds, which produce spears for fifty years, are using this vegetable in many delicious dishes such as an asparagus omelet or this simple but elegant salad.

To Steam the Asparagus
Allow *⅓ to ½ pound fresh asparagus spears per serving.* Trim the spears by laying them on a cutting board, then with a sharp knife gradually work up the spear, from bottom to top, to a point where the blade easily cuts through the spear. Rinse spears, then tie each serving into a small bunch with strong kitchen twine; stand the bunches upright in a deep 2½-quart kettle and sprinkle them with salt if you wish. Pour enough boiling water in the kettle to have about 2 inches of liquid; cover and steam 12 to 15 minutes or until the spears are tender but still crisp. Remove from the kettle, plunge in cold water and refrigerate until well chilled.

To Prepare the Salad
Arrange each serving of chilled asparagus on a *lettuce leaf* and spoon as much *Cream Mayonnaise* (recipe follows) over all, as desired.

Cream Mayonnaise

4 hard-boiled egg yolks	2 cups heavy cream
2 teaspoons powdered sugar	1 teaspoon prepared mustard
1 teaspoon salt	1 teaspoon minced fresh parsley
1 teaspoon ground pepper (preferably white)	1 tablespoon plus 1 teaspoon lemon juice

In a bowl, using the back of a spoon, rub the egg yolks into a fine powder, then add the sugar, salt, and pepper and rub all together until blended and smooth. Whip with a metal whisk half of the cream until soft peaks form; set aside. Work the remaining unwhipped cream drop by drop into the egg-yolk mixture, then work in the mustard, next the reserved whipped cream a spoon or so at a time

JANE WATSON HOPPING

and parsley, and finally the lemon juice, a few drops at a time. Chill before using. *Makes 2½ cups or enough to dress 6 to 8 asparagus salads.*

Stuffed Veal Leg Roast with Sour Cream Sauce

Old-time farm cooks knew how to cook this light-pink colored meat. They learned from experience that it had to be handled carefully so as not to dry it out and toughen the fiber. Since veal is more moist than other meats and is very lean, recipes tended toward braising or roasting after coating with flour, or they would call for baking it in a pastry wrap. Basting with the sour cream sauce makes the surface of the meat a nice rich color.

1 (4- to 5-pound) leg of veal (have your butcher remove the bone)	Black pepper
	Finely chopped fresh thyme
	Sour Cream Sauce (recipe follows)
Stuffing (recipe follows)	
⅓ cup butter, melted	Sweet paprika for dusting
Salt	

Preheat oven to 350°F. Make the stuffing. Loosely pack the cavity where the bone was with the stuffing and tie with strong kitchen twine to close the opening. Rub the outside of the meat with the butter, then season the meat evenly with salt, pepper, and thyme to taste. Let stand about 2 hours, then place on a rack in a large, shallow roast pan and bake uncovered in the oven about an hour. Pour *1 cup* of the sour cream sauce over the meat, dust with sweet paprika, covering well. Continue basting about every 15 to 20 minutes until the internal temperature of the meat reads 175°F on a meat thermometer, if you like your meat well done. (*Note:* Because of the delicacy of the texture and flavor of veal, many people prefer it cooked rare to medium done; for rare, *total* baking time will be about 2 hours, for medium, *total* time will be about 2½ hours.) *Makes about 6 to 8 servings.*

Stuffing
A combination of rich, coarse grain breads—rye and a heavy bread like pumpernickel—and even corn bread give this dressing character. Leave the crusts on and tear into small pieces.

1 cup chopped onions
1 cup chopped celery
¼ cup butter, melted
3 cups dark variety bread, crusts on, torn into pieces
1 cup white bread cubes
1½ teaspoons salt
1 teaspoon marjoram, finely crushed
1 teaspoon oregano, finely crushed
1 teaspoon basil, finely crushed
½ teaspoon black pepper
About 1 to 1½ cups Homemade Chicken Broth (see page 11)

In a skillet, sauté the onions and celery in the butter until they are clear, then place mixture in a large bowl. Add the bread cubes, salt, marjoram, oregano, basil, pepper, and enough stock to moisten, stirring until the stuffing binds; mixture should be fairly moist. Turn onto a greased casserole dish and bake in oven during the last hour the veal is roasting. *Makes about 6 cups stuffing.*

Sour Cream Sauce
2 cups dairy sour cream
¼ cup all-purpose flour
1 teaspoon minced fresh thyme

Combine all ingredients in a bowl, mixing well to make a paste or sauce. *Makes 2 cups basting sauce.*

Rack of Young Lamb with Fresh Mint Sauce

1 rack (about 3 to 4 pounds) of young lamb (less than a year old), trimmed
2 tablespoons butter
Salt
Black pepper
Fresh Mint Sauce (recipe follows)

Preheat oven to 325°F. Rub the lamb with the butter, then season it with salt and pepper, place on a rack in a roasting pan and bake until internal temperature reads 175°F, allow 45 minutes per pound. Lamb may be roasted rare, medium, or well done, according to your preference. (Many old-timers thought meat was not good unless it was well done; Europeans, though, like lamb slightly rare.) Serve with mint sauce on the side. *Makes about 4 servings.*

Fresh Mint Sauce
Very finely chop *3 tablespoonfuls of mint leaves* and place in a bowl. Add *2 tablespoons powdered sugar*, mixing well. Stir in *6 tablespoons white wine vinegar*. Let stand at least ½ hour at room temperature before serving. *Makes about ½ cup sauce.*

Winter-Parsnip Puffs

On farms, parsnips are planted shortly after Christmas and grow slowly all through the year. In late summer or early fall the main crop is harvested, and some are left in the garden for the winter. Then in spring, when they can be dug, the roots are large, often six to ten inches in diameter. The flesh of these parsnips stays mild and sweet until the warm weather comes, which makes them grow woody and inedible. Winter parsnips are pan-fried or mashed as in this recipe.

2 eggs, beaten
1½ cups hot or cold unseasoned parsnips, which have been cooked and mashed like potatoes
⅓ cup grated colby cheese
3 tablespoons hot milk

1 tablespoon finely chopped or grated onions
1 teaspoon finely chopped fresh parsley
¼ teaspoon salt
¼ teaspoon sweet paprika
2 tablespoons butter, softened

Preheat oven to 350°F. Combine the eggs, parsnips, cheese, milk, onions, parsley, salt, and paprika, blending well. Mound the batter in 6 or 8 puffs on a greased pan about 1½ inches apart. Brush top with the butter. Bake until lightly browned and well heated through (puffs will spring back to the touch), about 20 minutes. *Makes about 6 to 8 puffs.*

Fancy Rolls

All old-time women prided themselves on being able to make light, good-flavored dinner rolls, which they served with sweet-cream butter.

1 package dry or granulated yeast
¼ cup milk, lukewarm (105°F to 115°F)
2 cups milk, scalded

6 cups all-purpose flour
½ cup butter
½ cup sugar
2 eggs, well beaten
1 teaspoon salt

In a bowl, dissolve the yeast in the lukewarm milk. In a separate bowl, make a batter of the scalded milk and *3 cups* of the flour; stir to blend. Add the yeast and beat well to develop gluten. Cover with a dry towel and set in a warm place to rise. The mixture (we call it a "sponge") is ready when bubbles rise to the surface and occasionally break, in about 45 minutes. Meanwhile, in a separate bowl, cream together the butter, sugar, eggs, and salt.

When the sponge is ready, stir it down and add the sugar-butter mixture to it. Work in the final 3 cups of flour to make a moderately stiff dough. Turn out onto a floured surface and knead until very smooth. Shape into a ball and put in a clean, greased bowl. Cover with the towel again and let rise again for about 1 hour, until it doubles in bulk. Form into balls about the size of a large egg. In a well-greased 13x9x2-inch pan, tuck the rolls close together and snug against the sides of the pan and let them rise again. Bake in a pre-heated 375°F oven until golden brown, about 25 to 30 minutes. Serve immediately. *Makes about 2 dozen rolls.*

❧❀MOTHER'S FAVORITE EASTER CAKES

On Easter, sometimes on birthdays, too, Mother made this duo of huge cakes. The giant angel food, frosted with whipped cream, was the party cake; the sponge cake an after-everyone's-gone bedtime treat.

Big Fluffy Angel Food Cake

This cake gets its lightness from air incorporated into egg whites through beating. For an excellent texture, use eggs warmed to room temperature, 75°F; scrubbed and scalded equipment, a deep bowl, and either an electric beater or a hand beater such as a whisk. Grease or even a little moisture can reduce the volume of stiffly beaten egg whites, which should be 2½ to 4 times their original volume.

To prevent accidents when separating eggs, break one at a time into two small bowls, then put yolks and whites into their respective containers, a cup for the yolks and a large- or medium-size bowl with deep sides for the whites. Stiffly beaten egg whites will be glossy and will stand in firm, soft, elastic peaks.

10 egg whites
½ teaspoon salt
1 teaspoon cream of tartar
1½ cups sugar
1¼ cups cake flour, sifted 3
    times
1 teaspoon vanilla extract
    Whipped cream, optional
    (recipe follows)

Preheat oven to 350°F. Beat the egg whites with the salt until frothy; add the cream of tartar and beat just until stiff but not dry. Fold in the sugar, 1 tablespoon at a time. Gradually fold in the flour, then the vanilla. Pour into a large 10-inch angel cake pan and bake until firm to the touch, about 1 to 1½ hours. Remove from the oven and immediately turn pan upside down on a wire rack, letting cake stay in pan until thoroughly cooled. Then carefully take the cake out of the pan and frost with whipped cream, if desired. *Makes 1 tube cake.*

Whipped Cream
1 cup heavy cream   1 teaspoon vanilla
¼ cup sugar

Beat the cream until it is well fluffed and begins to mound. Add the sugar a little at a time, beating after each addition. Add the vanilla and beat a few times to blend. Continue beating as necessary until the cream is glossy. Serve in dollops on desserts. For thicker cream, beat a little longer, but pay close attention to the texture you are developing, stopping the beater now and then to pull it out of the cream. When thick whipped cream is ready, the beater will come out leaving a pretty firm hole in the cream. Such cream is used as a frosting or in pastry cases. When overwhipped, the cream will taste greasy. *Makes 2⅓ cups.*

Giant Egg-Yolk Sponge Cake

1 dozen egg yolks
2 cups sugar
1 cup boiling water
3 cups cake flour
4 teaspoons baking powder
½ teaspoon salt
1 tablespoon lemon juice
    Lemon Sauce (recipe follows)

Preheat oven to 350°F. In a very large bowl, beat the egg yolks until light with a rotary beater or whisk. Gradually add the sugar, then the hot water, beating all the while. Into a separate bowl, sift together the flour, baking powder, and salt, and add to the egg-yolk mixture, beating thoroughly. Stir in the lemon juice. Turn into a 10-inch angel food cake pan and bake until it springs back when lightly pressed, about 1 hour. Remove from the oven and turn the cake, pan and all, upside down on a wire rack to cool thoroughly. Then gently remove cake from the pan and place on a large cake plate. Serve unfrosted or spoon lemon sauce over each slice as it is served. *Makes 1 tube cake.*

A Simple Old-fashioned Lemon Sauce

½ cup sugar
1 tablespoon cornstarch
⅛ teaspoon salt
1 cup boiling water

2 tablespoons butter
2 tablespoons lemon juice
Grated rind of 1 lemon
1 egg yolk, beaten

In the top of a double boiler, combine sugar, cornstarch, and salt. Pour boiling water slowly over dry ingredients, stirring constantly. Over medium heat cook 5 minutes; remove from heat; add butter, lemon juice, and grated lemon rind. Remove from heat, pour ½ cup of hot lemon sauce over the egg yolk; return egg mixture to the remaining sauce; cook 1 minute more. Remove from heat, turn into a bowl; cool. *Makes 1½ cups lemon sauce.*

Note: Recipe may be doubled if you need more sauce. Serve this delicious sauce over plain cakes, gingerbread, or puddings.

From MAY IN VERMONT

Jest take an apple tree that leans
    A little towards the sun,
And have it have a twisty trunk
    And limbs that spread and run;
And lots of branches there and here,
    And twigs in thick array,
And then jest have the time of year
    Along around in May:

Such lovely loads of blessed bloom!
    That pink amongst the white!
A chandelier of trees like that
    Would light the world at night;

'Twould dim the silver on the moon
　　And make the stars look gray—
I'd move to Europe pretty soon
　　If 'twan't, by George! for May.

Don't bring me 'round no earthen pots
　　Or dooryard dabs of bloom,
I want an apple tree that's out
　　To give my eyesight room;
No meaching sweet pea plants for me,
　　With nothing much to say,
I want a whole-souled apple tree
　　Along around in May.

　　　　　　　　—*Daniel L. Cady*

MAY

Fresh Herbs and Candied Violets

On farms, in meadows, and throughout the woodlands, May is one of the most beautiful months of the year. The intense heat of summer has not yet begun; everywhere trees and grass are lush and green. Wild flowers such as shooting stars, yellow violets, pinks and their domesticated counterparts, blue, yellow, and white violets, jack-in-the-pulpits, anemones, hepaticas, forsythias, and dogwoods—are in full bloom.

The glorious early days of May are lit with sunshine and warmth, and yet temperatures stay mild enough to be invigorating. May Day baskets of flowers, cookies, and candies are in order!

MAY DAY BASKETS

On the eve of May Day—the first of May—children picked wild flowers. Then on kitchen tables all throughout the countryside, they made baskets out of bits of paper and filled them with the flowers, and sometimes cookies and candies. Secretly that night they hung them on door handles for old folks, widows, loved aunts, bachelors, and teachers to find the next morning.

Mrs. Fern Mecham recalls those days and an early morning May Day basket excursion:

While it was the custom to take flower-filled May Day baskets out late in the evening before the holiday, our mother, who put cookies and candy in with the flowers, sent us out on the morning of May first. She thought cats or varmints might get into the food in the baskets if they were left out all night. So early in the morning, we all went to gather fresh flowers—primroses, shooting stars, and lilacs.

When the baskets were filled and a little bit of ribbon was tied to the handles, my brothers and sisters and I took the baskets to folks who lived within a mile or so of our farm. My older brother and I usually took one to Mrs. Wilton who lived in back of our place.

She was about eighty years old and lived alone. To get to her house we ran through the dewy-wet field, breathlessly laying out our strategy for secretly putting the basket on her door knob. It really was only a matter of running up on the porch, knocking loudly on the door and then scurrying off the porch to hide in the lilac bushes, but to us then, it was a grand scheme.

As she came to the door, we were beside ourselves. It was as though she knew how to delight us. We knew that she could not see very well, but now I think she exaggerated her fumbling for the basket, to add suspense to the occasion. When she had it in her hand, she called out to us in a squeaky old voice, "I know you children is out there!" and she would peer right at us while we held our breath. She'd wait a minute, than start looking for the cookies in the basket—her favorite was Mother's Apple Butter Drops. The minute she found them, she would eat one, and then another—just like my little brother Roy, at home, who could not leave the cookies alone.

Years have passed, but I have never forgotten those early morning runs, and neither has my brother. He is quite old now and visity, not like he was as a boy—large for his age and quiet. It's strange, but all these years he has never admitted how much he really loved to take May baskets to Mrs. Wilton, not until last year.

Apple-Butter Drops

When jams, jellies, and butters are left over from one season to the next, farm women put them in cakes or cookies so as not to waste the sugar that had been used to make them.

¼ cup butter or margarine
½ cup, packed, light brown
  sugar
1 egg, beaten
½ cup spiced apple butter
1 cup whole-wheat flour
½ teaspoon baking soda

½ teaspoon baking powder
½ teaspoon salt
2 tablespoons heavy cream
1½ cups rolled oats
½ cup chopped walnuts
½ cup seedless raisins, finely
  chopped

Preheat oven to 350°F. In a large bowl, cream the butter and sugar until light. Add the egg and apple butter, blending until smooth. In a separate bowl, sift together the flour, baking soda, baking powder, and salt; add this and the cream to the sugar mixture, stirring well. Stir in the oats, walnuts, and raisins. Drop the batter by teaspoonfuls onto a greased cookie sheet about an inch apart. Bake 10 to 12 minutes or until lightly browned . Immediately remove drops from cookie sheet and cool on a wire rack. Store in an airtight container. *Makes 2½ to 3 dozen drops.*

Dried-Fig-Filled Cookies

Mother, like other women of her day, was a good provider. She dried peaches, pears, figs, and any other fruit she could obtain for winter use in pies, cakes, or in cookies like these. At my house, our all-time favorite is a date-filled version.

1 cup butter or margarine
1 cup, packed, light brown
  sugar
2 eggs, slightly beaten
  About 2¾ cups whole-wheat
  flour

1 teaspoon salt
½ teaspoon baking soda
  Dried-Fig Filling (recipe
  follows)

In a large bowl, blend together the butter, sugar, and eggs until light. Stir in the flour, salt, and soda. Shape the dough into 2 rolls about 1½ to 2 inches in diameter and about 6 to 8 inches long. Wrap in heavy waxed paper (or aluminum foil) and refrigerate for at least 3 hours.

Meanwhile, prepare the filling and let it cool, then chill.

To bake, preheat oven to 350°F. Unwrap each roll of dough and cut it in half lengthwise; lay it out on a floured surface and roll with a floured rolling pin into a rectangle, about 8 inches long, 3 inches wide, and ¼ inch thick. Spoon half of the filling down one side of the dough; spread the filling over that half of the dough to within ½ inch of the edge. Then, with a spatula, lift the other half of the dough over the filling. Seal the edges by pressing lightly together, forming a ½-inch border. Using a ruler to guide you, trim the sealed edge with a sharp knife to give the rectangle a nice even edge and cut crosswise into 2-inch-long bars. Place ½ inch apart on an ungreased baking sheet. Bake until golden brown on the bottom and light brown on top, about 10 to 12 minutes. Remove from oven and transfer to wire rack. Cool completely; store in an airtight container. *Makes about 3 dozen cookies.*

Dried-Fig Filling

1½ cups finely chopped dried figs (or dried dates)

¾ cup, packed, light brown sugar

¾ cup water

Dash of ground cinnamon

Combine all the ingredients in a medium-size saucepan and bring to a boil, stirring constantly. Reduce heat to medium and cook until syrup begins to thicken slightly on a spoon, about 1 to 2 minutes. Remove from heat and set aside; cool thoroughly before using. *Makes about 2½ cups filling.*

Old-fashioned Sea-foam Candy

Old-time cooks knew that brown sugar brought enough acid to their candy making so that a recipe such as this could be called "never-fail candy."

About 1 tablespoon cornstarch to prepare pan

1 pound box of light or dark brown sugar

½ cup water

2 egg whites

2 cups finely chopped pecans or salted peanuts

A drop or 2 vanilla extract

Lightly grease an 8x8x2-inch cake pan, then dust with about 1 table-spoonful cornstarch; set aside. Grease the sides of a large saucepan; in the pan combine the sugar and water, stirring to dissolve the sugar. Cook over medium heat to a "soft" crack stage (270°F–290°F), a candy thermometer will read 264°F. Meanwhile whip the egg whites until stiff peaks form. When the syrup is ready, pour it in a thin stream over the beaten egg whites, whipping all the while. Let cool until thick, then fold in *1½ cups* of the pecans. Pour into the prepared pan and garnish with the remaining *½ cup* pecans. Let sit overnight in a cool spot; don't refrigerate.

The following morning, cut the candy into 1-inch squares, remove from pan, and place pieces (not touching) on waxed paper or aluminum foil to let dry for 2 or 3 hours until firm and dry to the touch. Then layer in a can or box with a tight lid, placing each layer on a shim of waxed paper. *Makes approximately 1 pound.*

🌿 QUEEN OF MAY

To celebrate the arrival of May, old-time people often set up a May-pole decorated with streamers of ribbon or brightly colored cloth on local school grounds. Boys and girls gathered blossoms from the woods and fields to trim the pole. Girls wore their prettiest dresses for the May Day festivities, each girl hoping to be chosen queen of May. After the choice was made, the queen, in a little dimity or lawn dress, danced lightly with her subjects around the Maypole, weaving the streamers round and round in a brilliant pattern.

Light, beautiful dishes, such as cakes with marshmallow frosting and candied-violet confections adorned May Day tables.

Candied Violets

These delicate edible confections can be used as decorations on cakes or simply put out for nibblers on a glass candy plate. Both scent and flavor are exotic.

Whip *1 egg white* until it is frothy but does not stand in peaks. Gather perfect *violets and their leaves;* wash them gently and quickly in cold water and drip dry. When dry, dip each violet or leaf in the egg white and roll it quickly in *granulated sugar* to coat evenly, taking care not to get the sugar on too thick. Lay out on waxed papers to dry, well separated. In several hours or a day the blossoms will be quite crisp and can keep for several months without losing fragrance or flavor. Store in an airtight tin, layered between waxed paper. *Makes dozens.*

Hazelnut Cake with Honey Marshmallow Frosting

On many farm properties, hazelnuts grew wild along the creek banks. The trick was to beat the squirrels to them as they ripened. Assuming you brought home the fruits of the victor, you had the makings of a delicious cake.

Waxed paper, to prepare pan
1½ cups butter
2 cups sugar
6 eggs
1 cup milk
1 teaspoon lemon extract
3½ cups all-pupose flour, sifted
3 cups dry roasted, toasted, and chopped hazelnuts, plus additional finely chopped hazelnuts to garnish top of cake
½ teaspoon cream of tartar
¼ teaspoon salt
Honey Marshmallow Frosting (recipe follows)

Preheat oven to 275°F. Grease a 10-inch tube pan. Set the pan on a piece of waxed paper; draw a liner to fit the bottom; with scissors cut the paper to fit the pan; then fold the circle into quarters and with the scissors snip off the point to make an inner circle large enough to fit over the center cone of the pan. Slip the doughnut-shaped liner into the pan. Press down to line the pan bottom with waxed paper and grease again.

In a large bowl, cream the butter, then gradually beat in the sugar. Separate the eggs one at a time, and as you do so, mix each egg yolk into the butter mixture, beating after each addition until light. (Reserve the egg whites.) In a small bowl, combine the milk and lemon extract and alternately add it and the flour to the butter mixture. Fold in the hazelnuts. In a separate bowl, beat the egg whites with the cream of tartar and salt until stiff but not dry, then gently fold the egg whites into the batter. Spoon batter into the prepared pan and bake until the cake tests done, about 2 hours. (To test doneness, insert a toothpick in the cake; if it comes out clean with no batter clinging to it, the cake is done.) Remove from oven and let cake cool in the pan (set on a wire rack) for 30 minutes. Then remove cake from pan and finish cooling it on the rack or on a cake plate. When thoroughly cool, frost top and sides. Garnish with the reserved finely chopped hazelnuts. *Makes 1 tube cake.*

Honey Marshmallow Frosting

1 cup honey   2 egg whites

In a medium-size saucepan, boil the honey over medium high heat for about 10 minutes, stirring occasionally. Remove from heat and cool. Meanwhile, beat the egg whites until they form stiff peaks. Add the honey in a thin stream to the egg whites, beating the mixture constantly until it is thick enough to spread. Let frosting cool to room temperature before icing the cake. *Makes enough frosting for a large tube cake.* Recipe may be halved if it is to be used on top of the cake and partially down the sides.

Rhubarb Crunch

We love our old "pie plants," which yield so abundantly before fruits are ready for harvest. The stalks can be made into pies, puddings, jelly, wine, or this time-honored rhubarb crunch dessert.

1 cup sugar   4 cups chopped rhubarb, peel
3 tablespoons all-purpose flour   first if stalks are tough

Oatmeal Topping
½ cup, packed, light brown   ½ cup butter or margarine
    sugar   ⅓ cup all-purpose flour
½ cup rolled oats

Preheat oven to 350°F. In a small bowl, combine the sugar and flour, mixing well. Place the rhubarb in a large bowl, and add sugar and flour mixture, tossing until all pieces are coated. Place in a 9x9-inch casserole; set aside.

In a small bowl, combine all the topping ingredients, stirring until mixture is crumbly. Sprinkle topping evenly over the rhubarb mixture. Bake for 45 minutes. When done, rhubarb is tender, juices are thick and bubbling, and topping is lightly browned and crusty. *Makes 6 to 8 dessert servings.*

OLD-FASHIONED ROSES

They ain't no style about 'em,
  And they're sorto' pale and faded,
Yit the doorway here, without 'em,
  Would be lonesomer, and shaded
    With a good 'eal blacker shadder
      Than the morning-glories makes,
    And the sunshine would look sadder
      Fer their good old-fashion' sakes.

I like 'em 'cause they kindo'—
  Sorto' *make* a feller like 'em!
And I tell you, when I find a
  Bunch out whur the sun kin strike 'em,

It allus sets me thinkin'
  O' the ones 'at used to grow
And peek in thro' the chinkin'
  O' the cabin, don't you know!

And then I think o' mother,
  And how she ust to love 'em—
When they wuzn't any other,
  'Less she found 'em up above 'em!
    And her eyes, afore she shut 'em,
      Whispered with a smile and said
    We must pick a bunch and putt 'em
      In her hand when she wuz dead.

But, as I wuz a-sayin',
  They ain't no style about 'em
Very gaudy er displayin',
  But I wouldn't be without 'em,—
    'Cause I'm happier in these posies,
      And the hollyhawks and sich,
    Than the hummin'-bird 'at noses
      In the roses of the rich.

—James Whitcomb Riley

🌿 FROM ALL ABOUT THE FARM

From all around the farm, from secret dark corners of the plant and animal kingdoms and from the pots and buckets of pungent plants that cluster about our kitchen door, come teas, herbs, cosmetics, and other aromatic products. Even the delicate clover blossom gives up its light fragrance.

RED CLOVER BLOSSOM TEA

This popular tea of the 1800s is simple to prepare and inexpensive. For each cup of tea, you will need a *generous handful of freshly picked red clover blossoms* and *1 cup of boiling water*. To make tea, wash the blossoms quickly in a small amount of cold water. Put in a small kettle and add the hot water. Simmer for about 3 minutes, remove from the stove, cover, and steep 1 minute. Strain into a cup and serve immediately. For stronger tea, add other delicately flavored herbs, such as lemon mint or rose geranium, and honey, which both sweetens the tea and flavors it. *Makes 1 cup tea.*

HERBAL SALT SUBSTITUTE

About the farm there are many plants that when dried and pulverized yield enough salt to make a flavorful, natural salt substitute.

One natural salt substitute is *3 ounces of dried sweet basil, 2 ounces each of dried savory, celery seed, and sage, 1 ounce each of thyme and marjoram.* Add *½ ounce powdered sassafras (gumbo filé)* leaves. Then powder all herbs until fine. Sprinkle lightly on food using less than you would of salt. *Makes about 12 ounces.*

Other common sources of natural salt are beet, carrot, and radish leaves, all of which may be combined with herbs and powdered sassafras leaves.

CREAM SKIN SOFTENER

To keep the skin soft, women washed their faces in milk or smoothed into the skin *1 tablespoon of thick cold cow's cream* thirty minutes before bathing. The cream washed off in the bath without the use of soap, leaving the skin smooth and soft.

HOME-EXTRACTED FLORAL OILS

To remove oil from flowers, hang leafy herbs or blossoms upside down in a clear wine bottle. Cork the bottle and hang it right side up in the sun so that the heat will break the oil cells within the plant matter, releasing what's called "essential oil." Pour off the few drops of essential oil that collect in the bottom of the bottle. Lavender and roses both give up their oil this way. Use in bath or pat on wrist, throat, or behind the ear.

LEMON AND MINT SACHET BAGS

Pick a large bouquet of mint and dry enough to yield *2 cups dried leaves.* Use only the leaves. Grind or mince the peels of *about 4 lemons.* Place on a cookie sheet and dry in the oven at 250°F. Remove from oven and add several drops of *lemon oil* (purchased at a drugstore or health food store). Put in a jar and let stand for several days to let fragrances marry.

Make lime-green satin bags or light-yellow velvet bags about 3 inches square or 3 x 4-inch rectangles, if you wish, leaving one side open. Fill bags loosely and hand-stitch opening closed. Decorate with lace and mint-green velvet ribbon. This scent will last for a long while and is a nice small Christmas or spring gift. *Makes about 2 sachet bags.*

ROSARY BEADS

These beads were commonly made for rosaries but sometimes women strung them in intricate patterns to make curtains. They could even be washed, and after washing the fragrance of the curtains permeated the whole house.

Grind *2 gallons fresh rose petals* in a food grinder or food processor until a smooth dough is formed. Before the last 2 or 3 grindings, knead *several teaspoons of rose oil*, which contains some perfume, into the petal dough. So that the beads are equal in size, roll out the dough ¼ inch thick. Cut dough into circles with a standard sewing thimble and roll each circle in the palm of the hand to form a bead. String on a hat pin (or florist wire) which makes a hole in the bead, and set aside to dry for several days. When completely dried the beads will decrease one third in size. When thoroughly dry, remove beads from the hat pin and polish them by placing them in *olive oil or rose oil, preferred,* to cover halfway; soak them for a couple of hours, rolling them about occasionally to soak all sides. Wipe beads with a clean cloth, then string on dental floss, putting 3 small ceramic or steel beads between each rose bead. *Makes about 1½ to 2½ cups flower dough.*

Note: Ceramic and steel beads can be purchased in hobby shops.

✤ MOTHER'S DAY

Although several attempts were made around the turn of the century to establish a national Mother's Day (first in 1872 by Julia Ward Howe, author of the "Battle Hymn of the Republic," and again in 1904 by Franklin E. Hering of South Bend, Indiana), it was not until 1907 that Anna Jarvis's lifelong effort to have a day set aside to honor mothers was rewarded.

Growing up as she did—during a time when motherhood was a sacred calling, and cared for by a devoted mother whose influence Anna felt all her life—this sensitive woman was determined to see that mothers were given public and private credit, respect, and a show of love for the difficult tasks they performed.

It was she who selected the second Sunday of May and who originated the custom of wearing a carnation to honor mothers living and dead. Anna Jarvis urged citizens throughout the nation to honor "the best mother that ever lived"—their own.

On farms and homesteads across the nation, customs have grown up around this lovely day in May. One of the nicest is a family trip to a nearby marsh to watch baby goslings and duckings paddle around before they are big enough to fly away. In the old days the trip could be quite an experience. One could hardly drive two minutes on roads —hardly more than ruts—that connected the marsh with dry land without having to stop to let mother and baby waterfowl pass.

To top off the delightful trip to the marsh, families often picnicked in the shade of some giant tree. Girls, by turns giggling and serious, worked secretly before the holiday, baking ham and treats and desserts. Jars of pickles or bits of dried fruit left in the tins would be snatched out of the pantry at the last minute. Usually a thoughtful father would take his wife to town to visit a friend for the day, or, if the children were small, the mother would simply sit outside in the sunshine and answer questions about cooking in such a way that she did not appear to guess what was going on in her kitchen.

Mock Coleslaw with Cream Dressing

Made of large spring turnips, this mild-flavored salad is often be-lieved to be coleslaw (made of cabbage) with a special or "secret" seasoning.

2 cups peeled and shredded
   mild-flavored turnips
1 cup peeled and finely chopped
   celeriac (root celery)
1 cup peeled and chopped
   apples (Red Delicious are
   very good)

2 tablespoons minced onions
¼ cup Cream Dressing (recipe
   follows) or mayonnaise
Salt
Black pepper
Celery seed

In a large bowl, combine the turnips, celeriac, apples, and onions. Stir in the dressing, then season with the salt, pepper, and celery seed to taste. Chill well before serving. *Makes about 4 cups.*

Cream Dressing

½ cup heavy cream
2 tablespoons cider vinegar
   About 2 tablespoons sugar

Salt, optional
Black pepper, optional

Stir together the cream and vinegar in a small bowl. Add the sugar (start with 2 tablespoons, taste, then add more if you like). Season with salt and pepper, if desired. *Makes about ½ cup dressing.*

Mother's Rusk

These rolls are light and delicate in flavor. Excellent when hot, hard to beat when cold, they are very easy to make.

2 cups milk
½ cup butter
1 package dry or granulated
   yeast
½ cup lukewarm water (105°F
   to 115°F)

2 eggs, beaten until very light
½ cup sugar
Salt
About 6 cups all-purpose
   flour, plus flour for kneading

Scald milk; cool to lukewarm and add butter. Soften yeast in luke-warm water. Beat eggs, separately, then together with sugar and salt; stir in the milk-butter mixture, yeast, and about 4 cups flour to make a pancakelike batter. Set in a warm place and let rise until light in texture and foamy. Add the remaining flour to form a soft dough that is stiff enough to knead; do not add too much flour. Cover and let rise until double in bulk. Then with melted butter on fingers, make smooth balls a little larger than an egg and place just touching each other in well-greased 15x11x2-inch pans. When very light and airy, bake in preheated oven (350°F) until golden brown, about 25 to 30 minutes. Serve piping hot. *Makes about 2 dozen rusks.*

Angel Kisses

We whimsically call these cookies "angel kisses" because they are so pure in color, airy, and sweet.

3 egg whites	6 tablespoons all-purpose flour
1 cup sugar	1 teaspoon vanilla extract
1 cup shredded unsweetened coconut	¼ teaspoon salt

Preheat oven to 325°F. Beat the egg whites into soft mounds, gradually add the sugar and continue beating until stiff peaks are formed. Add the coconut, flour, vanilla, and salt; fold in until well blended. Drop the batter by teaspoonfuls onto a greased cookie sheet about 1 inch apart, since cookies spread. Bake 10 to 12 minutes but do not brown. Let cool on the cookie sheet. (The cooled kisses will be chewy but firm.) *Makes 3 dozen kisses.*

Honey Raisin Bread Pudding

Honey as a sweetener has always been considered a special treat, because it was costly and none too available, except on farms where bees were kept. In the old days women often tended the bees, and even took charge of robbing the hive to extract the honey.

¾ cup honey	5 eggs
2 tablespoons butter	1 tablespoon vanilla extract
2 tablespoons water	¼ teaspoon salt
4 cups white bread cubes, crusts left on (Either fresh or stale bread works nicely.)	Dusting of freshly grated nutmeg
½ cup golden raisins	Whipped cream, optional (page 61)
1 quart milk	

Preheat oven to 350°F. Grease a large baking pan (use a 12x8x2-inch or 11x9x2-inch pan) and set aside. In a medium-size skillet, combine ½ *cup* of the honey with the butter and water; heat until honey is dissolved; add the bread cubes and toss to coat the bread, then turn into the prepared baking pan. Sprinkle the raisins over the top, and stir enough to blend; set aside.

In a large bowl, combine the milk, eggs, vanilla, salt, and the *remaining ¼ cup* honey; whip with a metal whisk until well blended. Pour over the bread mixture and dust top with the nutmeg. Bake until a knife inserted into the center of the pudding comes out clean, about 45 minutes to 1 hour. Serve as is or with whipped cream. *Makes 6 to 8 servings.*

Death comes alike to ev'ry man
  That ever was borned on earth;
Then let us do the best we can
  To live fer all life's wurth.

Ef storms and tempusts dred to see
  Makes black the heavens ore,
They done the same in Galilee
  Two thousand years before.

But after all, the golden sun
  Poured out its floods on them
That watched and waited fer the One
  Then borned in Bethlyham.

Also, the star of Holy Writ
  Made noonday of the night,
Whilse other stars that looked at it
  Was envious with delight.

The sages then in wurship bowed,
  From ev'ry clime so fare;
O, sinner, think of that glad crowd
  That congergated thare!

—James Whitcomb Riley

⚜ DECORATION DAY

Decoration Day (Memorial Day) originated during the Civil War, when Southern women gathered large bouquets of spring flowers and scattered them over the graves of soldiers, honoring the Northern dead alongside their own.

In 1868, General John A. Logan named May 30 as a special day for honoring Union soldiers who had died in battle. He was commander in chief of the Grand Army of the Republic, an organization made up of veterans who fought for the Union in the War Between the States. This organization had charge of Memorial Day celebrations in the North for many years. In the South other days were set aside for honoring Confederate soldiers.

On Decoration Day it is traditional to have military parades and special programs, to read Lincoln's Gettysburg Address, and to put flowers and flags on graves.

In rural areas, country folk often took flowers to the cemeteries on Memorial Day eve. Since there were no caretakers for the graves, family members brought along small tools to weed the plots and vases of flowers for decoration. After tidying and sprucing up, they returned home to share some cake and coffee and talk of bygone days and ancestors, loved but not forgotten.

General Robert E. Lee Cake with Lemon Filling and Lemon-Orange Frosting

Memories of the Civil War ran fresh for many years after the conflict. Aside from the family tragedies that left widows and orphans, there was terrible destruction of the farm economy. Various forces tried to mend and heal these rifts, one being the national grange.

This recipe may be halved for smaller families. The cake is like a pound cake in texture, as it depends entirely on eggs for leavening.

Juice from 1 to 1½ lemons	10 eggs, separated
(¼ cup)	2 cups all-purpose flour
Grated rind of 1 lemon	1 teaspoon salt
2¼ cups sugar	

Preheat oven to 350°F. In a medium-size bowl, add the lemon juice and rind and *1 cup* of the sugar to the egg yolks; beat until thick and lemon-colored. Sift *1 cup* of the flour plus the salt over the mixture and fold it in; sift and fold in the *remaining 1 cup* flour. In a separate bowl, beat the egg whites until foamy; gradually add the *remaining 1¼ cups* sugar, beating to form fairly stiff peaks. Spread the egg-yolk mixture over the egg-white mixture and gently fold together. Bake in three greased and very lightly floured 9-inch layer pans until light brown, about 30 to 35 minutes (test with a toothpick). Cool in pans for about 5 minutes, then turn onto a wire rack. *Makes one 3-layer cake.*

Note: Prepare Lemon Filling while cake is baking; set it aside to cool, then refrigerate to chill. Do not make frosting until both cake and filling are completely cooled; then make frosting and assemble cake.

To assemble the cake: Spread filling between layers and frost top of cake. (The filling is light and may soak into the cake.) Or, if you wish, cut each layer in half horizontally, creating 6 thin layers. Place one layer, cut side up, on a cake plate; with a spatula, spread slightly more than ⅓ cup of the filling over the top. Put another layer on top, spread with filling, and cover with the next layer. Continue adding filling and layers until only 1 top layer remains. Put it in place and frost the top of the cake. (Do not put filling over the final layer.)

Lemon Filling

6 tablespoons sweet butter, cut into bits
¾ cup sugar
½ cup fresh lemon juice, strained
¼ cup cold water
6 egg yolks
2 teaspoons fresh lemon peel, finely grated

In the top of a double boiler, combine the butter, sugar, lemon juice, water, and egg yolks. Cook over boiling water, stirring constantly until the mixture thickens enough to heavily coat the back of a spoon. Do not let the filling boil or the yolks will curdle. Remove from heat; immediately spoon filling into a small bowl and stir in the grated lemon peel. Cool to room temperature, then chill. *Makes about 1 cup.*

Lemon-Orange Frosting

4 tablespoons butter, softened to room temperature
3½ cups (1 pound box) confectioner's sugar
2 tablespoons fresh lemon juice, strained
¼ cup fresh orange juice, strained
1 egg yolk
2 teaspoons fresh lemon peel, finely grated
3 tablespoons fresh orange peel, finely grated

In a large bowl, cream softened butter, beating with a spoon until it is light and fluffy. Alternately, beginning with 1 cup of the confectioner's sugar, blend in the sugar and combined lemon and orange juice, beating well after each addition. Last, beat in the egg yolk, grated lemon, and orange peel. *Makes about 2 cups.*

Federal Loaf

Lightly sweetened and flavored bread was often served with coffee or tea in place of cake. This old recipe is simple to make and delicious.

1 package dry or granulated yeast
1 cup warm water
1 cup milk
¼ cup sugar
¼ cup butter, melted
1 teaspoon salt
4 egg yolks, beaten
1 teaspoon grated lemon rind
1 teaspoon grated orange rind
6 cups all-purpose flour, plus additional flour for kneading
4 egg whites
Butter

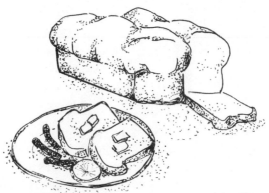

Preheat oven to 400°F. Set the yeast to proof in the warm water. Meanwhile, in a small saucepan, scald the milk; remove from heat; add the sugar, buttter, and salt and stir until butter melts and sugar dissolves. Let mixture cool to lukewarm, then pour it into a large bowl. Add the yeast, egg yolks, lemon rind, and orange rind. Stir in 4 cups of flour to make a batter, cover and let rise until light and bubbly. Then add remaining 2 cups of flour to make a soft dough. In a separate bowl, whip the egg whites until stiff but not dry and fold into the dough. Spoon the dough into 2 greased and floured 9x5-inch loaf pans. Cover with a dry towel and let rise in a warm place for 45 minutes to 1 hour. Bake until light brown, about 35 to 45 minutes. Let cool 10 minutes, remove from pan, and turn top side up. Serve at room temperature thinly sliced, with butter. *Makes 2 loaves.*

Old Folks' Cookies

1 cup sugar
½ cup butter
    Rind from 1 lemon, grated
2 eggs
½ teaspoon salt
½ teaspoon freshly grated
      nutmeg
½ cup milk
    Juice from 1 lemon
    About 3 to 4 cups all-purpose
      flour
1 tablespoon baking powder
1 teaspoon baking soda

Preheat oven to 375°F. In a large bowl, cream the sugar and butter together. Add the lemon rind, eggs, salt, and nutmeg and beat well. Stir in the milk and lemon juice. Into a separate bowl, sift together the flour, baking powder, and baking soda. Gradually add to the sugar-butter mixture and stir to form a soft dough (start with 3 cups flour and add more if needed). Turn onto a floured surface and roll dough ½ inch thick. Cut out with a large-size cookie cutter and place on a lightly greased cookie sheet about 1 inch apart. Bake until lightly browned, about 10 minutes. When cool store in an airtight container. *Makes 2½ to 3 dozen cookies.*

Ginger Cake

This old-fashioned cake was a favorite; it was served with tea and jam.

1 cup light molasses	1 large egg
1 teaspoon baking soda	4 cups all-purpose flour
¾ cup butter or margarine	2 teaspoons ground ginger
1 cup buttermilk	1 teaspoon baking powder
1 cup, packed, dark brown sugar	½ teaspoon salt

Preheat oven to 300°F. Put the molasses in a large bowl and place bowl over a large saucepan of boiling water until molasses is warm. Remove from heat. Add the baking soda and beat until mixture foams. Stir in the butter, buttermilk, sugar, and egg. Into a separate bowl, sift together the flour, ginger, baking powder, and salt. Stir dry ingredients into the wet ingredients. Spoon into 1 large, 13x9x2-inch loaf pan or into two 9x5-inch bread pans. Bake until a toothpick inserted comes out clean, about 35 to 45 minutes. Cool large loaf cake in pan; cool those in bread pans 10 minutes, then turn out on rack to finish cooling. Serve unfrosted hot or cold. *Makes 1 large loaf cake or 2 smaller cakes.*

A BOY'S SONG

Where the pools are bright and deep,
Where the gray trout lies asleep,
Up the river and o'er the lea,
That's the way for Billy and me.

Where the blackbird sings the latest,
Where the hawthorn blooms the sweetest,
Where the nestlings chirp and flee,
That's the way for Billy and me.

Where the mowers mow the cleanest,
Where the hay lies thick and greenest,
There to trace the homeward bee,
That's the way for Billy and me.

Where the hazel bank is steepest,
Where the shadow falls the deepest,
Where the clustering nuts fall free,
That's the way for Billy and me.

Why the boys should drive away
Little sweet maidens from the play,
Or love to barter and fight so well,
That's the thing I never could tell.

But this I know, I love to play
Through the meadow, among the hay;
Up the water and o'er the lea,
That's the way for Billy and me.

—*James Hogg*

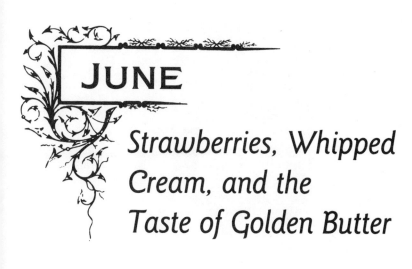

JUNE

Strawberries, Whipped Cream, and the Taste of Golden Butter

In the country, the June sun draws spring to a close and sets summer aglow. With the heat, blossoms pop out, turning hedgerows into a riot of color, and wild single-petaled pink roses splash color throughout the fields and over the hillsides. Along the road, apple seedlings promise a small apple of delicious flavor. Summer vegetables are up and growing strong for fall harvest; meanwhile spring beets, turnips, and sweet leaf lettuce are ready to be picked.

Rhubarb, strawberries, and cherries are in season and jam making begins in earnest. Evening meals and Sunday dinners are brightened by the addition of colorful fruit desserts.

Fresh meat is becoming plentiful, offering a relief from winter stores. Farm cooks, faced with an abundance of spring poultry, draw on all of their skills—frying, broiling, fricasseeing, simmering, and baking—to create endless chicken delicacies. From sparkling streams and clear lakes men bring home creels of freshly caught trout for similar treatments.

There is a quiet joy in the land as the age-old promise of renewal is fulfilled—summer is near!

THE BROOK SONG

Little brook, sing to me:
Sing about a bumblebee
That tumbled from a lily bell and grumbled mumblingly,
Because he wet the film
Of his wings, and had to swim,
While the water-bugs raced round and
laughed at him!

Little brook—sing a song
Of a leaf that sailed along
Down the golden-braided centre of your current
swift and strong,
And a dragon-fly that lit
On the tilting rim of it,
And rode away and wasn't scared a bit.

And sing—how oft in glee
Came a truant boy like me,
Who loved to lean and listen to your lilting melody,
Till the gurgle and refrain
Of your music in his brain
Wrought a happiness as keen to him as pain.

—*James Whitcomb Riley*

In the old days, boys and girls large and strong enough to work were kept home from school by their parents. There were fields to plant and gardens to weed. Baby pigs had to have rings put in their noses so they could run but not root in the lush alfalfa patches with their mothers. Summer lambs, those whose mothers rejected them or those that were one of three born to a fruitful mother, had to be bottle-fed.

The young and those not needed for labor at home were left in the classroom, waiting impatiently for summer. For them the wonder-working weather of late May and early June addled the mind, making "learnin' difficult if not near' impossible." On lazy late spring days, thoughts wandered to trout holes, deep cool-shaded woods, and games unending. Summer's call was so strong that teachers could not hold them—the wiggling body was present, but the wandering mind was already gone.

Then, finally, school was out!

Effie's Favorite Chicken with Homemade Egg Noodles

On farms, spring chickens grown large by summer were sometimes made into this succulent dish. Rich homemade egg noodles dressed with cream or butter were served as an accompaniment.

1 (4- to 5-pound) young fryer (or 2 smaller chickens), boned and cut into bite-size chunks (reserve bones and neck for making the broth)
About 1 teaspoon salt, plus ½ teaspoon for broth
About ¼ teaspoon black pepper, plus ⅛ teaspoon for broth
2 tablespoons butter
¼ cup water
1 cup reconstituted wild mushrooms, sliced before drying (or ½ pound sliced, store-bought mushrooms)

2 medium-size tomatoes, peeled and finely chopped (remove seeds if you find them objectionable)
¼ medium-size onion, very finely chopped
1 teaspoon minced fresh thyme
About 1 tablespoon all-purpose flour
¾ cup dairy sour cream
1 sprig fresh parsley, minced, optional
Homemade Egg Noodles (recipe follows)
2 tablespoons sesame seed, optional
1 tablespoon slivered almonds, optional

At least 30 minutes before putting the chicken on to cook, make the chicken broth: Place the reserved chicken bones and neck in a medium-size kettle, cover with about 2 cups water, and simmer with ⅛ teaspoon salt and ⅛ teaspoon pepper for at least 30 minutes. Then make the noodles up to the point of cooking; at this point the noodles will be heavily dusted with flour and rolled up like a jelly roll.

When the broth is ready (let it continue simmering until needed) and the noodles made, preheat oven to 350°F. Season the chicken pieces with salt and pepper. Heat the butter in a large skillet and brown the chicken on all sides, but do not cook it through. Pour the ¼ cup water around the chicken and bring to a boil; lower heat, cover, and simmer until meat is tender and all water has evaporated out of the skillet, about 20 to 25 minutes. Remove the chicken from the skillet (set unwiped skillet aside) and arrange chicken evenly in a 13x9x2-inch lightly greased baking dish. Cover and set in a warm place, such as on top of the stove, while making the sauce.

Next, scrape the browned residue loose from the bottom of the skillet used for browning the chicken. Add to the skillet the mushrooms, tomatoes, onion, and thyme and sauté 3 to 4 minutes. Sprinkle *1 tablespoon* of the flour over the vegetables, stirring well. Cook 1 to 2 minutes, stirring constantly. Drain 1 cup of broth off the chicken bones and add the 1 cup to the skillet, stirring until smooth. (Strain the remaining broth and use in another recipe.) Remove sauce from heat and blend in the sour cream. Adjust the seasoning with salt and pepper; set aside.

If the chicken needs heating to bring it to serving temperature, heat it in the preheated 350°F oven. Cook and dress the noodles.

Place skillet containing the sauce over a very low heat and cook until sauce is thick and bubbly, about 3 minutes. Remove from heat and pour sauce over the warm chicken. Garnish with parsley, sesame seeds, and/or slivered almonds, if desired. Serve immediately with the egg noodles. *Makes 6 to 8 servings.*

Homemade Egg Noodles

2 eggs	½ cup light cream
2 tablespoons water	1 tablespoon minced fresh
About 2 cups all-purpose	parsley
flour, plus flour for kneading	½ teaspoon poppy seed
Boiling water for cooking	Salt
noodles	Black pepper

Beat the eggs with the 2 tablespoons water in a large bowl. Add enough flour to make a very stiff dough (start with 1½ cups, then add more if needed). Knead and roll out paper thin. Cover the dough with a dry towel and let stand without handling for 30 minutes, then dust the top of the dough heavily with flour and roll it up like a jelly roll. Jelly roll may now be sliced and cooked, or noodles may be sized and hung to dry for later use. Jelly roll may be left unsliced, covered with a dry cloth, for about 1 hour.

When ready to cook noodles, bring a large pot of lightly salted water to boil. Then cut off thin slices of noodles and unroll the noodles; stretch them a little and drop in the boiling water. Cook just until tender, about 15 minutes, stirring occasionally. Drain well in a colander and return noodles to pot. Add cream, return to low heat and cook, stirring in a folding motion, until the cream is incorporated. Remove from heat, salt and pepper to taste, and serve immediately. *Makes 6 to 8 servings.*

Calico Slaw

Mother's summer slaw changed hues according to whichever bright vegetable was available to add to the spring-grown Golden Acre cabbage. One favorite combination—made in June—was tender green spinach and cabbage, brightened with coarsely shredded carrot and flavored with the first apple of the season, a crisp, tart summer-pie apple called June Red.

1½ cups shredded fresh, tender green spinach leaves
1½ shredded cups Golden Acre cabbage
1 cup peeled, coarsely grated carrots
¼ cup minced tops of chives or whole, finely cut green onions

1 tart summer pie apple, finely chopped (try to get June Red)
1 sprig fresh parsley, minced
½ cup mayonnaise
½ cup buttermilk
Salt
Black pepper
A sprinkling of celery seed or toasted sesame seed

In a large bowl, combine the spinach, cabbage, carrots, chives, apple, and parsley; refrigerate until ready to dress. In a small bowl, blend together the mayonnaise and buttermilk; add salt and pepper to taste, mixing well; refrigerate if making ahead. Just before serving, dress the slaw and sprinkle on a very light dusting of celery or sesame seed. *Makes 6 to 8 servings.*

Grabbled Potatoes

By late June or early July, spring-planted potatoes are about half to full grown. Grabbled—dug out of the sides of the hills with the fingers, removing only those large enough to eat—the young tubers are tender and still smell and taste of the earth. Such potatoes traditionally are boiled with the jackets on and served with fresh butter or sour cream to which minced fresh parsley or sometimes a mild herb like fresh basil, or even a little freshly grated horseradish, has been added. The dressing should be lightly flavored so as not to spoil the earthy new-potato flavor

Wash freshly grabbled potatoes gently so as not to damage their tender, thin skin. *Allow 1 medium-size potato per serving for women and children and 2 for men.* Put the potatoes in a large kettle and cover with cold water; boil lightly until potatoes are tender enough to be pierced with a fork, then pour off the cooking water. Over a low heat, shake the potatoes in the bottom of the pan just until they are dried. If desired, serve lightly seasoned butter or sour cream (described above) on the side. Serve piping hot.

Gone-in-a-Minute Strawberry Pudding

This light, airy dessert captures the flavor of ever-bearing strawberries, varieties that produce fruit of excellent flavor from spring until frost.

1 cup mashed strawberry pulp
1 egg white
¼ cup powdered sugar
   Whipped cream (page 61)
   About 2 teaspoons brightly
     colored strawberry
     preserves, optional
   Additional fresh whole
     berries, optional

Place the strawberry pulp, egg white, and sugar in a bowl and beat with a rotary or electric beater 10 to 15 minutes, or until stiff. Pile in four sherbet glasses and chill. Just before serving, spoon on a generous amount of whipped cream and top each serving, if you wish, with a fresh whole berry or ¼ to ½ teaspoon strawberry preserves for color. *Makes 4 servings.*

Honey Marshmallows

When bees swarmed early in June, guaranteeing a good supply of honey for the following winter, old-time mothers were happy to use some of the stored sweetener to make marshmallows for youngsters just out of school.

Cornstarch to flour baking pan
1 tablespoon unflavored gelatin
1 cup water
1 cup granulated sugar
1 cup honey

About 1 cup powdered sugar, or more as needed
Grated toasted coconut, shaved chocolate, or hot butterscotch, optional

Lightly grease a square 8x8-inch cake pan and liberally dust it with cornstarch; set aside. In a large bowl, sprinkle the gelatin over ½ cup of the water and let sit to soften for 3 minutes.

Grease the sides of a large saucepan and in it combine the granulated sugar, honey, and the remaining ½ cup water. Cook to a soft-ball stage over medium-high heat (234°F to 240°F on a candy thermometer) without stirring, then pour the hot syrup over the softened gelatin and stir well; let sit until it cools to the consistency of egg white. Whip mixture with a wire whisk, a rotary beater, or an electric mixer until it stands in stiff peaks. Pour into prepared pan and let sit for 8 to 12 hours, uncovered, at room temperature, to allow the marshmallows to become firm and dry on top.

Then turn onto a flat, smooth surface that has been liberally dusted with powdered sugar. Cut into 1-inch squares (or 2-inch if preferred). Roll each square liberally in powdered sugar. Lay finished marshmallows out on a large piece of waxed paper to dry at room temperature before storing in an airtight container. Before storing, dust liberally again with powdered sugar. If you wish you may roll these in grated, toasted coconut, or in shaved chocolate, or turn them into Scotch Kisses by dipping them in melted butterscotch morsels.

❧ A Country Wedding

Out in the country, a wedding was—and is—a high point in the social calendar, celebrated lavishly and with vigor. Heavy-duty summer work was set aside as much as possible so that many hands could help with the preparations. Friends and relatives came from far and near, leaving someone at home to do chores or had-to-be-done work, or getting a neighbor to help out.

The sentimental bride often took her mother's wedding dress out of a trunk and fitted it to herself for the momentous day; lucky the girl who could wear her grandmother's handmade Irish-lace gown, particularly one brought from the old country.

As she stitched a bit of new lace on the garment or fitted it, her friends sat about her and finished up bits of sewing on the linens she had been working on for her new home. Older women, great-grand-mothers, despite their age and sight, often put the last stitches on the quilts the couple would need—three made of gingham and calico often pieced together with flour-sack muslin squares, and one made of scraps of satin, velvet, and silk in a broken glass pattern, embroi-dered with an array of fancy stitches around each irregular piece.

To get ready for the gala affair and the many guests who would come to it, some to stay several days, the men—father and brothers of the bride—killed the "fatted calf" and butchered a young pig for pit roasting.

Aunts and women friends arrived with supplies and skills. Promises came for special cakes and pies, for spiced pickled pears, cherries, and peaches, someone's special sweet chunk-cucumber pickle. Many were the offers for jars of chow-chow, Dixie and India relish, and piccalilli. The wedding feast itself would be something to talk about!

When the excitement was at high pitch and the day had arrived, folks gathered either at the church or at the home of the bride's parents. Farmers, always looking a bit awkward at dress-up affairs, sometimes came to the wedding empty-handed. Seven or eight children would pile out of each wagon, a wife, and sometimes parents. But if you watched carefully, you would see them sidling up to the groom to tell him that they had "a yella Jersey cow or a few feeder pigs that he ought to come over and get fer his new place."

To everyone's delight, the house was beautiful, decorated with June flowers; the yard was neat as a pin; the bride beautiful, the ceremony short but tender, with serious talk of God's blessing on this new couple, and the feast and dancing in the yard were a great success.

When it was over, and everything settled down, older folks, exhausted with the pleasure of the day, sat and talked a bit while young people huddled in groups, planning the evening's shivaree, that rowdy, boisterous mock serenade that young country people loved. By nightfall the air was electric with excitement, all of the kettles, horns, bells, banjos, Jew's harps, and white lightnin' had been tested. Silly songs had been practiced, those with which to tease the bride and groom.

About dark, everyone so inclined, including children who were still up playing, wandered over to stand under the bride's bedroom window—young couples seldom went to their new home on their wedding day, sometimes because the distance was too far, other times because they did not want to miss the rest of the celebration. When the couple had been called to the window, the singers, already in high spirits, quickly became loud and full of rollicking good humor. Young men usually called to the groom, asking if he needed any help, which generally set off a round of guarded joking since women were present.

The groom was thought to have handled himself in a manly way if he fielded these jests adroitly. Some men made a reputation for themselves as a wit on their wedding night. And they established themselves as the protector of their hearth and home by disbanding the revelers, who left amid rowdy shouting and goodwill wishing. The knot had been tied!

Fruit Basket Salad with Strawberry Cream Dressing

In June, summer fruit is just beginning to ripen; rhubarb is in full harvest as are cherries and strawberries. Country women, skilled at combining products in season, work any fruits that come to hand into pies, cobblers, puddings, compotes, or a fruit salad like this one.

1 cup cubed rhubarb
½ cup water
   About ½ cup sugar, or more, to taste
1 tablespoon quick-cooking tapioca
1 cup strawberries, hulls removed

1 cup Royal Ann cherries, or another golden-colored, sweet variety, stems and pits removed
1 cup Bing cherries, stems and pits removed
   Strawberry Cream Dressing (recipe follows)
1 sprig fresh mint, optional

In a medium saucepan, cook the rhubarb, water, *½ cup* of the sugar, and the tapioca over a medium heat until a thin sauce is formed, stirring frequently. Remove from heat and make a puree, using a blender or sieve. Let cool.

Reserve about 6 pieces of each type of fruit (select the most attractive ones) for decorating the top of the salad. Fold the remaining strawberries and cherries into the rhubarb mixture and sweeten with more sugar if you wish. Spoon into a serving bowl, cover, and refrigerate until chilled. Just before serving, top with freshly made Strawberry Cream Dressing, which should be liberally mounded over the fruit base, and arrange reserved fruit on top. Add a sprig of mint for color, if you wish. *Makes 6 to 8 servings.*

The Strawberry Cream Dressing may be served on the side to be liberally spooned on top of each portion.

Strawberry Cream Dressing
This fruit salad dressing is also delicious if used as a topping on unfrosted cakes.

1 cup chopped strawberries
1 cup mayonnaise
¼ cup heavy cream, whipped to form soft peaks

Sugar to sweeten dressing, optional

In a medium-size bowl, fold the strawberries into the mayonnaise, then gently fold in the whipped cream. Serve immediately. If a sweet dressing is desired, add a little sugar but be sure to wait until just before using the dressing, since sugar will draw juice from the fruit, making the dressing thinner. *Makes 2¾ cups dressing.*

German Potato Salad with Cabbage

Served hot, this old-time salad is delicious with pork.

Water for cooking potatoes
6 medium-size potatoes, peeled
½ pound sliced bacon, cut into bits
¼ cup cider vinegar
1 tablespoon honey
2 teaspoons salt
½ teaspoon celery seed
1 cup finely chopped cabbage
¼ cup finely chopped dill pickles
1 tablespoon minced fresh parsley
3 hard-cooked eggs, finely chopped

Bring 1½ inches of water to boil in a medium-size kettle. Add the potatoes and cook until barely fork tender, about 20 minutes. Drain, cut into about ⅛-inch slices, and keep warm.

In a large skillet, fry the bacon until crisp. Add the vinegar, honey, salt, and celery seed and bring to a boil. Remove from heat. Add the potatoes to the skillet and toss gently to coat well but not break up potato slices. Add the cabbage, which should be slightly warm but crisp, and pickles, folding carefully so as not to mash the potatoes. Turn the salad out into a large bowl or casserole dish with a lid, which will keep the salad warm until it can be served. Sprinkle top with the parsley and chopped eggs and serve immediately. *Makes 6 to 8 servings.*

Roasted Suckling Pig with Onion Dressing and Fresh Horseradish Sauce

On old-time farms, piglets were born in late winter and late summer, each sow having from seven to ten babies, sometimes as many as eighteen. This abundance was a mixed blessing since farmers, by necessity, had to thin the herds to equalize the pig and feed suppy. Unlike today, pigs were butchered from very small size upward to maturity, and often roasted in quarters, halves, or whole, depending on the size. Such meat was a tender delicacy, often prepared for festive occasions.

Today people in rural areas still roast suckling pigs, weighing from 10 to 12 pounds. Such pork yields about 1 large, more small servings per pound of uncooked meat.

1 (10- to 12-pound) pig
Butter or margarine as
   needed
1 teaspoon salt, ¼ teaspoon
   black pepper, ¼ teaspoon
   marjoram per pound of meat
1 carrot, unpeeled
1 whole onion, peeled
2 stalks of celery, uncut
1 each orange and apple, whole
   or halved, unpeeled
½ cup or more flour for dusting
½ cup water

1 cup cream (half-and-half will
   do nicely) or 1 cube melted
   butter or margarine with ½
   cup water added
1 small apple (June Red
   preferred)
2 blueberries or cranberries; if
   unobtainable use maraschino
   cherries
1 large bunch fresh parsley, to
   garnish platter
20 small red potatoes for boiling

Preheat oven to 350°F. Rub the outside of the pig with butter, sprinkle it generously inside and out with salt, pepper, and marjoram. Fill the cavity with the vegetables and fruit. Put the pig on a rack over a 15x11x2-inch roast pan, or one that is even larger, with its feet under it, braced with skewers so that it remains upright. (The legs may be braced, front legs forward, hind legs back, if that is easier.) Roll the ears in pieces of greased cloth or cover with aluminum foil, and put a small 3x3x1-inch block of wood in the mouth to hold it open so that an uncooked apple can later be put in it. Dust the back generously with flour, which coats the meat and takes up fat. Pour water in the drip pan. Roast in a moderate oven, basting often with cream until a meat thermometer stuck in the thigh reads 170°F or "well done," 3 hours or more. (Remember, though, that such pork is young like spring lamb, so check on it occasionally. Cook well done, but don't overcook.)

When the pig is done, carefully move it to a large turkey platter; remove the ear coverings, put the apple in its mouth, and blueberries (or other small fruit) in its eyes. Arrange parsley and small red potatoes, which have been boiled whole in their jackets and are still hot, around the base of the meat. Serve immediately, carving at the table. *Makes about 12 to 16 servings.*

Onion Dressing

2 cups onion, chopped
2 cups celery, chopped
½ cup pan drippings, more if
   needed for seasoning
6 cups dark variety breads,
   including about 2 cups corn
   bread, broken into small
   pieces

2 cups white bread, broken into
   small pieces
1 level tablespoon salt
1 teaspoon black pepper
2 teaspoons marjoram, finely
   crushed
2 teaspoons oregano, finely
   crushed

2 teaspoons sweet basil, finely crushed	1 quart Homemade Chicken Broth (page 11) plus boiling water, as needed

In a large skillet, sauté the onion and celery in ½ *cup* pan drippings until they are clear. Put them and the bread into a large mixing bowl. Add salt, pepper, herbs, and broth to moisten. Stir until the dressing binds; it should be fairly moist or the finished product will be dry. Taste, add additional salt, pepper, and herbs to taste.

Do not stuff the pig; the meat cooks more evenly when the cavity is only slightly filled with fruit and vegetables (which moisten and flavor the meat). Our objection to stuffing such meat is that large amounts of dressing stuffed into the cavity cook last and therefore lie warm and uncooked during most of the cooking time, during which toxins may develop, causing food poisoning.

Instead, grease two large 13x9x2½-inch baking pans or one 15x11x2-inch pan and turn the dressing into it. Bake dressing along with the pork, when possible, during the last hour that the pig roasts. When done, it should be well plumped and browned. Serve as a side dish. *Makes 12 to 16 servings.*

Any leftovers may be reheated or frozen for later use with chicken or pork.

Fresh Horseradish Sauce
Dig fresh horseradish, a small amount at a time, wash, scrape (or peel with a potato peeler), and grind it. If you don't have it in your garden, buy whole horseradish and prepare. Add white vinegar to moisten and salt. Seal in a jar and store in the refrigerator.

For a sauce, stir into the sour cream enough drained horseradish to please your palate—about one-third cup for each cup sour cream. Add sugar, black pepper and salt to taste; ½ teaspoon caraway seed and one medium apple, peeled and finely shredded, to each cup of sauce.

Auntie's Duckling with Raisin Bread Stuffing

Richly flavored with fruit and spices, this special treat is just right for serving at a party.

1 (5- to 6-pound) domestic duckling
Water to parboil duck
¼ cup butter, as needed
Salt
Black pepper

Raisin Bread Stuffing (recipe follows)
Ground ginger
Freshly grated nutmeg
About ¼ cup orange marmalade

Preheat oven to 350°F. Rinse the duck well and wipe it dry. Remove any visible fat. Parboil for about 30 minutes in enough water to cover. Drain duck well and transfer it to a large casserole dish with a lid (or you can use a small roasting pan with a lid). Rub the butter over the duck's surface, then season with salt and pepper, inside and out. Place the duck, breast side up, and fill the duck with stuffing; cover the casserole or pan and bake for 2 hours. Remove the lid, sprinkle a little ginger and nutmeg over the duck and brush lightly with the marmalade. Continue baking, uncovered, to set the glaze and brown slightly, about 25 minutes. *Makes 4 to 6 servings.*

Raisin Bread Stuffing

1 cup chopped celery
1 medium apple, peeled and chopped
¼ cup butter or margarine
6 slices raisin bread, cubed, with crusts on
About ¼ cup orange marmalade dissolved in ½ cup boiling water (see Note)

½ teaspoon salt
½ teaspoon ground cinnamon
¼ teaspoon freshly grated nutmeg
1 egg, beaten

In a large skillet, sauté the celery and apple in the butter until tender but not browned. Remove from heat. Add the bread cubes and enough of the marmalade mixture to make a moist stuffing. Stir in the salt, cinnamon, and nutmeg, then fold in the egg. *Makes about 8 servings, or enough to stuff one duckling.*

Note: This is a delicious stuffing, so everyone will want more. Make two batches. From the first batch, fill the duck, using 2 or 3 cups of the stuffing, pack loosely. Then add remainder of the first batch to a second batch and turn into a greased 13x9x2-inch baking pan. During the last 45 minutes of roasting time (for the duck) bake until puffed and lightly browned. Serve as a side dish. *Makes about 8 servings, in addition to stuffing in the duckling.* (Freeze any leftover stuffing and serve with pork chops.)

Oven-Baked Mountain Trout with Parsley and Lemon Butter

Cold, high lakes yield up fat, richly flavored trout in summer. When baked and dressed with parsley and lemon butter, they are fit for a king.

4 to 6 (12- to 16-ounce) whole trout, or other fresh fish, with heads, gutted and scaled
½ cup sweet butter, melted

2 tablespoons minced fresh parsley
Juice and rind, finely grated, from 1 lemon
Salt
Freshly ground black pepper

Preheat oven to 350°F. If trout are larger than 16 ounces, fillet. In a pan or dish large enough to hold 1 piece of trout, combine the butter, parsley, lemon juice, and lemon rind, mixing well.

Lay the fish out on a piece of waxed paper or aluminum foil. Lightly salt and pepper each trout, inside and out, then spoon a little of the butter mixture inside each cavity, and dip the fish in the butter to coat; place trout on a greased cookie sheet and pour any remaining butter over the fish. Bake just until the fish flakes, about 30 minutes. *Makes 4 to 6 servings.*

Snow-White Rolls

Old-time people believed that bread was the staff of life and they ate rolls or thick slices of sturdy bread at every meal. Holidays and special occasions were times when ladies showed off their skills at bread making. These light snow-white rolls or their kin appeared at even the smallest gathering.

2½ teaspoons salt
2½ cups milk, scalded and cooled to lukewarm
½ cup butter
¼ cup sugar, plus 2 tablespoons to activate yeast

¼ cup lukewarm water (105°F to 115°F)
1 package dry or granulated yeast
About 5 to 5½ cups all-purpose flour

Add the salt to the milk, stirring until salt is dissolved. Cream the butter and ¼ *cup* of sugar together in a large bread bowl or mixing bowl and stir in the warm milk. Pour ¼ *cup* lukewarm water over the yeast, add *2 tablespoons* sugar to activate the yeast. Let set 10 minutes to form a "head." Add the yeast to the milk mixture and stir to combine; add *5 cups* flour and beat until smooth. Add more flour if necessary to form a moderately stiff batter. Cover with a dry towel and let rise in a warm place until doubled in bulk, about 1 hour. Stir down the dough, then spoon into 24 greased muffin cups (each will be about half full); cover again with the towel and let rise until doubled in bulk, about 45 minutes. Bake in a preheated 425°F oven until lightly browned on top and bottom, about 15 to 20 minutes. *Makes 2 dozen rolls.*

Note: To test for doneness, take one roll out of the pan and look at the bottom. When it is well browned, rolls are done.

Golden Egg Bread or Cloverleaf Rolls and Fresh Butter

These fancy braided loaves or cloverleaf rolls, turned golden by the rich yolks of Bantam chickens and dusted with poppy seed or sesame seed were show-off breads and were religiously served with freshly churned butter.

2 packages dry or granulated yeast
½ cup lukewarm water (105°F to 115°F)
1 cup milk, scalded and still hot
⅓ cup honey
1 tablespoon salt
1 cup heavy cream

3 eggs, well beaten (5 eggs if you use eggs from Bantam chickens)
About 6 to 7 cups unbleached all-purpose flour
1 egg, beaten with 2 tablespoons water
About 1 tablespoon poppy seed, caraway seed, or sesame seed, optional

Dissolve the yeast in the warm water; set aside.

In a large bowl, combine the milk, honey, and salt. Stir in the cream. When the mixture cools to lukewarm, add the yeast and the 3 eggs, beating well. Stir in just enough flour (about 3 cups) to make a starting batter (it should be a little thicker than pancake batter); whip the batter hard for about 3 minutes to develop the gluten. Cover with a dry towel and put it to rise in a warm place for about 1 hour; then stir it down and add the *remaining 3 cups* flour. Turn onto a floured surface and knead until the dough is elastic, about 20 minutes. Wash the mixing bowl and grease it. Place the dough in the bowl, then invert dough so top is greased; cover with a dry towel, set in a warm spot, and let it rise for about 1 hour or until it is about double in bulk. Turn onto a floured surface.

For bread: Gently divide dough into 2 equal portions. Divide each portion into 3 more equal portions, so there are 6 in all. Separate the strands so that simple braiding can begin: Begin with 3 strands, working both ways; first, from the middle of the strands, braid one end of the loaf and turn the end pieces under, then braid the other end and turn those ends under. Now flip the braid over and lay the other three strands lengthwise on top of it. Repeat the sequence, braiding each end from the middle and turning under so that you have another complete braid. Now pinch the ends of the first and second braids together to form your double-braided loaf. Glaze lightly with the beaten egg and water mixture; discard unused portion. Sprinkle with poppy, caraway, or sesame seed—or a mixture—if desired.

Place loaves on a greased cookie sheet and bake in a preheated 400°F oven for 20 minutes; then reduce oven setting to 350°F and continue baking until the loaf is golden brown, hollow when tapped, and has turned loose from the pan, about 35 to 40 minutes more. Remove from the oven; let the bread sit on the cookie sheet for about 10 minutes to cool; remove from pan, then put on a wire rack to finish cooling. *Makes 1 double-braided loaf.*

For rolls: Pinch off enough to make 72 (6 dozen) small balls the size of walnuts. Roll dough into smooth balls with hands; place 3 dough balls in each of 24 well-greased muffin cups. Bake at 400°F until golden brown, about 25 minutes. *Makes 2 dozen rolls.*

Bride's Cake with Cream Cheese and Brandy Frosting

An old-fashioned bride expected to have a fancy fruitcake for her wedding. This one, containing almonds and citron peel, is both delicate and attractive. Traditionally it was iced with a boiled frosting, but I prefer it with this good and easy-to-make cream cheese frosting.

1 cup butter or margarine	½ cup blanched chopped
1 cup sugar	almonds
5 eggs	½ cup shredded candied citron
¼ cup brandy	peel (preferred) or ¼ cup
2 cups all-purpose flour	candied orange peel, finely
1½ teaspoons baking powder	chopped
1 teaspoon salt	Cream Cheese Frosting
¼ teaspoon ground mace	(recipe follows)
2 cups golden raisins	

Preheat oven to 350°F. In a large bowl, cream together the butter and sugar. Separate the eggs, and as you do so, add each egg yolk to the butter mixture; beat each egg yolk in before adding another one. Stir in the brandy. In a separate bowl, combine the flour, baking powder, salt, and mace, mixing well; blend into the egg-yolk mixture. Fold in the raisins, almonds, and citron peel. In another bowl, whip the egg whites to stiff peaks and fold them into the batter. Turn batter into a greased and lightly floured 10-inch tube pan. Bake until golden and firm to touch, about 1 hour and 15 to 20 minutes. Remove from the oven and let the cake pan sit about 10 minutes on a wire rack before turning cake out of the pan. Cool thoroughly before frosting. *Makes 1 tube cake.*

Cream Cheese Frosting
1 (16-ounce) package cream cheese, softened

1½ cups powdered sugar
1 tablespoon brandy

In a medium-size bowl, beat all the ingredients together until smooth. Frost the cake lightly just before serving. *Makes enough frosting for 1 tube cake.*

Wedding Punch

Country women have combined rhubarb and strawberries in many different recipes through the years; the strawberries provide flavor, the rhubarb tartness and body. This richly colored punch sparkles with character and needs no flavoring agent to buoy its spirit.

2 quarts washed and chopped rhubarb
2 quarts hulled strawberries

2 quarts water
2 cups sugar

Place the rhubarb and strawberries in a large kettle Add the water and sugar. Bring to a boil, then reduce heat to a gentle simmer and cook just until the rhubarb is soft and has given up its juice. (*Note:* Since strawberry flavor is delicate, you may cook the rhubarb for a few minutes, then add the strawberries and just return to boiling. A light touch is required here!) Remove from heat, cover, and let sit for 10 to 15 minutes. Strain (discard pulp) and refrigerate. Serve icy cold. *Makes about 2 quarts.*

Dandelion Wine

This bright yellow flower grows wild over lawns and meadows. It was brought to America from Europe by early colonists. The young leaves can be used for salads and greens, like spinach. And an old-fashioned wine is made from the tender young flowers.

1 gallon (16 cups) dandelion
   blossoms
1 gallon water
   Juice from 2 lemons
1 used tea bag, which is used
   to obtain tannic acid

½ teaspoon wine yeast
   (purchased in hobby shops)
2½ pounds sugar

Dip the blossoms in cold tap water to rid them of insects and to freshen them. Do not soak them. Remove and discard all green parts; place the blossoms in a large kettle and pour fresh water over them; drain in a colander—don't let them soak. Return blossoms to the kettle.

In a separate kettle, heat *½ gallon (8 cups)* of the water until it is hot to the touch; pour the hot water over the blossoms; let mixture steep until cool. Then drain the liquid from the petals into a freshly scrubbed and sterilized 2-gallon crock, squeezing petals to yield as much liquid as possible. Discard the petals.

To the crock add half the sugar, and the lemon juice, tea bag, and yeast. Cover with a clean dish towel and let the mixture ferment at room temperature. (It will be bubbling steadily and a little foam will be on top.) Every 3 to 4 days, add 1 cup more sugar until the sugar is used up. (If you add the sugar too fast you may kill the yeast.) When the wine has fermented for about 2 weeks, pour off the sediment into 1-gallon jugs and cork with a tight ball of cheesecloth. Let the wine sit for about 30 days, then rack (pour off the sediment) again. In 6 months, pour it carefully into freshly scrubbed and sterilized pint- or quart-size bottles and label; cork. Let the wine set for a week or more before serving. Flower wines are usually served during the first year they are in storage; they do not particularly improve with age. *Makes about 1½ gallons.*

From THOUGHTS FER THE
DISCURAGED FARMER

They's been a heap o'rain,
But the sun's out today,
And the clouds of the wet spell
Is all cleared away,
And the woods is all the greener,
And the grass is greener still;
It may rain again to-morry,
But I don't think it will

Some says the crops is ruined,
And the corn's drowned out,
And propha-sy the wheat will be a failure,
Without doubt;
But the kind Providence
That has never failed us yet,
Will be on hands onc't more
At the 'leventh hour, I bet!

—*James Whitcomb Riley*

✤ First Haying of the Season, Hayride, and a Nighttime Picnic

About mid-June, when the first cutting of hay was at hand, farmers were always skeptical of the weather. They grouched a lot about "getting it rained on" but there was a thrilling side to beating Ol' Mother Nature to the punch! For the farmers who fought the rain and won, there was plenty of boasting down at the general store, talk about reading the signs, and giving advice about how "it didn't do no harm to mow when one storm was jest leaving, 'cause usually you could get the hay up 'fore another one come in."

However, not one of them would admit to the excitement he felt when he saw black clouds riding swiftly in on the wind, nor the surge of energy and power that set his heart to pounding and his body to sweating. Taciturn to the core, he could not let anyone know the pure

sweet satisfaction that he got from standing in the barn, looking out at the rain pouring over his empty hay fields, or the pleasure he took when every deep breath was sweetened by the fragrance of sunshine left in the dried hay about him.

When days were sunny and nights balmy, young folks began to plan a hayride and nighttime picnic. Then one evening when chores were done, fellas and their girls, a few older folks, and half-grown youngsters, musicians, and drivers piled into a great hay wagon filled with dried, soft grasses and jounced along over unpaved country roads, told stories, laughed, sang sentimental and silly songs, and pitched a little woo.

When the twilight began to darken, the wagon—its lanterns dancing like fireflies—turned into the farmyard with its load of riotous passengers for a hot dinner on trestle tables. The party might be moved inside if the house was large enough and if there were enough lamps to see by, but if not, it was held in the yard around a bonfire. Little ones who had stayed home now were allowed to join the party.

Dilled Cucumbers in Sour Cream Dressing

2 cucumbers, peeled and sliced ¼ inch thick	3 tablespoons minced fresh dill Pinch of celery seed
1 cup boiling water Ice water	Sour Cream Dressing (recipe follows)

Place the cucumber slices in a heatproof bowl. Pour the boiling water over them and let stand for 5 minutes. Drain, plunge into ice water and let the slices chill. Drain well and place in a serving bowl. Sprinkle the dill and celery seed over the slices and add the dressing, tossing until all slices are well coated. Refrigerate until well chilled before serving. *Makes 4 servings.*

Sour Cream Dressing

1 cup dairy sour cream	1½ teaspoons salt
1 tablespoon lemon juice (preferred) or cider vinegar	¼ teaspoon black pepper About 1 teaspoon sugar

Combine the sour cream, lemon juice or vinegar, salt, pepper, and *1 teaspoon* sugar, mixing well. Taste for sweetness and add more sugar, if desired. *Makes 1 cup dressing.*

Baked Beans with German Sausage

Cranberry, red kidney, or white Navy beans are old-time favorites for these baked beans.

1 pound dried beans, soaked
  overnight and drained
  (cranberry, red kidney, or
  white Navy beans
  preferred)
Cold water for cooking
  beans
½ cup, packed, dark brown
  sugar
½ teaspoon salt
½ teaspoon black pepper

1 teaspoon butter
1 teaspoon dry mustard
4 ounces lean salt pork,
  chopped
1 tablespoon light molasses
1½ pounds smoked, precooked
  German sausage,
  Bratwurst, Knockwurst, or
  other similar type pricked
  with a fork to prevent
  bursting

Preheat oven to 325°F. Pick over the beans, removing any refuse or defective beans. Wash, drain, cover with cold water, and let soak overnight.

The next morning drain the beans. Place the beans in a large heavy saucepan or Dutch oven and cover with water; cook slowly until the skins crinkle and break. Drain, reserving the liquid. In a heavy ovenproof bean pot, layer the ingredients in thirds, beginning with a layer of beans. When everything is in the pot, add enough reserved bean liquid to cover the beans. Bake, tightly covered, in a preheated 325°F oven for 5 hours or until almost done. Remove lid and lay German sausages on top of the beans. Add boiling bean liquor or water if necessary, cover and cook until beans are tender. *Makes 4 to 6 servings.*

Spiced Apples with Cider

Some apples like Early McIntosh, Gravenstein, and Spitzenberg are good for making sauces and pies, but do not hold their shape as well as a Cortland, Golden Delicious, Late McIntosh, Rome Beauty, or Winesap, all of which are good-flavored apples that hold their essence during cooking, and which I prefer to use for this recipe. This makes a delicious side dish with pork.

6 tart cooking apples (select Cortland, Golden Delicious, Late McIntosh, Rome Beauty, or Winesap, if possible)
4 cups apple cider
2½ cups sugar
1 stick cinnamon
12 whole cloves
6 whole allspice
¼ teaspoon ground ginger
Juice from 1 lemon

Wash, peel, core, and quarter apples and set aside. In a saucepan, mix together the remaining ingredients. Bring to a boil and boil for 10 minutes. Add the apples and simmer slowly until soft. Transfer apples to a heated platter that has a good lip. Boil the syrup until thick, then strain it and pour over the apples. *Makes 6 to 10 servings.*

Sunshine Cake

In warm weather, people with milk cows whip up one or two freezers of ice cream for almost any occasion. This light, spongelike cake is a popular one to serve with rich, creamy homemade ice cream (page 128).

4 eggs, separated
3 tablespoons cold water
1½ cups sugar
½ cup boiling water
1 teaspoon salt
1 teaspoon lemon juice
1⅓ cups all-purpose flour, sifted
½ teaspoon cream of tartar

Preheat oven to 325°F. In a large bowl, beat the egg yolks with the water until foamy; add the sugar and beat until light and creamy. Add the boiling water, salt, and lemon juice, stirring until well blended. Add the flour, mixing well. In a separate bowl, whip the egg whites and cream of tartar until mixture is stiff enough to stand in peaks, then fold into the batter. Bake in an ungreased 9-inch tube pan until firm to the touch and light golden brown; will be lightly cracked on top; about 1 hour. Remove from the oven, turn the pan upside down on a wire rack, and cool the cake in the pan. Serve unfrosted as is or with your favorite homemade ice cream. *Makes 1 tube cake.*

JULY

Ice Cream, Firecrackers, and Fresh Corn

July, hot and breathless. Without this searing month, the seasonal clock would stop. From its dust and heat, and from the sweat and bent backs of farmers comes the harvest. As the summer reaches its peak, the weather is clear, rain is almost unknown, and the air is dry. By the end of the month unirrigated fields on farms have turned brown, and grass and leaves throughout the countryside have lost their freshness.

Where there is irrigation, plants thrive. Poppies, dahlias, sweet peas, and nasturtiums are in full, brilliant bloom. This is still the season of abundant life. The air is full of the hum of insects and birds darting everywhere in search of food. For farmers the tempo of the season quickens. Field work begins in earnest and with it the promise of a successful harvest.

THE BUMBLEBEE

You better not fool with a Bumblebee!—
Ef you don't think they can sting—you'll see!
They're lazy to look at, an' kindo' go
Buzzin' an' bummin' aroun' so slow,
An' ac' so slouchy an' all fagged out,
Danglin' their legs as they drone about
The hollyhawks 'at they can't climb in
'Ithout ist a-tumble-un out agin!
Wunst I watched one climb clean 'way
In a jim'son-blossom, I did, one day,—
An' I ist grabbed it—an' nen let go—
An' *"Ooh-ooh! Honey! I told ye so!"*
Says The Raggedy Man; an' he ist run
An' pullt out the stinger, an' don't laugh none,
An' says: "They *has* ben folks, I guess,
'At thought I wuz predjudust, more or less,—
Yit I still muntain 'at a Bumblebee
Wears out his welcome too quick fer me!"

—*James Whitcomb Riley*

❧ FRESH OUT OF A SUMMER GARDEN

On the farm, a meal in summer means a trip to the garden with a bucket or basket in which to pick a few fresh cucumbers, corn, crookneck squash, a snippet of basil, and muskmelon if they are ripe. Grateful for the abundance and lack of want, one cannot help but agree with the unknown poetic writer who once wrote: "In the garden, humid with dew lifting off tall, tassled corn, surrounded by glistening, great squashes and multi-colored peppers tucked amidst deep, green leaves, one catches a glimpse of Paradise Lost . . . "

String Beans, New Potatoes, and Bacon

My family always raised Kentucky Wonders—a prolific, old variety of pole bean. Grandpa cut four willow poles and stuck them in a square about two feet across around each of his hills of beans; then he tied the tops together. Sometimes his poles took root and bright flags of willow green topped his tent of bean leaves. As a child, I felt a special wonder when reaching inside his verdant tent to pick the long, straight-hanging beans.

2 pounds tender, young string beans
2 pounds new potatoes
Salt
Black pepper

4 slices lean raw bacon
Water to cover beans
Strips of fried bacon for garnish, optional

Clean, top and tail the beans, or leave the tails on, if you wish. Place the beans in a large Dutch oven. Peel the potatoes by rubbing the skins off, or wash them well and leave the skins on. Arrange the potatoes on top of the beans and salt and pepper the beans and potatoes to taste. Cover the potatoes with the raw bacon. Add just enough water to cover the string beans, then cover the pot. Cook over medium to low heat until the beans are tender and the potatoes are steamed done. Transfer to a heated serving platter. If desired, garnish the platter with strips of cooked bacon or crumble cooked bacon and sprinkle it over the top of the beans and potatoes. Serve immediately. *Makes 6 to 8 servings.*

Wilted Lettuce

This recipe uses old-fashioned "cut-and-come-again" leaf lettuce. Pull or pinch off lettuce leaves, bring them into the house right away, and wash, drain, and dry them. In the springtime, add 1 or more chopped young, green onions.

6 slices bacon, cut into small
   pieces
2 tablespoons cider vinegar
2 tablespoons water
1 teaspoon light brown sugar
½ teaspoon salt
   Dash of black pepper, about
   ⅛ teaspoon
   A wooden salad bowl heaped
   full with freshly picked and
   cleaned leaf lettuce

Fry the bacon in a large skillet until crisp; drain on paper towels and keep hot. Set aside skillet with the hot bacon fat still in it.

Combine the vinegar, water, sugar, salt, and pepper in a bowl. From the reserved skillet, pour off all but about 3 tablespoons of hot fat. Carefully pour the vinegar mixture into the skillet, taking care not to let it splatter and burn you. Place skillet over high heat and bring mixture to a boil. Remove from heat and pour over the lettuce leaves. Garnish with the bacon and serve immediately. *Makes 6 servings.*

Fried Squash Blossoms

From either the winter or summer varieties of squash, pick up the fallen male blossoms from the ground shortly after they close—the female blossom is turning into a squash. *Allow about 3 blossoms per serving.* Open each blossom and remove all but the petals and enough of the stem to hold the flower together. Carefully wash, drain, and dry. Fold the flowers closed again. Dredge each blossom lightly in *flour* (the flour makes the batter cling to the blossom). Then dip the blossom in *batter* (recipe below) and deep-fry in oil or sauté in butter until golden brown. Drain and serve immediately. Salt and pepper lightly at the table. Serve as a vegetable. *Makes 4 to 6 servings.*

Batter

1 cup all-purpose flour, slightly more for a thicker batter, if desired
1 cup light cream
1 egg
1 teaspoon baking powder
½ teaspoon salt

Combine all the batter ingredients in a bowl. *Makes about 1½ cups batter.*

Corn Fritters

Country cooks use corn as a starch with their meals throughout most of the summer until potato harvest, then, for "meat and potato" men, spuds grace the table.

6 eggs, separated
1⅔ cups cooked fresh corn, cooled and cut from cob
¼ cup all-purpose flour
½ teaspoon salt
Pinch of black pepper
6 tablespoons bacon fat

In a large bowl, whip the egg yolks until light and lemon-colored. Add the corn, flour, salt, and pepper, stirring until well blended. In a separate bowl, beat the egg whites until stiff and fold them into the corn mixture. Heat the fat in a heavy skillet until hot. Drop the batter by spoonfuls into the hot fat and cook until brown on both sides and done. Drain on paper towels. Serve as a side dish alongside meat, or serve with crisp bacon as a main dish. *Makes 6 side-dish servings or 4 main-dish servings.*

Sausage-Stuffed Onions

We use large sweet Bermuda or sweet Spanish onions for this delicious main-course supper dish. Serve them with new peas and baked potatoes.

4 large sweet onions (preferably Bermuda or Spanish)
Water for parboiling
½ pound pork sausage
½ cup very fine dry breadcrumbs
Boiling water for around base of onions
Salt
Black pepper
2 slices bacon
¼ cup toasted sesame seed, optional

Preheat oven to 350°F. Peel the onions and parboil them just until tender. With a knife, carefully remove some of the center; reserve for use in another dish, leaving at least ½-inch shell. In a bowl, combine the sausage with the breadcrumbs; stuff filling into the center of each onion. Arrange the stuffed onions snugly in a casserole and pour boiling water around the base of the onions to have about ⅓ inch liquid. Season tops of onions with salt and pepper and lay the bacon across the onions. Cover and bake until the sausage is cooked—firm to the touch or a meat thermometer reads "well done." (*Note:* Remove the cover for the last 10 minutes or so of baking time to brown the onions; if you are using sesame seed, sprinkle them on the onions as you start to brown them.) Serve immediately. *Makes 4 main-dish servings.*

THE FLAG GOES BY

Hats off!
Along the street there comes
A blare of bugles, a ruffle of drums,
A flash of color beneath the sky:
Hats off!
The flag is passing by.

Blue and crimson and white it shines,
Over the steel-tipped, ordered lines.
          Hats off!
The colors before us fly;
But more than the flag is passing by.

Sea fights and land fights, grim and great,
Fought to make and save the State;
Weary marches and sinking ships;
Cheers of victory on dying lips;

Days of plenty and years of peace;
March of a strong land's swift increase,
Equal justice, right, and law,
Stately honor and reverend awe;

Sign of a nation, great and strong
To ward her people from foreign wrong;
Pride and glory and honor,—all
Live in the colors to stand or fall.

          Hats off!
Along the street there comes
A blare of bugles, a ruffle of drums;
And loyal hearts are beating high;
          Hats off!
The flag is passing by!

                              —*Henry H. Bennet*

FOURTH OF JULY CELEBRATION

When America was a land of small towns and rural countrysides, people were sentimental and patriotism ran high. There was the joy of a youthful nation that knew in its heart that it was *the best*. It was a time when people believed in country, family, God, and each other. A man's word was his bond; a handshake was binding. Back then, people thrilled to the sound of a school band playing "Columbia, the Gem of the Ocean" or "You're a Grand Old Flag." And on July Fourth, everyone—farmers, merchants, bankers, girls, boys, and dogs—

turned out for a celebration of freedom. This could mean a grand parade followed by a picnic in the park. There adults visited and gossiped and watched as boys in their knickers and girls in their sailor collars flew like kites across the lawn.

Sending one of the boys home early to do the chores, farm folk stayed in town after dark to watch the fireworks rain down over the lake and listen to the excited shouts of the crowd as a spectacular skyrocket exploded against the stars.

Pan-fried Rabbit

On farms, wild and domesticated rabbit was fried more frequently than chicken. This picnic fare is delicious.

1 (2-pound) young domestic rabbit, cut in pieces	½ teaspoon black pepper
½ cup all-purpose flour	Fat for pan-frying, either margarine or lard
1½ teaspoons salt	

Dredge the moist, freshly rinsed rabbit pieces in a paper bag containing a mixture of the flour, salt, and pepper. In a very large iron skillet heat about 3 tablespoons of fat just until it begins to smoke, then reduce the heat. Add more fat as needed to prevent sticking. Arrange the pieces of rabbit in the skillet; fry until the meat is golden brown on the bottom and the blood has come to the surface on top, then turn pieces and cook until well done (keep in mind that the thinner pieces will cook more quickly than the thick ones). Test with a fork; any liquid that oozes out should be clear. Transfer the meat to a platter and let it cool before serving. *Makes 6 to 8 servings.*

Vera's Pickled Eggs

Pickled eggs aged in the spring house or cellar were popular picnic fare in the past. The eggs should be prepared about three days ahead of time, thus making them won't conflict with frying chicken or rabbit and getting a fair half dozen children ready for a holiday.

You will need a 1-gallon glass jar and lid in which to store the eggs, both in perfect condition.

1 dozen eggs	4 cups white distilled vinegar
1 gallon (16 cups) boiled, cooled water to fill the jar	2 cups water
	½ cup sugar

6 bay leaves	1 teaspoon salt
3 cayenne peppers	1 teaspoon black pepper
1 medium onion, chopped	

Boil the eggs for a full 20 minutes, then shell them. Place a freshly scrubbed and sterilized 1-gallon jar (sterilize the cap, too) on a wooden surface or on folded dish towels and fill it to the very top with the boiled water, which is still hot; let it stand. Meanwhile, put the vinegar, water, sugar, bay leaves, hot peppers, onion, salt, and pepper in a saucepan and bring to a boil; remove from heat and cool until hot but not boiling hot. Empty the gallon jar and in the very hot jar place the eggs. Return the hot vinegar mixture to a boil, then pour it over the eggs. Cover lightly and set aside to cool at room temperature, then cap and date jar. Refrigerate for 3 days before serving; will keep about a week, but more than likely a family will finish them off in one day. *Makes 1 dozen pickled eggs. Caution:* Do not skip heating the gallon jar before pouring the hot vinegar mixture into it; pouring a hot liquid into a cold jar will break the jar.

Mother's Denver Biscuits

This dough improves with age—once it is kneaded it may be used immediately, or it may be refrigerated and baked into small batches of biscuits, as desired. For holidays, Mother often made the dough the day before she needed it, to lighten the work load on the special occasion.

1 quart milk, scalded and still hot	3 packages dry or granulated yeast
2 medium or 1 large potato, peeled and chunked (to yield 1 cup mashed potatoes)	3 tablespoons baking powder
	About 10 to 12 cups all-purpose flour, plus flour for kneading dough
1 cup butter	Melted butter, about ⅓ to ½ cup, to dip biscuits in before baking
1 cup sugar	
3 tablespoons salt	

In a medium saucepan, boil the potatoes; when cooked, drain, reserving *½ cup water*. With a potato masher or fork, mash the potatoes; measure 1 cup. Cool to lukewarm. In a large bread bowl, combine the hot milk, mashed potatoes, potato water, butter, sugar, and salt, mixing well. When the mixture is lukewarm, stir in the yeast and baking powder and enough flour (start with 4 cups) to make a batter.

Scrape down the sides of the bowl and cover with a dry towel. Set in a warm place and let rise until double in bulk. Then stir in enough additional flour to yield a good, soft bread dough that yields easily to the touch but does not stick to the hands. Turn onto a floured surface and knead until smooth and elastic. Use dough immediately, or cover well and refrigerate for later use.

To make the biscuits, pinch off a piece of dough the size of an egg, form it into an oval ball and dip it in melted fat. Fit biscuits snugly against each other and sides of a 2-inch deep greased baking pan (the biscuits should be crowded a little, as they need each other for support as they rise). Let rise uncovered until very light and double in bulk. Bake in a preheated 400°F oven until the rolls are golden brown, about 25 to 30 minutes. Serve piping hot. *Makes about 4 dozen biscuits.*

The summer winds is sniffin' round the bloomin' locus' trees;
And the clover in the pastur is a big day fer the bees,
And they been a-swiggin' honey, above board and on the sly,
Tel they stutter in theyr buzzin' and stagger as they fly.
The flicker on the fence-rail 'pears to jest spit on his wings
And roll up his feathers, by the sassy way he sings;
And the hoss-fly is a-whettin'-up his forelegs for biz,
And the off-mare is a-switchin' all of her tale they is.

—James Whitcomb Riley

TAKING DINNER INTO THE FIELD

No matter how much a man likes farming, sweating in the hot July sun tires the back and weakens the convictions. It's then that we take dinner into the field, to lift the spirits, and bring a jug of something cool to drink.

Ice-Cold Raspberry Nectar

In season, rich-red, golden, or deep-purple nectar was made by the gallon, the color depending on the variety of raspberries used.

3 quarts picked-over
    raspberries, rinsed and
    hulled (may substitute some
    blackberries or strawberries
    for variety)

4 cups water
1 cup sugar or more, to taste

Place the raspberries, water, and sugar in a large kettle and cook over high heat until the fruit bursts, just to a good rolling boil. Then let the berries set for 10 to 15 minutes in the kettle with the heat off. Strain but don't force the fruit solids through the strainer. Discard solids. Sweeten to taste. Bottle and cork lightly, just enough to exclude air, but not so tightly that fermentation would break the bottle before popping the cork. Use quickly (within a week) as nectar unsealed or lightly sealed will ferment. Store under refrigeration. Serve ice cold, out of the refrigerator, or over ice.

To keep for longer periods of time, pour boiling hot nectar into freshly washed and sterilized canning jars while they are still very hot, leaving ½ inch head room and seal tightly with new washed and scalded canning lids and thoroughly washed and scalded rings. Store in a cool dark place to preserve color. *Makes 3 to 4 quarts.*

Baked Fresh Salmon

Cooked at daylight on a wood-burning cookstove, salmon or other baked fish served cold was a favorite old-time summer treat, a change from the usual beef, pork, and chicken.

3 to 5 pounds salmon roast cut from tail of a large pink or red salmon that has been gutted and scaled (Pacific Coast or Alaskan salmon preferred)
Melted butter
1½ teaspoons salt
¼ teaspoon black pepper
1 tablespoon parsley, minced fresh or 1 teaspoon dried

1 teaspoon chervil, minced fresh or very light dusting of dried
½ teaspoon savory, minced fresh or very light dusting of dried
½ cup green onions, minced fresh tops

Preheat oven to 350°F. Brush the fish lightly on both sides with the butter and sprinkle with the salt, pepper, herbs, and onions. Turn over and season other side. Place in a well-buttered baking dish and cover loosely with buttered kraft paper—a brown grocery bag. Bake until the fish flakes or until the internal temperature in the thickest part reaches 140°F. (*Note:* Lean fish must be basted while cooking; fat fish, such as salmon taken from the mouths of rivers or from the ocean, need not be basted.) Serve immediately or cook slightly and refrigerate until well chilled. *Makes 6 to 8 servings.*

Mark's Bread with Dill Butter

At our house my son-in-law says, "Who needs cake!" as he carries around chunks of this bread.

2 packages dry or granulated yeast
½ cup plus 1 tablespoon sugar

½ cup hot water, temperature range 105°F to 115°F
½ cup heavy cream

1½ cups very hot water	About 6 to 8 cups all-
1 tablespoon salt	purpose flour
	Dill Butter (recipe follows)

In a large mixing bowl, combine the yeast, *1 tablespoon* of the sugar, and the *½ cup* hot water, stirring well. Let sit until yeast is totally dissolved. In a 2-cup measuring cup, put the cream and the *1½ cups* very hot water. Add water-cream mixture to the bubbling yeast; stir in the remaining *½ cup* of sugar and the salt. Add enough flour (start with *4 cups*) to make a thick batter. Beat briskly for 3 or 4 minutes to develop the gluten. Then add enough flour (you will probably need to add about *3 cups*) to make a soft dough. Turn the dough onto a surface floured with *1 cup* flour and knead enough of the flour in to make a fairly stiff dough.

Roll the dough into a log-shaped loaf. Lay the loaf diagonally from corner to corner across a greased cookie sheet. Make a deep lengthwise slice in the top. Cover with a dry towel and let stand in a warm place until double in bulk. Bake in a preheated 425°F oven for 15 minutes, then reduce oven setting to 350°F and continue baking until nicely brown, about 15 to 20 minutes more. Remove the bread from the oven. While still hot, rub the top generously with margarine or butter. Let cool on the cookie sheet for 15 to 20 minutes (assuming the family will wait that long). Serve with dill butter on the side. *Makes 1 loaf.*

Dill Butter

Serve this delicious butter—in a soft or melted state—with fish or spread on it on good bread (such as Mark's Bread, above).

2 hard-cooked egg yolks	½ teaspoon salt
½ cup butter, slightly softened	Ground pepper (white
1½ tablespoons minced dill weed	preferred)
and tender young dill seeds	

Press yolks through a sieve and place in a small bowl. Add the butter, dill weed, salt, and pepper, beating until light. Form into a ball or log. Chill to allow flavors to blend. *Makes about ½ cup butter.*

Ada Wilkins's Hermits

Like other farm women, Ada dried a lot of fruit in season. Many of her "special" recipes were made of dried fruit. A favorite in the community was this family cookie recipe.

1 cup honey	1 teaspoon baking soda
½ cup, packed, brown sugar	1 teaspoon ground allspice
½ cup butter	½ teaspoon salt
2 eggs, well beaten	1 cup chopped walnuts
3 tablespoons dairy sour cream	1 cup chopped dried apples
	1 cup seedless raisins
2¼ cups all-purpose flour, sifted	½ cup candied orange rind
1½ teaspoons ground cinnamon	

Preheat oven to 400°F. Cream the honey, sugar, and butter together in a large bowl. Blend in the eggs and sour cream. Sift together the sifted flour, cinnamon, baking soda, allspice, and salt and add to the honey mixture, mixing until a soft dough forms. Fold in the walnuts, apples, raisins, and orange rind. Spread the dough evenly over the entire bottom of a greased cookie sheet. Bake until lightly browned and firm to the touch, about 15 to 20 minutes. Remove from the oven and let cool to lukewarm on the cookie sheet, then, while still on cookie sheet, cut into 2 or 3 dozen bars. When chilled, bars will have set enough to break apart, or, if necessary, cut again. *Makes 2 to 3 dozen cookies.*

From SONGS O' CHEER

My Grampa he's a-allus sayin',
　"Sing a song o' cheer!"—
And, wunst I says "What kind *is* them?"
　He says,—"The kind to *hear.*—
'Cause they're the songs that *Nature* sings,
　In ever' bird that twitters!"
"Well, *whipperwills* and *doves*," says I,
　"Hain't over-cheery critters!"
"Then don't you sing like *them*," he says—
　"Ner *guinny-hens*, my dear—
Ner *peafowls* nuther (drat the boy!)
　You sing a song o' cheer!"
I can't sing nothin' anyhow;
　But, comin' home, to'rds night,
I kindo'-sorto' kep' a-whistlin'
　"Old—Bob—White!"

　　　　　　　　　—*James Whitcomb Riley*

❧ A Sweltering Evening's Supper

On Grandpa's farm in Missouri, where milk and cream flowed like water, and eggs were laid in a never-ending supply, ice cream—cranked in an old wooden freezer and sweetened by the many hands that made it—was a common Sunday night supper on hot days.

While Grandpa and the boys tended the cattle, horses, and swine, Grandma and the girls made the ice cream, often in several flavors. Then late, almost at dusk, families gathered for supper. Sometimes Uncle Frank's family came over from a nearby farm, but often the crowd was made up of the immediate family and assorted gangly youngsters who had come to visit during the day, then gone home for chore time and returned afterward for an ice-cream feed at Grandpa's.

Everyone ate great bowls of ice cream, sometimes with cookies such as Butternut Cookies (page 130), until they were surfeited or got a headache from the cold. Then people sat awhile to visit, and when the hot July day began to cool and darkness drifted slowly in, the country folks began to hit the hay, for the new working day in July came at daylight on old-time farms.

TO CHURN HOMEMADE ICE CREAM

To make home-churned ice cream, begin by checking the equipment. Carefully wash the can and dasher in hot soapy water and rinse. Allow them to cool thoroughly. Then prepare the ice cream recipe of your choice and churn it.

Prepare custard-base ice cream the day before you plan to churn it. This produces a smoother, finer-textured product; plus, a well-chilled custard will freeze faster.

Prepare fruit just before the ice cream is churned or while the initial churning is being done. Chill and add to the cream mixture when it becomes partially frozen.

Crack the ice and determine its weight (if it isn't precracked and weighed); measure out the correct amount of salt.

When making a *4-quart freezer can* of ice cream, use *about 20 pounds of crushed ice*, measure out *about 2½ cups of rock salt* for making the ice cream, and *another 2½ cups* for ripening it. When using *table salt*, use *1½ cups* for making the ice cream and *another 1½ cups* for ripening it.

Fill the freezer can only about three-fourths full of the chilled ice cream mixture. (Don't overfill it or the texture of the ice cream will not be as nice.) Set the can into the freezer pail and insert the dasher. Be sure the can is centered on the pivot in the bottom of the pail and that the dasher is correctly in place. Put the lid securely on the can; set the hand-crank unit in place over the top of the dasher and lock it in place.

To pack with ice and salt, first fill the bucket about one-third full of ice, sprinkle with salt, then add ice and salt in layers until the pail is full. More salt and ice may have to be added during the freezing period. After the bucket is full, wait about 3 to 4 minutes before starting to churn.

When using a hand-cranked freezer, turn slowly at first until a pull is felt, then triple the speed for about 5 to 10 minutes. About 20 minutes of steady cranking in all is necessary. When ice cream has frozen to the consistency of mush, it is ready.

If the ice cream freezes too quickly (if the crank is difficult to turn after a very short time), this means too much salt has been added. A solid layer has formed on the inside walls of the can, leaving the center unfrozen. To correct the situation, take the freezer apart, remove the dasher, stir the frozen ice cream back down into the unfrozen mixture, put the dasher back in place, and reassemble the freezer. Remove the salt and ice from the bucket, repack with the correct proportions of ice and salt, and start churning again. Be certain that the drain hole is clear.

Usually ice cream is then "packed" for at least two hours to harden it. (For immediate use, churn until the ice cream is a little harder.) To pack it, clean the salt and ice away from the top of the can, pour off the salt water from the bucket, and wipe off the lid. Carefully remove the lid and take the dasher out, being careful not to get any salt water in the ice cream. Scrape the ice cream down from the sides of the can and replace the lid. Place a cork in the hole of the lid where the dasher was. Repack the bucket with salt and ice, in the same proportions that were used for the initial packing, until the bucket is again full and the ice is piled up over the lid of the can. Cover the bucket with newspaper or 2 or 3 paper grocery bags. Throw a heavy piece of material (an old blanket will do) over the bucket and let it stand.

Mother's Uncooked Vanilla Ice Cream

At home, our mother could stir this recipe up in a flash. I think she sometimes used more cream than milk, giving the ice cream a richer, smoother texture.

4 eggs
2 cups sugar
1 quart milk
1 quart heavy cream

1 tablespoon plus 1 teaspoon
    vanilla extract
½ teaspoon salt

In a very large bowl, whip the eggs until light. Add the sugar and beat to blend. Add the milk and cream, mixing well. Stir in the vanilla and salt. Freeze in an ice cream machine as described on pages 128–29. *Makes about 3 quarts and is the correct amount for a 1-gallon freezer.*

Chocolate Custard Ice Cream

Rich, creamy dark chocolate ice cream was made only for special occasions like someone's birthday. It was much more everyday to have either vanilla or fruit ice cream, made with strawberries, peaches, or other fruits in season.

1 quart milk	4 eggs, beaten
4 squares unsweetened	1 quart heavy cream
chocolate	½ teaspoon ground cinnamon
2 cups sugar	¼ teaspoon salt

In a medium-size saucepan, combine the milk and chocolate. Heat slowly over low heat until the chocolate is melted; don't overheat it. Add the sugar, stirring until dissolved. Remove from heat and cool to room temperature. Add the eggs and cream, stirring to blend. Add the cinnamon and salt, blending thoroughly. Freeze in a hand-cranked ice cream freezer as described on page 128. *Makes enough to fill a 1-gallon freezer three-fourths full.*

Fresh Peach Ice Cream

Use peaches that are firm but well ripened.

1 quart heavy cream	½ teaspoon salt
2 cups sugar	4 cups peach puree (made in a
4 eggs, beaten	blender) *or* 4 cups peeled
2 teaspoons brandy flavoring	and finely chopped firm,
(brandy may be substituted)	well-ripened peaches

Bring the cream and sugar to a boil in a medium-size saucepan. Remove from heat. Place the eggs in a large bowl. While the cream is still hot, gradually add it to the eggs, stirring constantly. Cool, then chill overnight. When ready to churn the ice cream, add the brandy flavoring and salt. Then freeze in a hand-cranked ice cream freezer as described on page 128. The fresh peaches may be added when the mixture becomes mushy, only partially frozen. If using the puree, add it when you add the brandy flavoring and salt. *Makes about 3 quarts.*

Butternut Cookies

Most farm women had a few nuts of various kinds in storage at all times for their cooking. Such nut meats were off limits to all nibblers, large and small alike.

1 cup butter
1 cup, packed, light brown
   sugar
1 tablespoon vanilla extract
2 eggs

2½ cups all-purpose flour
1 teaspoon salt
2 teaspoons baking powder
1 cup chopped butternuts

Preheat oven to 350°F. In a large bowl, cream together the butter, sugar, and vanilla. Add the eggs, beating well. Sift the dry ingredients into the butter mixture and blend well. Stir in the butternuts. Drop by spoonfuls onto a lightly greased cookie sheet. Bake until lightly browned, about 10 minutes. Remove from oven, transfer to wire rack, cool thoroughly, and store in an airtight container. *Makes about 3 dozen cookies.*

From THERE IS EVER A SONG SOMEWHERE

There is ever a song somewhere, my dear,
  Be the skies above or dark or fair,
There is ever a song that our hearts may hear—
There is ever a song somewhere, my dear—
  There is ever a song somewhere!

There is ever a song somewhere, my dear,
  In the midnight black, or the mid-day blue;
The robin pipes when the sun is here,
  And the cricket chirrups the whole night through;
The buds may blow, and the fruit may grow,
  And the autumn leaves drop crisp and sere;
But whether the sun, or the rain, or the snow,
  There is ever a song somewhere, my dear.

There is ever a song somewhere, my dear.
  Be the skies above or dark or fair,
There is ever a song that our hearts may hear—
There is ever a song somewhere, my dear—
  There is ever a song somewhere!

—*James Whitcomb Riley*

AUGUST

Jams, Pickles, and County Fairs

By August the longest days of summer have already passed. Although afternoons and evenings are still warm, nights tend to be cooler than those of July. In more northern regions and in higher elevations, dew falls and nighttime temperatures drop, sometimes even bringing a nipping frost—a warning that summer is coming to an end. In the woods and fields, insects are noisier and more numerous than in any other month. Bird nests stand empty as flocks begin gathering to fly south.

Farmers are endlessly busy with field crops ready for harvest. Blueberries, blackberries, raspberries, early apples, and peaches are ripe. Potato tops have lain over and turned yellow, the tubers are ripening in the earth and will have to be harvested before rains come, often in September. String beans are in full harvest as is summer corn. Tomatoes are ripening and so are melons. In the yellowing fields, goldenrod and wild asters—tall-growing flowers—add bits of color here and there, testifying to the maturity of the season.

From OUR HIRED GIRL

Our hired girl, she's 'Lizabuth Ann;
   An' she can cook best things to eat!
She ist puts dough in our pie-pan,
   An' pours in somepin' 'at's good and sweet,
An' nen she salts it all on top
With cinnamon; an' nen she'll stop
   An' stoop an' slide it, ist as slow,
In th' old cook-stove, so's 'twon't slop
   An' git all spilled; nen bakes it, so
   It's custard pie, first thing you know!
     An' nen she'll say:
   "Clear out o' my way!
   They's time fer work, an' time fer play!—
     Take yer dough, an' run, Child; run!
     Er I cain't git no cookin' done!"

—*James Whitcomb Riley*

134

JANE WATSON HOPPING

🌿 SUMMER FRUIT:
SWEET AN' JUICY

In every corner of the kitchen, on porches, and in sheds are boxes, buckets, and pans of early fruits and berries. A few peaches trickle in from the orchards, then become a flowing stream of juicy golden-red fruits. Apples are still hard, but ready for applesauce and pies.

Women and girls begin early each morning by washing canning jars. By nightfall they will have as many as one hundred jars of deep-purple and golden jams, bright-red jelly, richly spiced applesauce, and neatly packed sliced peaches and apples for pies.

And for supper there will be a sweet an' juicy dessert.

Blueberry Crisp

While quite delicious all by itself, a blueberry crisp often had thick cream off the top of milk—icy cold from the spring house—spooned over it.

4 cups washed and stemmed blueberries
¼ cup hot water
1 slightly rounded tablespoon tapioca

½ cup butter
½ cup all-purpose flour
½ cup sugar
Heavy cream, optional

Preheat oven to 400°F. In a medium-size bowl, combine the blueberries, water, and tapioca; set aside. In another bowl, cream the butter. Add the flour and sugar, blending to form crumbs. Spoon the blueberry mixture into a greased 13x9x2-inch baking pan, then sprinkle the flour and sugar mixture evenly over the top. Bake until the berries are tender and the top is browned, about 40 to 45 minutes. Serve immediately as is or with cream spooned over the top. *Makes 4 servings.*

Raspberry Snow

This quick, easy dessert can be whipped up by a little girl—even one who has been helping all day with canning. I like to serve it in glass dishes to show off the pretty raspberry color.

¾ cup mashed raspberries
   Sugar to sweeten the
     raspberries

3 egg whites
¼ cup sugar to sweeten egg
   whites

Lightly sweeten the raspberries to taste with sugar; set aside. In a medium-size bowl, beat the egg whites until stiff; add the ¼ cup sugar and beat a few strokes to blend. Fold in the raspberries. Spoon into 4 glass dessert dishes, serve immediately. *Makes 4 servings.*

Sour Cream Peach Pie

This fresh peach dessert may be topped with whipped cream, but at our house we prefer it plain with extra peaches piled on top.

½ cup all-purpose flour
¾ cup sugar, plus 2 tablespoons
   for peaches on top of pie
½ teaspoon salt
2 cups dairy sour cream
3 eggs, well beaten

1 cup peeled, sliced peaches,
   plus 1 to 1½ cups extra
   slices for top
¼ teaspoon vanilla extract
1 (9-inch) baked pie shell, a
   Flaky Crust (see page 28)
   Whipped cream, optional (see
   page 61)

Note: If slicing the peaches ahead, mix them with *1 tablespoon lemon juice.*

In the top of a double boiler, combine the flour, sugar, and salt. Stir in the sour cream and cook over boiling water until thick, stirring constantly. Remove double boiler from heat, leaving the pan sitting over the hot water.

Place the eggs in a bowl and very gradually add ⅓ cup of the hot sour cream mixture, stirring quickly to blend, then add this egg mixture to the remaining hot sour cream mixture, stirring quickly until smooth and well blended. Return to double boiler over heat. Continue cooking about 3 minutes longer to set the eggs, stirring constantly. Remove from heat and cool. Fold in the 1 cup peaches and the vanilla. Spoon into the baked pie shell and chill thoroughly. Just before serving, lightly sweeten another 1 to 1½ cups slices with 2 tablespoons sugar and arrange them over the top of the pie. Top with whipped cream if you wish. Serve immediately. *Makes one 9-inch pie.*

🌿 WILD BLACKBERRY SUMMER

Everywhere in farm country there are wild patches or thickets of fruits or nuts; but most abundant are the wild blackberries, growing in hedgerows, along creek banks, in pastures, and along slow- and fast-moving streams. By August, the blackberries are in full season, some of them as big as your thumb, hanging thickly in clusters and providing an abundant harvest for wild critters, birds . . . and for folks, too, down on their luck.

A neighbor, Mrs. Edna Billings, remembers a time when she, her younger brothers and sisters, and their mother were grateful for such wild provender. She recalls:

It was durin' the Depression. It was bad, in 1930, in our area. My father went off looking for work and we never heard from him again. Mama thought maybe he'd been killed or something. We didn't have much, but Mama always kept us fed and kept us some place to live.

Then in the summer of '32, we was really up against it. So, we give up the house we was renting and went out into the hills and camped near a berry patch and a clear stream. We took some flour and sugar with us, and some other stuff, and Mama had her cannin' kettles and her jars. So us kids picked berries and caught fish, and did some tradin' with farmers around about.

We did all right, we made some jam and put up some berries for the winter. We was barefoot, and we played a lot. Folks seem to think it must have been awful, livin' out like we done, but it was nice, there was water for swimmin' and games to play. We laughed a lot that summer. When Mama was old, she used to say it was God and love that pulled us through those times.

Old-fashioned Blackberry Pie

Some women combine the raw blackberries, sugar, and cornstarch in a medium-size bowl, turn them into an unbaked pie shell, cover with a top crust, and bake. Others like to make a filling out of cooked berries thickened with cornstarch, and then assemble the pie. Either way, wild blackberries baked in a crisp, flaky pie crust are a treat "fit for a king."

4 cups picked-over blackberries
½ cup sugar
    About ¼ cup water
¼ cup cornstarch dissolved in
    ⅓ cup cold water

Double-Crust Pie Pastry
(recipe follows)

Preheat oven to 425°F. Place the blackberries and sugar in a saucepan and add just enough water (about ¼ cup) to keep the berries from sticking to the pan bottom until they make their own juice. Heat to boiling, stirring frequently but gently, since overstirring breaks up the berries. Add the dissolved cornstarch, stirring quickly to blend; continue cooking, stirring only as needed to keep berries from sticking until the juice is thickened. Remove from heat and let cool. While filling is cooling, prepare pastry. Refrigerate until needed.

When filling and pastry are cold, divide into 2 portions, one slightly larger than the other; roll out the large one and line the pie pan with it; fill the shell with berry filling; moisten the edges and cover with rolled out top crust. Crimp the edges and cut vents in the top crust. (*Note:* Berry pies often spew over, so set a baking sheet underneath them in the oven to catch the dripping; one that can be scrubbed up between pies.) Bake until crust is nicely browned, about 45 to 50 minutes. Let pie set up about 1 hour before serving. *Makes one 9-inch pie.*

Double-Crust Pie Pastry

2 cups all-purpose flour, plus
    flour for rolling out dough
1 teaspoon salt
¾ cup cold butter or margarine
¼ cup cold water

About 2 tablespoons heavy
    cream (milk may be
    substituted)
Sugar to sprinkle on top

In a medium-size bowl, combine the flour and salt. Cut in the butter until the mixture resembles grains of corn. Sprinkle the water over the mixture and mix thoroughly with a fork until all particles cling together to form a ball.

Blackberry Cobbler with Two-Egg Cream Cake Crust

Old-time cobbler recipes such as this one often called for a cream-cake batter for the crust. A simple butter-cake batter may be used if you prefer.

Preheat oven to 350°F. Fill a large (2-quart) casserole dish or flat 13x9x2-inch baking pan half full with about *4 cups* ripe, picked-over blackberries sweetened with *about ½ cup sugar* to taste. Make the simple Two-Egg Cream Cake Batter (recipe follows) and spoon the batter over the berries, spreading it evenly over filling with a spoon. Bake until the crust is cooked through and browned, about 1 hour. (The toothpick test is most accurate to determine the crust's doneness since cobblers sometimes look brown but are not cooked clear through: Push a toothpick midway into the cobbler crust and bring it back out; if the toothpick comes out clean, not sticky with uncooked batter clinging to it, the cobbler is done.) Serve hot or cold, with *1 tablespoon* of *cream* over the top of *each* serving, if desired. *Makes 1 cobbler.*

Two-Egg Cream Cake Batter

Cream in the old days varied considerably in its fat content, not only from cow to cow but at different times of year. Therefore, old-time cooks learned to judge the fat content according to the thickness of the cream. If the fat content was higher than they wanted for a particular recipe, they would dilute the cream with milk. Nowadays, most people buy cream in stores, which is fairly consistent in its fat content.

2 cups all-purpose flour	1 teaspoon salt
1 cup sugar	2 eggs
1 slightly rounded tablespoon baking powder	1½ cups heavy cream
	1 tablespoon vanilla extract

Into a large bowl, sift together the flour, sugar, baking powder, and salt. Make a hollow in the dry ingredients and pour the eggs, cream, and vanilla into it. Beat very well. *Makes enough crust for 1 cobbler.* Once the batter has been made it is used in the main recipe above, which gives instructions for its use.

Wild Blackberry Jam

About one quarter to one third of the blackberries that Mother put in her blackberry jam were underripe, which increased the acid content of the jam and also improved its texture. So use about 7 cups ripe ones and about 2 cups underripe ones.

9 cups picked-over firm, blackberries (preferably wild, store-bought will do)	1 cup water
	7 cups sugar

Wash the berries well and drain them. Discard any bruised berries or ones that show any signs of imperfection. Remove stems and caps. Put the berries in a deep stainless-steel or unchipped enamel preserving kettle that is large enough that the jam won't boil over. Add the water and bring to a boil; boil for 10 minutes, watching carefully and stirring frequently. (After this 10-minute boiling time, if you object to seeds in jam, put the berries through a sieve and then return the pulp to the boiling point.) Add the sugar and continue boiling rapidly until the temperature of the jam reads between 222°F and 224°F on a candy thermometer or until the mixture is thick and clear. Immediately ladle or pour the hot mixture into very hot half-pint- or pint-canning jars. (*Note:* Use new lids and jars and rings in perfect condition; sterilize and keep them hot until ready to fill.) Wipe the rims well with a clean, damp cloth and seal; cool, label, and date. Store upright in a dark, cool, and dry place. Refrigerate after opening. *Makes 8 to 10 half pints or 4 to 5 pints.*

⇒☙ THE COUNTY FAIR

The moment school was out, our children began to plan on going to the fair for a whole day and an evening. They could hardly wait for wild blackberry season to begin so that they could start picking, to earn fair money. Hard work would bring as much as $7.50 each, to be splurged on cotton candy, indigestible food, rides on a Ferris wheel and other contraptions that whirled and twirled and thrilled you beyond measure.

Little did they know or care about the practical side of those fairs. Early-day farmers, eager to improve their products—to raise cattle that gave more milk, hogs that produced more and meatier young, garden produce and field crops that yielded larger vegetables and more tons—responded overwhelmingly to farm societies. One such organization, the grange, organized and sponsored the first exhibitions of useful new farm inventions and the best examples of farm products, giving prizes to local exhibitors for excellence. Soon county and state fairs followed their example, and still do, so that while children spent their pennies at the fair, farmers were gathering to show off and compare their produce and livestock.

Even so, with the enthusiasm of youth the children shared in the educational purpose of the county fair. As we all walked up and down the aisles of the agricultural shows, seeing amazing sights like thirty-pound cabbages, huge peppers, tall sunflowers, yellow eggplants, and four-hundred-pound baking squashes and pumpkins, the children too

marveled. All of us found the new varieties of beans and grains and the literature about new farming methods (provided by seed and implement companies) interesting.

After looking at the prizewinning vegetables and fruits, we all went down to the stock barns where the prizewinning animals—those that could be used for breeding and thus would improve the herds—were on display. Like other men, my husband remained in the stock barn, talking about breeding and milk production. Marketing information passed back and forth and deals were struck. We knew that the only thing that would pull him away from the barns was the horse race or the display of new machinery.

So, the boys raced off to take a grand tour of the fairgrounds and the girls and I went to look at the women's exhibits. On display were prizewinning canning, cooking, baking, and the products of other homemaking skills. On tables were cakes and pies, numerous types of bread, lovely cookies, glittering jars of jams, relishes, and pickles, and good-looking jars of salmon, string beans, peaches, and pears. There were lovely pieces of crocheted work in intricate patterns—tablecloths, lace-trimmed pillowcases, yokes for dresses and nightgowns. The tatted lace seemed almost unreal it was so finely wrought. Quilts worked in wedding ring and double wedding ring patterns hung on frames. There were crazy quilts, too, and those worked in many other appliquéd patterns.

Usually we spent some time looking at the homemaking exhibits before we started off to the flower pavilion. Then all of us—women, irrespective of age—delightedly strolled among the floral displays where the scent of roses hung heavy on the air and where perhaps a waterfall cascaded down over an intricate, handmade embankment, giving one the feeling of deep woods. Marveling at the skill of such displays, we made secret plans to brighten up the farm at home.

By late afternoon, all were tired and hungry. We rested and picnicked in the park before going back to the fair for the evening. Then, as the day cooled and the lights glittered everywhere and the raucous sound of carnival music seemed louder, we began to watch the evening displays—square dancers, pulling contests, and the tree-climbing, log-splitting, ax-throwing displays of local timbermen.

The boys dashed back and forth sharing news about wondrous rides, leaving with me prizes they had won at darts or in shooting contests. The girls with great deliberation decided on the jewelry they would buy, selecting real gold-plated wire pins, delicately worked into their very own names, right in front of their eyes.

Near midnight, the gates closed and we left, tired but happy, filled with new ideas and good memories of a lovely day.

Aunt Margaret's Crispy Oatmeal Cookies

Perhaps these cookies have never won a prize at the county fair, but their winning the hearts of children and adults alike for over thirty-five years should count for something.

1 cup butter or margarine	1 teaspoon baking soda
1 cup granulated sugar	3 cups quick-cooking oats
1 cup, packed, light brown sugar	½ cup chopped walnuts
	½ cup seedless raisins
2 eggs, well beaten	Powdered sugar, about
1 teaspoon vanilla extract	½ cup or slightly more
1½ cups all-purpose flour	About 1 tablespoon ground
1 teaspoon salt	cinnamon, optional

In a large bowl, cream the butter and sugars. Add the eggs and vanilla, beating until blended. Into a separate bowl sift together the flour, salt, and baking soda and add to the creamed mixture, mixing well. Fold in the oats, walnuts, and raisins. Divide dough into 2 equal portions and form each into a ball; then shape into logs 2 inches in diameter and about 6 to 8 inches long. Dust powdered sugar (flavored with ground cinnamon, if desired) on a flat surface and roll each dough ball in it until well coated. Wrap each portion in waxed paper and refrigerate until thoroughly chilled. Then slice ¼ inch thick and place on an ungreased cookie sheet. These cookies spread out, so allow two inches or more between them. Bake in a preheated 350°F oven for 8 to 10 minutes, or until light brown and crisp. Store in an airtight container. *Makes about 5 dozen cookies.*

Prizewinning Sauerkraut in a Jar

Give or take a little on the amount of salt added to this kraut depending on the recipe, women for years have made jars of it, tucked them under sheds or into storerooms where they would not freeze or be forgotten as they fermented. Then in midwinter, when the palate cried out for tart foods, the kraut was retrieved and served as it was —raw—or cooked into various pork dishes.

Wash *green or white cabbage* well and trim any signs of decay or blemishes. Core, trim, and shred the cabbage. Pack it tightly into freshly scrubbed and sterilized 1-quart canning jars. Add *1½ tablespoons salt* to each jar; fill to the top with *cold water*, making sure all cabbage is submerged in liquid; cover the entire surface with a clean *grape leaf* and seal with a brand new self-sealing lid, screwing the ring on as tightly as possible. Put the jars upright in a medium-warm place to ferment (set them on folded newspaper as some leak during fermentation). Label and date jars. The sauerkraut will be ready to eat in three to four weeks. (When proper fermentation has taken place, the lid will stay on tight.) Store jars upright in a cool, dark, and dry place.

When opening a jar, do not worry if the lid is not on tight. Instead, check contents which should be white and crisp; yellowed or softened kraut should be thrown away. Mishaps in making this sauerkraut can come from reducing the amount of salt used (salt is part of the fermentation process), setting the kraut to ferment at too low a temperature (70°F is ideal), or storing the kraut at too low a temperature that allows it to freeze.

Mother's Stuffed and Pickled Bell Peppers

In winter when fresh vegetables were hard to come by, these crisp peppers, filled with delicious cabbage relish, perked up many a meal.

24 large, perfect-shaped green bell peppers	2 tablespoons salt
2 cups salt	3 tablespoons mustard seed
1 gallon (16 cups) water	1½ tablespoons celery seed
6 quarts finely chopped green cabbage	5 cups white distilled vinegar
	5 cups sugar

Wash bell peppers well and trim any blemished areas.

Slice off the stem end of the peppers, cutting down about ¾ inch from the top; reserve tops. Cone and seed the peppers. Put the peppers and their tops to soak overnight in a mild brine (made of the 2 cups salt mixed with the 1 gallon water); weight peppers and tops down so they are completely submerged in the liquid.

The following day, drain and rinse the peppers and tops in cold water; drain and set aside.

Prepare the relish: In a very large bowl, sprinkle the cabbage with the 2 tablespoons salt. Stir to mix well, then let stand at room temperature for 3 hours, covered with a clean dry towel. Squeeze the cabbage, draining off as much moisture as possible. Add the mustard seed and celery seed, stirring thoroughly. Stuff the relish into the peppers, place the tops on, and fasten shut by wrapping each pepper and top several times around with a white cotton thread.

Wash and scald 12 wide-mouth canning jars; wash and scald lids and rings. Fill jars with very hot water; let set until you are ready to pour boiling liquid over the peppers; then pour the water out (putting boiling liquid into cold jars can break the glass). Pack the peppers into the jars, 2 large stuffed peppers or 3 smaller ones in each jar.

Then in a medium-size saucepan, bring the vinegar and sugar to a boil, and simmer 5 minutes. Immediately pour the boiling hot liquid over the peppers and promptly seal the jars. Label and date jars. These peppers will be ready to use in 2 to 3 weeks. Refrigerate after opening. *Makes 8 to 12 jars*, depending on size of peppers.

Grandma's Watermelon Rind Pickles

At every county fair, there are numerous entries of watermelon rind pickles. The farm women have always seemed to think they were "somethin' fancy."

Rind from 1 medium-size watermelon (a thick rind makes a better pickle)
1 cup salt
Cold water
Boiling water, about 1 gallon
2 teaspoons powdered alum
2 tablespoons whole cloves
2 broken sticks cinnamon

2 tablespoons whole allspice berries
½ nutmeg seed
9 cups sugar
7 cups cider vinegar
1 (6-ounce) jar maraschino cherries (reserve liquid), halved, *or* 1 cup candied citron, candied pineapple, or candied ginger

Cut the melon into thick slices. Peel the green skin and any red meat from the rind, leaving only the white part of the rind. Cut rind into fancy shapes—diamonds, circles, strips, and such. Place shaped pieces in a large bowl. Sprinkle the salt over them and add enough cold water to cover. Let stand overnight.

Wash and rinse the rind pieces; drain well since the rind gives off water that will dilute the syrup. Place the rind in a large kettle. Add the alum to the boiling water and pour enough over the rind to cover. Cook until tender when tested with a fork, then drain. Rinse under cool water and drain well.

Place the cloves, cinnamon, allspice, and nutmeg in a cloth bag and tie closed. Place the sugar, vinegar, and spice bag in a large kettle and boil until a thick syrup is formed, about 20 minutes. Remove the spice bag and add the drained rind. Simmer until clear, about 5 to 8 minutes more. Remove from heat and add the halved cherries and their juice or the candied citron, pineapple, or ginger. Let rind stand in syrup overnight at room temperature. The following day, pour off the syrup into a saucepan; bring to a boil, then pour it over the drained rind that has been attractively arranged in freshly scrubbed and sterilized pint or half-pint canning jars that are still hot. Fill the jars up to ½ inch from the rims, making sure all pieces of rind are submerged in liquid. Promptly wipe rims with a clean, damp cloth and place hot lids on top with sealing compound down; screw on metal rings firmly. Label and date jars and store upright in a cool, dark, and dry place. Store at least two weeks before using. Refrigerate after opening. *Makes 6 pints or 12 half pints.*

Honey-Apple Marmalade

5 to 6 medium-size tart apples (Jonathan preferred)	chopped
1 cup water	Juice from 2 lemons, finely chopped
Rind from 2 lemons, finely	Honey

Put peeled (or leave unpeeled if you wish) and chopped apples in a 6-quart kettle; add water, and cook until apples are tender. Test with a fork and watch closely. Add lemon rind and juice, stir to blend. Remove apple-lemon pulp from kettle, measure; return to kettle and add half as much honey as fruit pulp. Cook until thick, about 20 minutes or more; check often. Put into freshly scrubbed and sterilized jars (use new lids), wipe the tops, and seal. *Makes 6 to 8 half pints.*

(Note: Put lids in a pan of hot water; bring to a boil. Turn off heat; put lids on jars while still hot.)

✑❀ CAKEWALK

In late August, just before school opened, country parents were often faced with a shortage of books in their district. A cakewalk to earn money sometimes remedied the situation. The cakewalk was originally an elaborate step or walk performed by blacks in the South in competition for a prize cake. Subsequently it developed into a strutting dance and then into a game played in farm communities all across the nation.

To prepare for this social occasion with a serious purpose, women got out their very best recipes and decorated huge three-layer cakes with elaborate frostings called "seafoam" or "seven-minute."

On the appointed evening, folks from miles around gathered at the school. A committee secretly assigned a number to each cake that came in. Then when the musicians were set up and after people had had time for a bit of visiting, foot-square cards with numbers on them were placed in a ring about a schoolroom now devoid of its desks.

Eager players paid a dime and picked a card to stand on. When the ring was complete, the music began. Then amid much laughter the men, with heavy-booted feet more accustomed to furrows than foolishness, pranced around the ring in a high stepping, strutting cakewalk until the music stopped.

One of the tall cakes was brought out for display and a number called. The person standing on the matching square had won the cake. Usually that person did not play again, but bachelors and widowers laughed and made jokes and pestered the women for a chance to win another one of their cakes.

By the end of the evening, everyone had had a good time, the school had books, and as old-timers said, "No one was hurt," meaning the cost to each family was small.

French Chocolate Cake with a Fluffy Chocolate Frosting

Since chocolate was never a staple commodity on old-time farms, women prized a good chocolate cake recipe and baked it only for special occasions.

½ cup unsweetened cocoa powder
1½ cups sugar
⅓ cup hot water (more if needed to make a smooth paste)
½ cup butter or margarine

1 cup sour milk or buttermilk
3 eggs, slightly beaten
1 teaspoon vanilla extract
2 cups all-purpose flour
1 teaspoon baking soda
Fluffy Chocolate Frosting (recipe follows)

Preheat oven to 350°F. In a small bowl, combine the cocoa, *½ cup* of the sugar, and the hot water, stirring it into a paste. In a large bowl, cream the *remaining 1 cup* sugar and the butter; then mix in the milk, eggs, and vanilla. Sift in the flour and baking soda, beating until light. Spoon into 2 greased and floured 9-inch cake pans. Bake until the cake springs back when pressed lightly with the fingertips, or until a toothpick inserted in the center comes out clean, about 30 to 35 minutes. Remove from oven and turn out on a wire rack to cool thoroughly, then frost. *Makes one 2-layer cake.*

Fluffy Chocolate Frosting

3 ounces unsweetened chocolate
3 tablespoons butter or margarine

1½ cups sifted powdered sugar
1 teaspoon vanilla extract
Pinch of salt
2 egg whites

In the top of a double boiler, melt the chocolate over hot (not boiling) water; cool before adding to other ingredients. In a mixing bowl, cream the butter until light and fluffy. Add *¾ cup* of the sugar and blend well. Stir in the chocolate, vanilla, and salt.

In a separate bowl, beat the egg whites until stiff but not dry. Beat in the *remaining ¾ cup* sugar, about 2 tablespoons at a time, beating well after each addition. Continue beating until mixture peaks, then gently fold in the chocolate mixture, taking care not to reduce volume. *Makes enough frosting for one 2-layer cake.*

Burnt-Sugar Cake with Caramel Marshmallow Frosting

To prepare her Burnt-Sugar Syrup, Mother put ½ cup granulated sugar in a frying pan over low heat, warming it until the sugar softened, then melted, and finally began to bubble and brown. When the sugar had turned very dark but was not burned or smoking, she removed the pan from the heat and poured ½ cup boiling hot water into the pan with the sugar to make a molasses-colored syrup. Once cooled, she bottled the syrup and stored it in the refrigerator for later use. This amount (about ½ cup) was sufficient to flavor 3 cakes or pies.

½ cup butter or margarine	2½ cups all-purpose flour
1½ cups sugar	2 teaspoons baking powder
2 egg yolks, slightly beaten	2 egg whites, beaten until soft
1 cup water	peaks form
2 teaspoons Mother's Burnt-	Caramel Marshmallow
Sugar Syrup	Frosting (recipe follows)
1 teaspoon vanilla extract	

Preheat oven to 350°F. In a large bowl, cream the butter and sugar. Add the egg yolks, water, burnt-sugar flavoring, and vanilla; beat until blended and light. Stir in *2 cups* of the flour. Beat a few strokes, then sift in the *remaining ½ cup* flour and the baking powder; beat several more strokes. Gently fold in the beaten egg whites, being careful not to reduce their volume. Spoon batter into 2 greased and floured 9-inch cake pans. Bake until the sides of the cake have pulled away from the pan and the top feels firm to the touch, about 30 to 35 minutes. Turn out on a wire rack, cool thoroughly, then frost. *Makes one 2-layer cake.*

Caramel Marshmallow Frosting

2 egg whites	2 teaspoons Mother's Burnt-
Pinch of salt	Sugar Syrup
¾ cup light corn syrup	1 teaspoon vanilla extract

In a medium-size bowl, beat the egg whites until stiff but not dry; mix in the salt. In a small saucepan, heat the corn syrup to boiling. Slowly pour the hot syrup over the beaten egg whites, stirring constantly; continue beating until the frosting is fluffy and soft peaks form. Add the Burnt-Sugar Syrup and vanilla, stirring to blend. *Makes enough to frost one 2-layer cake.*

Champion Silver Cake with Snow Peak Frosting

High, light-textured three-layer cakes were the beauts of old-time cake making. Standing tall, sliced in great chunks, such cakes took prize after prize at farm-country county fairs. This old champion can be dressed in Snow Peak Frosting (see below), or iced with rich swirls of thick whipped cream.

1 cup butter
3 cups sugar
2 cups milk
2 teaspoons vanilla extract
5 cups cake flour
1 tablespoon plus 1 teaspoon baking powder
½ teaspoon salt

6 egg whites, well beaten until soft peaks form
Snow Peak Frosting (recipe follows)
1 cup sweetened shredded coconut, for sprinkling on top of cake

Preheat oven to 350°F. In a very large bowl, cream the butter and sugar until very light in texture. In a small bowl, blend the milk with the vanilla. Add the milk mixture and *4 cups* of the flour alternately to the butter mixture, beating until well blended between additions; be sure to beat thoroughly. Then sift in the *remaining 1 cup* flour and the baking powder and salt. Beat again. Gently fold in the egg whites, taking care not to reduce their volume. Bake in 3 greased and floured 9-inch cake pans until lightly browned and springs back when touched, about 30 to 35 minutes. Remove from oven, let sit 10 minutes in pans, then turn out and cool thoroughly on a wire rack. Then frost the cake and sprinkle the coconut on top. *Makes one 3-layer cake.*

Snow Peak Frosting
1½ cups light corn syrup
4 egg whites

½ teaspoon salt
1 teaspoon vanilla extract

In a medium-size saucepan, heat the corn syrup to the boiling point. In a large bowl, beat the egg whites until stiff but not dry. Beat in the salt. Slowly pour the hot syrup over the egg whites, beating constantly until the frosting is light and soft peaks form. Fold in the vanilla. *Makes enough to frost one 3-layer cake.*

Gentleman's Choice Served with Whipped Cream

This rich old-time cake is baked in a single-layer pan, cut into squares, and served with whipped cream.

½ cup sugar	½ cup hot water
½ cup molasses	1½ cups all-purpose flour
2 tablespoons butter or margarine	½ cup unsweetened cocoa powder
3 eggs, well beaten	Whipped cream (see recipe page 61)
1 teaspoon baking soda	

Preheat oven to 350°F. In a large bowl, combine the sugar, molasses, butter, and eggs, mixing well. Dissolve the baking soda in the hot water and add to the sugar mixture, blending well. Then sift in the flour and cocoa and beat until well mixed. Turn into a greased 11x7-inch cake pan (2 inches deep). Bake until a toothpick inserted into the center of the cake comes out clean, about 40 to 45 minutes. Cool in the pan. Cut into squares and top each serving with a heaped tablespoonful of whipped cream. *Makes one 1-layer cake or 8 to 10 servings.*

Sand Cake

Women who like to cook have always enjoyed novelty recipes. This sand cake, made with cornstarch instead of flour, passed from hand to hand until it came to me. It is a delightful cake.

1 cup butter or margarine	5 eggs
1 teaspoon salt	1½ cups cornstarch
1 cup sugar	1 teaspoon lemon extract

Preheat oven to 350°F. In a large bowl, combine the butter and salt, mixing until butter is creamed. Add the sugar by tablespoonfuls, beating constantly. Separate the eggs and as you do so, add 1 yolk at a time to the butter mixture, beating after each addition; place egg whites in a separate bowl. Add the cornstarch one tablespoonful at a time to the butter mixture, beating between additions. Stir in the lemon extract. Beat the egg whites to a froth and fold them in. Spoon the batter into a 9x9x2-inch greased and paper-lined loaf pan with top of paper greased, too. Bake until light brown, about 45 minutes. Test by inserting a toothpick into the center of the cake; if it comes out clean, cake is done. Serve unfrosted. *Makes one cake.*

Simnel Cake with Almond Filling

This almond-flavored cake has won many "ooh's and ah's" wherever it has been taken. We call it a holiday cake.

¾ cup butter
¾ cup sugar
2 cups flour
1 teaspoon baking powder
¾ teaspoon salt
4 eggs, well beaten
½ teaspoon almond extract
2 cups sultana raisins
½ cup slivered almonds
½ cup chopped candied citron
  Almond Filling (recipe
    follows)

Preheat oven to 350°F. In a large bowl, cream the butter and sugar together until light. Into a separate bowl, sift the flour, baking powder, and salt. Add the eggs, almond extract, and flour mixture to the butter mixture, beating until well blended. Fold in the raisins, almonds, and citron; set aside.

Make the filling. Line a greased 13x9x2-inch loaf cake pan with waxed paper and grease top of paper, too; spoon half of the cake batter into the pan. Then spread half the filling mixture evenly over the batter. Cover the filling evenly with the remaining half of the cake batter.

Bake for 45 to 50 minutes or until the cake is about two-thirds done. Then spread the top of the cake with the remaining almond filling. Continue baking until the cake tests done, when a toothpick is inserted in the middle, about 25 minutes more. *Makes one loaf cake.*

Almond Filling
2 cups powdered sugar
½ cup ground almonds
2 eggs, well beaten
1 teaspoon almond extract

Mix all the ingredients together in a medium-size bowl until well blended. *Makes about 1½ cups.*

THE BAREFOOT BOY

Blessings on thee, little man,
Barefoot boy, with cheek of tan!
With thy turned-up pantaloons,
And thy merry whistled tunes;
With thy red lip, redder still
Kissed by strawberries on the hill;
With the sunshine on thy face,
Through thy torn brim's jaunty grace;
From my heart I give thee joy,—
I was once a barefoot boy!
Let the million-dollared ride!
Barefoot, trudging at his side,
Thou hast more than he can buy
In the reach of ear and eye,—
Outward sunshine, inward joy:
Blessings on thee, barefoot boy!

Oh for boyhood's painless play,
Sleep that wakes in laughing day,
Health that mocks the doctor's rules,
Knowledge never learned of schools,
Of the wild bee's morning chase,
Of the wild flower's time and place,
Flight of fowl and habitude
Of the tenants of the wood;
How the tortoise bears his shell,

How the woodchuck digs his cell,
And the ground mole sinks his well;
How the robin feeds her young,
How the oriole's nest is hung;
Where the whitest lilies blow,
Where the freshest berries grow,
Where the groundnut trails its vine,
Where the wood grape's clusters shine;
Of the black wasp's cunning way,
Mason of his walls of clay,
And the architectural plans
Of gray hornet artisans!
For, eschewing books and tasks,
Nature answers all he asks;
Hand in hand with her he walks,
Face to face with her he talks,
Part and parcel of her joy,—
Blessings on the barefoot boy!

—*John Greenleaf Whittier*

SEPTEMBER

Bumper Crops and Canning Kettles

September, the age-old harvest month or barley month,* is a time of overflowing boxes, baskets, buckets, and pails. All through September the seasonal movement is relentless. The weather cools, evenings grow chill, and the promise of fall is in the air. And by the end of the month, the earth is stripped of crops.

The land seems rich and pregnant. In the woods and orchards there is the incessant drop of acorns and nuts—the flitting, dancing tails of silver-gray squirrels as they dart out of cover to snatch goodies off the ground for their growing winter hoards. Bits of fluff fly about through the air, carrying seeds to distant corners of the farm.

Toward the end of the month, a last burst of summer comes, forcing late roses to bloom in the front yard. Touches of golden haze hang on the land. The tide turns, the pace slows, dusk comes earlier, and nights have a nip to them. Fall is at hand and children return to school.

* September was called barley month by Anglo-Saxons because it was the month in which they harvested that grain.

There were no frills in old-time schools. Children learned reading and how to figure or cipher (do arithmetic). Penmanship was an art a child practiced diligently. Recess was pure joy, a release for farm children accustomed to being free and active. Older children played rough and tumble games like crack the whip while the smaller ones enjoyed hide and seek, farmer in the dell, and London bridge.

Lunches were carried to school in a lard pail or sometimes simply wrapped in a large napkin or piece of paper tied with string. Food was usually leftovers, such as cold fried chicken or ham, with thick slices of home-baked bread. In season, green onions or apples might be included. And there were always endless cookies, sweet breads, and cakes to brighten the no-nonsense days.

In most families, education took a backseat to survival. When our grandmother died in childbirth, all of her children, except the youngest, who was only four, were already in school. It was a trying time for the family; survival meant getting the spring work done. Everyone worried about the little one and his sorrow over losing his mother, so the teacher of the one-room school near them kindly let four-year-old Freddie come to school with the other children. Shortly, she had him working on his alphabet and reading out of a primer.

On the other hand, Uncle Arch, who had been needed to help with the farming, didn't graduate from the eighth grade until he was seventeen. Eventually, when he could be spared at home, he and his sister, Mabel, moved twenty miles away to a town of only three hundred that had a two-year high-school, a rarity in small towns of the day.

Is it any wonder that teachers and some parents dreamed of a time when children would be able to start school in the fall and "finish out the term" without being kept home to help with the work.

Sorghum Gingerbread

Raised like corn, sorghum grows eight feet tall with a heavy head of rust-brown grain on top. When harvested, the stalks are stripped of leaves and the butt and seed ends are cut off. The lovely pastel-green juice is then squeezed out of the stalks by pressing them between two heavy rollers. When boiled into honeylike syrup, sorghum is delicious for use in baking or for eating on bread, like jelly.

2½ cups unbleached all-purpose flour	2 teaspoons ground nutmeg
	2 teaspoons ground cinnamon

2 teaspoons ground ginger	1 egg, well beaten
1½ teaspoons baking soda	1 cup sorghum
½ teaspoon salt	1 cup hot water
½ cup butter	Whipped cream, optional
½ cup, packed, light brown sugar	(see page 61)

Preheat oven to 350°F. Grease and flour a 9x9x2-inch cake pan. Into a medium-size bowl, sift the flour, nutmeg, cinnamon, ginger, baking soda, and salt. In a large bowl, cream together the butter and sugar. Add the egg and sorghum, stirring to blend. Alternately in thirds, add the flour mixture and the water, beating well after each addition. Spoon into the prepared pan and bake until the bread tests done with a toothpick, about 50 to 60 minutes. Cool 10 minutes before removing from the pan, then cut into squares and serve in sauce dishes, topped with whipped cream. *Makes 8 to 12 servings.*

Winter Squash Loaf

We raise huge winter squash, which store well. The thick-meated yellow and orange varieties—Golden Delicious, Hubbard, Sweet Meat, and Butter Nut—are excellent for use in this sweet bread.

1 cup butter	4 cups all-purpose flour
⅔ cup granulated sugar	2 teaspoons baking soda
1 cup, packed, light brown sugar	1 teaspoon salt
	2 teaspoons ground cinnamon
4 eggs	¼ teaspoon ground ginger
¼ cup water	¼ teaspoon ground cloves
2 cups baked squash pureed in a blender	¼ teaspoon ground nutmeg
	1 cup chopped walnuts

Preheat oven to 350°F. In a large bowl, cream the butter and granulated sugar until light and creamy. Add the brown sugar and beat until smooth. Add the eggs, one at a time, beating after each addition. Add the water and squash puree. Into a medium-size bowl, sift the flour, soda, cinnamon, salt, ginger, cloves, and nutmeg; gently fold together if necessary so spices are well blended. Add the flour mixture to the squash mixture, stirring until well blended. Then fold in the walnuts. Grease three or four 4x8-inch loaf pans, depending on whether three thick, or four thin, loaves are preferred; dust pans with flour. Spoon equal portions of the batter into the pans. Bake until a toothpick inserted into the center of the bread comes out clean, about 30 to 45 minutes depending on the size of the loaf. Place pans on a wire rack for 10 minutes, then remove bread from pans to finish cooling. When completely cool, wrap in foil or plastic wrap to retain moisture. This bread is delicious when aged overnight. *Makes 3 large or 4 small loaves.*

Buttermilk Doughnuts

All of his married life, Grandpa White talked about the nutmeg-flavored doughnuts that his mother made when he was a boy and which he had never tasted since. Grandma White and I worked at combining recipes all one summer until we finally settled on one that was close, this one for buttermilk doughnuts.

3 tablespoons heavy cream	¾ teaspoon freshly grated
1 cup sugar	nutmeg
3 eggs, well beaten	About 4½ cups all-purpose
1 cup buttermilk	flour
1 teaspoon lemon extract	Shortening or vegetable oil
1½ teaspoons baking powder	for deep-frying
½ teaspoon baking soda	Powdered sugar for dusting
½ teaspoon salt	doughnuts

In a large bowl, combine the cream and sugar, beating until smooth. Add the eggs, buttermilk, and lemon extract. Into a medium-size bowl, sift the baking powder, baking soda, salt, and nutmeg with *2 cups* of the flour. Add these dry ingredients to the liquid ingredients, mixing well. Add enough additional flour ½ cup at a time to make a soft dough, one that is just stiff enough to handle. Turn onto a floured surface, roll about ¾ inch thick, and cut out with a doughnut cutter. In a deep skillet or deep fryer, heat the shortening or oil to 365°F. Fry doughnuts in the hot fat until golden brown on both sides; do not crowd. Drain both sides on absorbent paper until the surface is dry, then dust with powdered sugar. *Makes 2 dozen doughnuts.*

Sweet Potato Pie with Egg Pastry

My grandfather raised fields of sweet potatoes in Missouri. These potatoes grew on the tops of ridges separated by wide, shallow valleys.

The year after my grandmother died, Grandfather and all of the six children were very sad. Early that summer he found his youngest children laughing and rolling over the green carpet of leaves, up and down the ridges of his sweet potato patch. This was something they had never done and something that had never been permitted. But this one time, he listened to the laughter, then turned and walked away.

Egg Pastry (recipe follows)

2 to 3 sweet potatoes (or enough to yield 1 cup cooked pulp), baked

¼ cup butter

½ cup, packed, dark brown sugar

3 eggs, beaten

⅓ cup light sorghum

⅓ cup milk

2 teaspoons vanilla extract

½ teaspoon salt

Whipped cream, optional (see page 61)

Preheat oven to 425°F. Line the pie pan with the pastry dough and refrigerate until ready to use.

Mash the 1 cup baked sweet potato pulp until smooth; cool slightly. In a large bowl, cream together the butter and sugar. Add the potato pulp and eggs, mixing well. Add the sorghum, milk, vanilla, and salt; stir to blend. Pour the filling into the prepared pie shell. Bake at 425°F for 10 minutes, then reduce oven setting to 350°F and continue baking until the top is browned and the pie is firm. Test with a knife blade: Insert in center; if blade comes out clean the pie is done, about 35 to 45 minutes more. Serve as is or topped with whipped cream, if desired. *Makes one 8-inch pie.*

Egg Pastry

½ cup butter or margarine

1 cup all-purpose flour, plus flour for kneading

½ teaspoon salt

1 egg

About 2 tablespoons cold water, more if needed

1 teaspoon cider vinegar

In a medium-size bowl, work the butter into the flour and salt until the mixture is coarse with lumps the size of peas. In a small bowl, beat the egg, water, and vinegar into a froth, then stir this into the flour mixture. Form the dough into a ball and place on a floured surface and knead only as much as is needed to form a smooth ball which can be handled without sticking to the hands. Roll out dough and line an ungreased 8-inch pie pan with it. Fill and bake as directed in the above recipe. *Makes one 8-inch pie shell.*

Grain that was in verdure waving,
Weareth now a hue of gold,
And the yellow heads are bending,
With the fruitage that they hold;
That the ripened fruit be gathered,
Speed the sickle to and fro;
For the countless hosts of kernels,
Snowy loaves ere long will show.

Not in vain the talk of plowing,
And the sowing of the seed,
For the wealth of golden kernels,
Shall supply the public need;
See the shocks as thickly scattered,
As the tents of soldier band;
Soon they shall be grandly builded,
Where the ricks shall towering stand.

Soon from out the noisy thresher,
There shall golden streams be pour'd.
That the farmer's heart will gladden,
And shall bring his just reward;
Smiles the land today with plenty,
Plenty for the needy throng;
Let all classes and conditions,
Join to swell the harvest song.

—Jas. L. Orr
—E. R. Latta

Cooking for the Threshing Crew

All women, young and old, did a great deal of cooking to keep large families and farm help well fed. Country girls learned to cook at an early age and took pride in being able to efficiently set a good table. By age fourteen or sixteen, girls were often conscripted by neighbor women who needed their help cooking for the threshers.

The threshing crews were men who traveled north as the grain matured for harvest, hauling huge equipment with them. Once a threshing machine was set up in the field or near the barns, the men settled down to stay on the farm, living and eating with the family until the job was done.

To maintain their strength, these men had to be fed great quantities of food. They were usually on the job early, came in at noon for a huge meal, after which they rested in the shade for an hour or two, then went back to work until dark.

For the farm women, these extra mouths to feed meant several days or weeks of heavy-duty kitchen work. Since the grain harvest was in late summer, when days were still hot, the additional cooking was quite a task, mostly done early in the morning hours while it was still cool. Cooking on wood-burning stoves, these women and girls prepared platters of meat, dozens of meat pies, kettles of stews, piles of yeast bread and biscuits, flavorful cakes, pies, and cobblers, and vegetables of every kind. Pitchers, jars, jugs, and vats were full of lemonade, tea, coffee, and milk.

When their work was done, the harvesters moved north from Missouri into Kansas, from Kansas clear to the Canadian border, always following the ripening grain. Often they took the hearts of a few country girls with them. And sweating again in the northern fields, they remembered the blue-eyed prairie flowers whose able hands had fed them and revived their exhausted bodies.

Coleslaw with Hot Bacon Dressing

Old-time cooks used bacon with some of its grease, vinegar, sugar, and water to make salad dressing. This coleslaw is a dressed-up version of Mother's slaw.

3 cups finely shredded cabbage
½ cup finely chopped celery
¼ cup minced red bell peppers
¼ cup minced green or yellow
  bell pepper
4 slices bacon, cut into ½-inch
  pieces

2 medium-size green onions,
  finely chopped
½ cup mayonnaise
¼ cup cider vinegar
1 scant tablespoon sugar
1 teaspoon salt
¼ teaspoon celery seed

Mix together the cabbage, celery, and bell peppers in a large salad bowl; set aside. In a heavy skillet lightly brown the bacon, transfer it from the drippings to drain. Sauté the onions in the drippings for about 1 minute, or just long enough to wilt them. Remove from heat. Return the bacon to the skillet and add the mayonnaise, vinegar, sugar, salt, and celery seed; stir together. Pour over the vegetable mixture and toss lightly. Serve immediately. *Makes 6 servings.*

Ada's Hot Potato Salad

6 medium-size potatoes
2 hard-cooked eggs, chopped
4 slices bacon
¼ cup chopped onions
1 egg, beaten
¼ cup cider vinegar

1½ teaspoons salt
  Black pepper
6 to 8 sprigs fresh parsley
1 celeriac (root celery),
  peeled, cubed and cooked,
  optional

Boil the potatoes until tender; drain, peel, and slice while still hot; place in a large bowl. Add the hard-cooked eggs and set aside. Fry the bacon in a skillet until crisp; drain bacon and crumble it, reserving skillet with bacon fat. Add the onions to the skillet with the bacon fat and fry until golden brown. Transfer onions to the bowl with the potatoes, reserving the bacon fat. Place the beaten egg in a small bowl and slowly add the bacon fat, beating constantly. Stir in the vinegar and salt and add pepper to taste. Pour over the hot potatoes, mixing lightly until well blended. Garnish with parsley and serve immediately. (*Note:* If necessary, reheat in a double boiler.) Celeriac may also be boiled in water until tender, then cubed and added, if desired. *Makes 6 to 8 servings.*

Swiss-Fried Chicken

This recipe was quite popular for using with chickens that were full grown but still young. It was also and still is a rather quick, on-top-of-the-stove method for frying chicken.

2 large (3- to 3½-pound) fryers
  Salt
  Black pepper
¼ cup onion juice

Melted butter
Batter (recipe follows)
Vegetable oil for deep-frying

Cover the chickens with lightly salted water and cook until fairly tender but the meat should not be falling away from the bone. Remove from broth, cool, and cut into pieces for frying. (Reserve broth for another recipe.) Then moisten them well with the butter. Sprinkle chicken pieces evenly with salt, pepper, and onion juice as desired. Let stand at least 2 hours in refrigerator to absorb flavors of the seasoning. Then dip in batter and fry in hot oil until coating is browned and chicken is heated through. Drain on paper towels and serve immediately. (*Note:* The backs and wings may be reserved with the broth for use in other recipes.) *Makes about 12 pieces.*

Batter

1 cup all-purpose flour
2 egg yolks, beaten
½ cup brandy

Milk as needed for a stiff
  batter, approximately
  2 to 3 tablespoons
2 egg whites, beaten until stiff
  peaks form

Place the flour in a medium-size bowl. Add the egg yolks, brandy, and just enough milk to make a stiff batter, mixing well. Fold in the egg whites. Let the batter stand for 1 to 2 hours at room temperature before using. *Makes about 1½ cups.*

Roasted Guinea Chickens

On farms, *guinea fowl*, dark-gray birds with white spots on their feathers, are called watchdogs of the poultry yard because they make such loud raucous cries when disturbed. Such birds, related to pheasants, are a bit quarrelsome and hard to raise, but the meat is considered a delicacy, and farm wives also welcome the small, spotted, thick-shelled eggs.

Very young birds, *squab guinea*, weigh from ¾ pound to 1½ pounds. *Guinea chickens*, often fried like domesticated chickens, weigh from 1½ to 2¼ pounds. Older birds, *guinea hens*, weigh from 2½ to 3 pounds and are braised with cooking time varying according to size. All of the meat, regardless of the guinea's size, is dark and mildly gamey, like pheasant, which is delicious.

2 (1½- to 2-pound) guinea chickens
Butter, softened, 1 or 2 tablespoons for each chicken
Salt
Black pepper
½ teaspoon dried sweet marjoram, pulverized
1 tablespoon dried chervil, pulverized
1 small onion, halved
2 small stalks celery, including leaves
2 sprigs fresh parsley
4 to 6 slices farm-style bacon
Flour
Honey Butter Glaze (recipe follows)
Freshly grated nutmeg for dusting

Preheat oven to 300°F. Wipe the guineas clean; rub them inside and out with butter, then sprinkle inside and out with salt and pepper. Next, rub the marjoram between your fingers and sprinkle it over the guineas inside and out; do the same with the chervil. In each cavity place 1 onion half, 1 piece of celery, and 1 sprig of parsley. Place the guineas breast up in a close-fitting pan with a lid. Arrange 2 or 3 slices of bacon across each guinea. Insert a meat thermometer in the breast of 1 of the guineas, cover, and bake until thermometer reads 170°F. (*Note:* If you suspect the bird to be an older one—a hen—add ¼ cup water to the pan before baking. Allow about 30 minutes total baking time per pound of bird: A 2-pound bird would require 1 hour, a 3-pound bird 1½ hours.) Remove the lid and discard the bacon. Sprinkle the guinea breasts lightly with flour. Resalt and pepper, if needed. Baste generously with Honey Butter Glaze and continue baking uncovered until the thermometer reads 180°F and the breast is lightly browned, about 20 minutes. Dust lightly with freshly grated nutmeg. Don't overcook or baste scantily or else the breast will dry out. *Makes 6 to 8 servings.*

Honey Butter Glaze

½ cup light honey (clover
    preferred)
½ cup hot water

¼ cup butter or margarine
Nutmeg for dusting

In a small saucepan, combine honey, water, and butter; heat over medium heat until butter has melted thoroughly.

Potato Biscuits

At our house, potatoes are always plentiful and therefore they are worked into many different recipes, including various breads such as these potato biscuits, which take a bit more time than most, but are very nice biscuits for company. (Using mashed potatoes left over from the night before makes them easier; the potatoes must be well chilled.)

2 cups unbleached all-purpose
    flour, plus flour for kneading
    dough
2 teaspoons baking powder
1 teaspoon salt
1 cup cold butter or margarine
3 eggs, lightly beaten

1 cup cold, smooth mashed
    potatoes
2 tablespoons heavy cream
1 tablespoon water
1 tablespoon caraway, sesame,
    or poppy seed

In a large bowl, combine the flour, baking powder, and salt. Using a pastry blender or rubbing it in with the fingertips, cut in the butter, taking care not to work the butter so much that it melts into the flour. Set aside *2 tablespoons* of the beaten eggs. Add the remaining eggs and the potatoes and cream to the flour mixture, stirring until a thick dough is formed. Turn onto a floured surface and knead half a dozen times. Roll dough ¼ inch thick and then fold it into halves, then over into quarters. Refrigerate for 30 minutes, then roll dough thin again and fold into quarters and refrigerate 30 minutes. Repeat this process of rolling, folding, and chilling the dough 3 more times. Meanwhile, preheat oven to 400°F. Finally, roll dough ¼ inch thick and cut into rounds with a floured biscuit cutter. Place on an ungreased baking sheet about 1 inch apart. Mix the reserved 2 tablespoons eggs with the water and brush mixture on tops of biscuit rounds. Sprinkle a generous pinch of caraway, sesame, or poppy seed evenly over the rounds. Bake until light brown, about 15 to 20 minutes. Serve while piping hot. *Makes 10 to 12 biscuits.*

Cornmeal Gems

When I was growing up corn bread was often made of white meal, but this old gem recipe puts aside the Southern prejudice that vows yellow corn is for hogs and white corn is for people. When baked in the decorated cups of an old-fashioned gem pan, this delicious muffinlike quick bread is a must for company.

1½ cups unbleached all-purpose flour	1 teaspoon salt
¾ cup yellow cornmeal	1 egg, beaten
¼ cup sugar	⅔ cup milk
1 tablespoon plus 1½ teaspoons baking powder	⅓ cup butter, melted

Preheat oven to 425°F. In a medium-size bowl, combine the flour, cornmeal, sugar, baking powder, and salt; mix thoroughly. In a small bowl, combine the egg, milk, and butter, stirring until smooth. Add the liquid to the dry ingredients, stirring only enough to dampen all of the dry ingredients. (The gem batter should be lumpy; overstirring will make tunnels form in the bread.) Spoon the batter into 24 greased muffin cups or gem pan cups, spreading batter out evenly. Bake until golden brown and firm to the touch, 15 to 25 minutes. Turn out, upside down. Serve hot. *Makes 2 dozen gems.*

Mahogany Cake with Fudge Frosting

Old-time people delighted in the richly hued world about them, in the color of nuts, berries, leaves, and the wood that they burned and built with. Some man or woman must have seen in the rich deep color of this chocolate cake the gleaming depths of polished mahogany.

1½ cups sugar	1 teaspoon baking soda
⅔ cup butter	2 teaspoons vanilla extract
3 eggs, well beaten	2 scant cups all-purpose flour
½ cup unsweetened powdered cocoa	Fudge Frosting (recipe follows)
1¼ cups milk	

Preheat oven to 350°F. In a large bowl, cream the sugar and butter. Add the eggs, stirring until well blended; set aside. Place the cocoa and *½ cup plus 2 tablespoons* of the milk in a small saucepan, blending well. Cook over low heat to the consistency of custard. Remove from heat and place pan in a large pan of cold water to cool the chocolate mixture to lukewarm. Add to the butter and sugar mixture, blending well. Dissolve the baking soda in the *remaining ½ cup plus 2 table-spoons* milk and stir into the butter and sugar mixture. Stir in the vanilla. Add the flour, beating well. Spoon the batter into 2 greased and floured 9-inch cake pans. Bake until a toothpick inserted in the center of the cake comes out clean, about 30 to 35 minutes. Turn layers onto a wire rack to cool thoroughly, then brush off any crumbs and frost. *Makes one 2-layer cake.*

Fudge Frosting

2 cups sugar	2 tablespoons light corn syrup
⅔ cup milk	2 tablespoons butter
⅓ cup sifted unsweetened cocoa	1 teaspoon vanilla extract

In a medium-size saucepan, combine the sugar, milk, cocoa, and corn syrup; stir until sugar is dissolved. Cook over medium heat until the syrup forms a very soft ball (230°F to 234°F) when a small quantity is dropped into ice water, stirring only enough to prevent burning. Remove from heat and stir in the butter; cool to lukewarm. Add the vanilla and beat until the frosting is creamy and of spreading consistency. *Makes enough frosting to ice one 2-layer cake.*

❧ BUMPER CROPS AND CANNING KETTLES

When I was a little girl, we depended for survival on the family garden, the milk cows, our "butcher beef," and on our pantry. It was the heart of the Depression. My father, a good worker, earned as much as he could, but it was our old-time farm skills that sustained us.

The pantry was small but well filled. When we were naughty we had to sit on a box in the pantry until we mended our ways. Once our tempers had faded, that room became a very cool, fragrant, and quiet place in which to spend a little time. It was stocked with bottles of juice and Worcestershire sauce; canning jars filled with pickles, jams, fruit, vegetables, and mincemeat. Burlap bags filled with carrots, apples, potatoes, turnips, and nuts stood about the room. On the floor and on the shelves there were boxes of raisins, tins of soda crackers,

and crocks of meat put down in lard. That pantry spoke of security, of summer days along the river playing in the sand while Mother worked in her garden, and of Grandpa, never far away.

Wild Plum Butter

In September, along the creek banks in southern Oregon, wild plums —perfuming the air—hang thickly on branches and drop in soft profusion on the ground to be eaten by raccoons and other varmints— and folks too who pick endless bucketsful off the loaded branches and turn the bounty into delicious wild plum butter. (If you don't have wild plums, store-bought will do.)

8 cups pitted and chopped plums	1½ cups water
	6 cups sugar

Note: Be sure to select unblemished plums, wash well and remove signs of decay or imperfections before chopping.

Place the plums in a saucepan large enough, about 4 quarts, so the jam won't boil over. Add the water and bring to a boil and continue boiling for about 10 minutes. Add the sugar and continue boiling rapidly until the jam is thick and clear, or until it registers 222°F to 224°F on a candy thermometer. Remove from heat, skim foam off the surface, and pour or ladle the jam into freshly scrubbed and sterilized half-pint canning jars with sterilized new lids and washed and scalded rings. Wipe the rims well and seal, cool jars upright, label and date them, and store upright in a cool, dark, and dry place. *Makes 8 half-pint jars.*

Rose Hip Honey

In hedgerows and in open fields, wild roses decorate the landscape with open single-petaled pale-pink flowers and leave behind a beauteous harvest of rose hips (seed pods). These hollow little pods contain large amounts of vitamin C and have been used for centuries—in both fresh and dried forms—for tea. They also can be made into this delicate honey, which is wonderful on pancakes or used to sweeten tea; it can also be made into a cold drink by simply diluting it with cold water.

1 gallon ripe wild rose hips, or enough to make 4 cups rose hip puree (Dried rose hips may be purchased in health food stores; reconstitute as directed, then follow cooking directions below)

1 cup water, ½ cup more if needed, for cooking rose hips
2 cups sugar
Juice from 1 lemon

Rinse the rose hips gently, being sure to check the inside of the pods for worms (wash them out of the pod). Simmer rose hips in 1 cup water until tender, add additional ½ cup only if needed, and puree. Then in a medium-size saucepan, boil the puree, sugar, and lemon juice together until a skin forms on the surface of a small quantity dripped onto a cold plate (refrigerate to chill if needed). Bottle or pour into washed, scaled half-pint canning jars while still hot and seal with new lids and clean rings. Label and store in a cool, dry place. Refrigerate when opened. *Makes about 4 or 5 half pints.*

Pickled Quince

During the Depression, Mother found a burned-out homestead on company property where quince trees grew. When the fruit was yellow-ripe, she had permission to pick it. In season, she made preserves, conserves, marmalades, fruit cheese—a sweetened fruit puree cooked until it becomes so thick it can be chilled into a cheeselike brick that is served sliced and laid on buttered bread like cheese—and pickles out of those strongly scented, softly fuzzed, apple-shaped fruits. And all that winter, she made delicious sauces and pies out of the fresh fruit she had stored in boxes and baskets in the pantry. (We, like others, never ate quince fresh—they have a sour flavor that puckers the mouth.)

I like to serve this pickled quince with roast pork or roast lamb.

1 gallon (16 cups) peeled and cored yellow-ripe quince	2½ cups boiling water
2 sticks cinnamon	2 cups white distilled vinegar
6 whole cloves	6 cups sugar
1 piece dried gingerroot the size of a quarter	Juice from 2 lemons

Slice the quince into wedges about ¾ inch wide; set aside. Place the cinnamon sticks, cloves, and ginger in a cloth bag and tie closed. In a large saucepan, combine the water, vinegar, sugar, bag of spices (if you don't have a spice bag, tie spices in a clean 6-inch square of cotton cloth and tie with kitchen twine), and the lemon juice; bring to a boil, then cook the quince a quart at a time in the syrup until it forks tender. Immediately pack hot quince into freshly scrubbed and sterilized pint jars, leaving ½ inch head room, wipe the rims well, and seal. Seal with hot new lids and sterilized rings. Process in a boiling water bath for 10 minutes. Cool upright, then test for an airtight seal by pressing down center of each lid; the lid should stay down. Label and date, and store in a cool, dark, and dry place. *Makes 8 to 10 pints.*

Sun-Cooked Peach Preserves

Peaches preserved in this old-fashioned way hold their shape and retain their fresh flavor. Whenever possible use only firm, tree-ripened, free-stone canning peaches such as Hale or Alberta.

Peel *peaches* and cut them in half. Dip the halves in a solution made of the *juice of 2 lemons* and *1½ quarts cold water*. Next, roll the halves in *powdered sugar*, coating them well; lay them in a single layer on a shallow glass baking dish or deep platter, seeded side up, and fill the seed cavity with more powdered sugar. Set the dish in the sun in a safe place. Cover dish or platter with a piece of plate glass or a glass pie plate. Keep the peaches in the hot sun for one whole day and that night bring them inside and refrigerate. The following morning, turn the peach halves over and sprinkle on more powdered sugar and set them in the sun again. Let the peaches sit overnight, then the next morning, pack them tightly (but do not crush), in sterilized and still very hot pint or half-pint canning jars leaving ½ inch head space.

Allow 2 medium peach halves to a half-pint jar or 3 to 4 medium peach halves to a pint jar, depending on the size of the peaches. Wipe the rims well and seal with hot new lids and sterilized rings. Simmer in a boiling water bath for 15 minutes. Label and date jars; store in a cool, dark, and dry place. (When kept out of the light these peaches have a good color for a long time.)

From SEPTEMBER DARK

The air falls chill;
The whippoorwill
Pipes lonesomely behind the hill;
The dusk grows dense,
The silence tense;
And low, the katydids commence.

Through shadowy rifts
Of woodland, lifts
The low, slow moon, and upward drifts,
While left and right
The fireflies' light
Swirls eddying in the skirts of night.

—James Whitcomb Riley

❧ HARVEST HOME SUPPER

Around September 23, the full moon that occurs nearest the vernal equinox of the sun appears. For several nights, this beautiful harvest moon rises at about the same time, shining so brightly that farmers in northern parts of the country can work in the fields until late at night, taking in the harvest.

The end of harvest late in September signals the onslaught of many social events, a fair or harvest festival, or a lovely harvest home supper. The first full moon after the harvest is a hunter's moon. It marks the beginning of the fall hunting season; thus venison is often featured at harvest dinners.

Fresh Tomato Relish

Chop together *4 to 6 large, ripe peeled tomatoes, 1 sweet onion, ¼ teaspoon garlic juice,* and *2 green bell peppers.* If long sweet yellow

JANE WATSON HOPPING

peppers are available, they are also delicious in this relish. Mix in *about 1 to 2 teaspoons minced fresh sweet basil, 2 tablespoons finely chopped fresh parsley, 1 tablespoon of good-quality cider vinegar*, and *3 tablespoons olive oil.* Add a *pinch of pepper*, and *salt to taste.* Refrigerate until well chilled. Serve alongside cold meats. *Makes about 4 cups.*

Venison Cutlets Stuffed with Fresh Pork Dressing

We remove all fat off the deer, believing that the bone marrow and fat, hair and such is what gives this meat an off flavor. When only the lean meat, moistened with fresh pork dressing, is used, there is no finer dish than venison.

Fresh Pork Dressing (recipe follows)	Black pepper
	Flour for dredging
2 pounds boneless venison, sliced into pieces about 4 ounces each, ¼ inch thick	¼ cup lard
	1 cup milk, beef stock, or thin beef or other meat gravy
Salt	

Preheat oven to 350°F. Prepare the dressing. Pound the venison about ⅛ inch thick. Then cut the meat into about 2x4-inch pieces. Place a mound of dressing on each piece, fold the venison over the dressing, and fasten closed with toothpicks or tie with a light string. Season the meat with salt and pepper and roll the venison cutlets in flour. Brown the meat on all sides in the lard. Arrange the venison birds in a casserole dish that has a cover. Pour the milk or stock or gravy over the venison birds. Cover and bake until done, about 1 hour. *Makes 6 to 8 servings.*

Fresh Pork Dressing

½ pound fresh ground pork sausage, unseasoned	½ teaspoon dried sweet basil, finely pulverized, more if desired
1 cup chopped onions	
1 cup chopped celery	About 2 cups hot water, or more as needed
1½ teaspoons salt	
½ teaspoon black pepper	3 cups dried and cubed dark variety breads, crusts left on
1 teaspoon dried marjoram, finely pulverized	
1 teaspoon dried oregano, finely pulverized, more if desired	1 cup dried and cubed white bread

In a heavy skillet, fry the sausage until well done, and the fat has been rendered out and is now liquid in the pan. Remove the sausage from the pan and drain the liquefied fat into a heatproof measuring cup. Return ¼ cup of the rendered fat to the skillet. Add the onions and celery to the skillet and sauté until clear. Transfer vegetables to a large bowl and add the reserved sausage and the salt, pepper, marjoram, oregano, and basil, mixing well. Swish the hot water (about 2 cups) around in the skillet to dissolve any sediment into the water, and pour enough over the bread cubes to form a moist dressing; stir until the dressing binds; add more water if needed. (The dressing should be fairly moist at this point or the finished dressing will be dry.) *Makes about 4 or 4½ cups.*

Shepherd's Sweet Potato Pie

Weathers—castrated males that have not been sold by their second year—become mutton. Such meat is roasted and made into ground mutton dishes.

1 pound lean ground mutton	¼ cup, packed, light brown sugar
½ cup very fine dry breadcrumbs	¼ cup heavy cream
½ teaspoon salt	2 eggs, lightly beaten
¼ teaspoon black pepper	1 tablespoon butter
3 cups hot mashed sweet potatoes (about 4 pounds whole raw potatoes)	Freshly grated nutmeg

Preheat oven to 400°F. In a medium-size bowl, mix together the mutton, breadcrumbs, salt, and pepper. Place in a 9-inch pie plate and pat with fingers to line the bottom and sides, like a pie crust. Refrigerate until well chilled. In a medium-size bowl, combine the sweet potatoes, sugar, cream, and eggs, mixing well. Spoon mixture into the prepared chilled meat shell, dot top with the butter, and dust with nutmeg. Bake until a knife blade inserted into the center comes out clean, about 45 minutes. *Makes 6 to 8 servings.*

Harvest Home Venison Pot Roast

During hunting season, shaggy-mane mushrooms can be found near old logging roads and in cutover parts of the forest after a rain.

Hunters often pick a few, taking home a hatful or a bundle of them tied up in a shirt, or stuffed into coat pockets.

This roast is wonderful with baby potatoes boiled with their skins on, then pan-fried with a little butter, and chopped fresh basil, parsley, and chives until potatoes are browned.

1 (4- to 6-pound) bone-in shoulder or haunch venison roast
½ to ⅔ cup all-purpose flour
¼ to ½ cup lard or margarine
2 cups tomato juice
2 medium-size onions, chopped
2 peeled and sliced medium-size carrots
2 large stalks celery (including leafy tips), cut into ½-inch slices
2 peeled garlic cloves, crushed
2 to 3 teaspoons salt
2 teaspoons oregano leaves
½ teaspoon black pepper
Cornstarch for thickening gravy
2 pounds shaggy-mane mushrooms
Butter for sautéing mushrooms
Minced fresh parsley for garnish

Trim excess fat from the roast. Coat the meat with the flour. Heat the lard in an 8-quart Dutch oven over high heat until hot. Carefully place the meat in the hot fat and brown on all sides to seal in the juices. Add the tomato juice, onions, carrots, celery, garlic, salt, oregano, and pepper. Bring to a boil. Cover and reduce heat to a simmer; simmer until meat is tender, about 3 to 3½ hours, turning the roast occasionally so it will cook evenly. Add boiling water if needed.

When the roast is done, transfer it to a platter; cover and keep warm. Remove the vegetables from the Dutch oven and skim off fat from the broth in the pot. Measure the skimmed broth and add *2 tablespoons cornstarch with just enough water to moisten per cup* of broth for a moderately thick gravy. Heat the broth and cornstarch mixture to boiling, stirring constantly until gravy has thickened; set aside. Sauté the mushrooms in a little butter; salt and pepper lightly, then pour liquid off the mushrooms into the gravy, stirring to blend. Slice the roast and place on serving plate. Top the meat slices with some of the gravy and spoon drained mushrooms on top. Garnish with parsley and serve immediately. *Makes about 10 servings.*

Late-Corn Pudding

During the late harvest, a few young ears of corn still hang on the stalks. Farm children run out to the garden for their mothers to salvage this last bit of summer goodness for supper or for harvesttime potluck dinners.

2 eggs
2 cups fresh, tender corn,
   parboiled, cut off the cob
2 cups milk, scalded and still
   hot

1½ tablespoons butter, melted
1 teaspoon sugar
  Pinch of black pepper
  About 1 teaspoon salt

Preheat oven to 325°F. In a large bowl, beat the eggs until light, then stir in the corn, milk, butter, sugar, and pepper; salt mixture to taste. Pour mixture into a 1½-quart greased casserole; set the casserole in a pan and fill pan with enough warm water to cover bottom half of casserole. Bake for 1 hour 15 minutes. Serve immediately. *Makes 6 servings.*

Apple Custard Pie

September and October bring on the apple harvest, and with it an endless number of apple dishes. This custard pie is a relief from the everyday apple and deep-dish apple pies. It also reflects the increased milk supply as dairy cattle "come up" on their milk production as cool weather arrives and late summer rain brings fall grasses.

Flaky Crust Pastry (page 28)
¼ cup all-purpose flour
1 cup, packed, light brown sugar
3 apples, peeled, halved, and cored

1 egg, beaten
1½ cups milk
½ teaspoon ground cinnamon
¼ teaspoon freshly grated nutmeg

Preheat oven to 450°F. Line an ungreased 9-inch pie pan with the pastry dough. Mix *2 tablespoons* of the flour and *¼ cup* of the sugar, blending thoroughly, and sprinkle evenly over the bottom of the pie shell. Arrange the apple halves, core side up, in the pie shell. In a medium-size bowl, combine the egg and milk; pour over the apples. In a separate bowl, blend the *remaining 2 tablespoons* flour with the *remaining ¾ cup* sugar and the cinnamon and nutmeg. Sprinkle over the apple halves. Bake at 450°F for 10 minutes, then reduce oven setting to 325°F and bake 30 minutes more or until custard is firm and a knife blade inserted into it comes out clean. *Makes one 9-inch pie or 4 to 6 servings.*

OCTOBER

Snow on the Mountain, Soups, and Hot Breads

During October on the farm, country men, women, and children begin to prepare for winter. The nights hold a promise of winter cold and crops must be brought in by mid-month. After the first bone-chilling night, frosts ice the ground, killing all remaining vines and insects in the garden, and birds—except for the hardy sparrow and chickadee—have left for a warmer climate.

On big and little farms alike, everyone is trying to save the last of the harvest, hauling it in from the fields and storing it away. Late apples and some grapes still hang on trees and vines, ripe for picking. Buildings, cellars, and pantries fill up with brightly hued jars of preserves and orderly rows of fruit and vegetables. The earthy aroma of potatoes and ripe apples fills the air.

After the frost, the weather often warms up again, Days can be hazy with fall sunshine, fresh with an autumn tang. In the woods the leaves change to brilliant crimson, russet, and gold, and fall flowers, such as wild asters and fringed gentian, bloom as beautifully as spring blossoms.

I love Old October so,
I can't bear to see her go—
Seems to me like losin' some
Old-home relative er chum—
'Pears like sorto' settin' by
Some old friend 'at sigh by sigh
Was a-passin' out o' sight
Into everlastin' night!
Hickernuts a feller hears
Rattlin' down is more like tears
Drappin' on the leaves below—
I love Old October so!

Can't tell what it is about
Old October knocks me out!—
I sleep well enough at night—
And the blamedest appetite
Ever mortal man possessed,—
Last thing et, it tastes the best!—
Warnuts, butternuts, pawpaws,
'Iles and limbers up my jaws
Fer raal service, sich as new
Pork, spareribs, and sausage, too.—
Yit, fer all, they's somepin' 'bout
Old October knocks me out!

—James Whitcomb Riley

END OF THE GARDEN

Before heavy rains or frost kill tender vegetables, we strip the crops, leaving only those that are too immature for picking in the field. Tomatoes and melons are picked when they are good-sized but still green, to slowly ripen in storage. Other vegetables, such as baking squash, must be fully mature and well seasoned on the vine or they will rot once picked. (Stems are always left on when vegetables are picked so that bacteria cannot enter.)

Everyone helps pick the garden clean, the family and sometimes neighbors who come over to give a hand. When the garden is cleaned out and boxes and buckets piled high, we haul all our bounty into the yard behind the house where it is sorted. Baking squash are wiped clean and packed loosely in boxes so that they have good ventilation;

ripe or perishable vegetables are set aside for immediate use in dishes such as home-canned vegetable soups and relishes. An assortment of the last of the summer squash, deep red-ripe bell peppers, ripe and not-so-ripe tomatoes, half a bucket of late-maturing string beans, cabbage, and a few ears of corn is set aside for upcoming family meals. Then a pile of winter squash and pumpkins (both high-yielding crops), often boxes of late corn, and any other vegetables that can be spared are put in the truck and taken to the Salvation Army, the Gospel Mission, or other charitable organizations.

Old-Country Cabbage and Meat with Old-Country Bread

The world over, cabbage, which grows abundantly even in cold climates, is a farm staple. Vera's friend George calls this stewlike dish Italian Cabbage.

1 large head cabbage, coarsely chopped
1 medium-size red onion, chopped
½ red bell pepper, chopped
½ pound lean ground pork sausage
½ pound lean ground beef
2 fresh basil leaves, minced

1 sprig fresh parsley, minced
1 tablespoon salt
1 teaspoon black pepper
1 quart canned whole tomatoes
1 cup tomato puree (or use another 1 quart canned tomatoes)
Old-Country Bread (recipe follows)

Place all ingredients except the bread in a large stew pot. Simmer until meat and vegetables are tender and flavors are well blended, about 45 minutes. Serve in soup bowls as a main dish with bread on the side. *Makes 10 to 12 main-dish servings.*

Old-Country Bread

2 tablespoons dry or granulated yeast
2 cups warm water
¼ cup sugar
2 teaspoons salt
5 to 6 cups unbleached all-purpose flour, plus flour for kneading and rolling out dough

1 egg beaten with 2 tablespoons water
Butter, minced herbs, or grated Parmesan cheese for top of bread, optional

In a large bowl, combine the yeast, water, and sugar; let mixture sit about 10 minutes. Add the salt and about half of the flour, or as much as necessary to make a cakelike batter; beat to develop the gluten. Cover with a dry kitchen towel, place in a warm spot, and let rise until quite light and doubled in bulk, about 45 minutes. Mix in the rest of the flour and turn onto a floured surface. The dough should be very stiff. Sprinkle on flour as needed until the dough is not sticky and can be handled, then knead until dough is elastic and smooth, about 10 minutes. Wash the bowl used to mix the dough and grease it; return the dough to the bowl and turn dough until all surfaces are greased. Cover with a dry towel and let stand in a warm place until doubled in bulk, about 35 to 40 minutes. Punch it down, turn it out on a lightly floured surface, and divide into 2 equal portions. Form each into a cigar-shaped, free-standing loaf. Place loaves on a greased cookie sheet and slash tops with a sharp knife. Brush the tops with the egg mixture and let rise again uncovered until the loaves are puffed and light, about 35 to 40 minutes. Bake for 10 minutes in a preheated 400°F oven, then reduce oven setting to 350°F and continue baking until the crust is lightly browned and the loaf sounds hollow when tapped, about 40 minutes more. Place loaves on a wire rack to cool or serve hot topped with butter, minced fresh herbs, or sprinkled with grated Parmesan cheese. *Makes 2 loaves.*

Corn Chowder with Fresh Pork Sausage

Mother often cooked half a pound of fresh-ground pork sausage in a frying pan to render out the fat and then added the meat to the corn chowder instead of the traditional salt pork or bacon. She thought the cooked meat made a more nourishing main-dish meal out of these end-of-the-garden vegetables than one that was only seasoned with salt pork or bacon.

2 tablespoons chopped salt pork, bacon, or ½ pound fresh pork sausage, precooked in a frying pan to render out the fat
1 large onion, chopped
2 cups boiling water for cooking the potatoes
4 cups peeled, chopped potatoes

Salt
Black pepper
6 (8-inch) ears of corn, shucked, the silk removed, and washed
Boiling water for cooking the corn
2 cups half-and-half
1 tablespoon finely chopped fresh parsley

In a skillet, cook the sausage or salt pork over low heat about 5 minutes. Add the onion and cook about 3 minutes more. Drain, removing as much fat as possible. Add the water and potatoes, and salt and pepper to taste; continue cooking until the potatoes are tender.

Meanwhile, ease the ears of corn into a pot of boiling water; boil for 5 minutes. Remove from heat. Drain and cool, then cut corn off the cobs and set corn aside. When the potatoes are tender, stir in the half-and-half and corn and heat to boiling. Remove from heat and sprinkle with the parsley. Serve immediately with a crisp vegetable on the side. *Makes 8 main-dish servings.*

End-of-the-Garden Uncooked Relish

In the fall when the garden was almost gone and before the first early frost, Mother went into the field to salvage whatever was left—a cabbage, cucumbers, peppers, green or ripened tomatoes, a few string beans, and anything else that would be good in uncooked relish. From the woodshed she collected a few onions. Then she cleaned all the vegetables and ran them through the large disc of a meat grinder.

Once the vegetables were ground, Mother stirred salt into them until they tasted slightly salty, and then let them stand for one to three hours until they made their own brine.

She poured the vegetables through a clean cloth, draining and squeezing them until all liquid was out of them. The dry vegetables were then put in a large canning kettle or soup pot. She stirred mustard seed (and sometimes celery seed) generously into them. Next she heated a pickling solution of half vinegar and half sugar to boiling. (For a sweet relish, she added more sugar than vinegar; for a tart one more vinegar than sugar was added.) Then she poured the hot solution over the vegetables and stirred to blend well. Enough pickling solution was added to moisten the relish well, but not to make it runny. The relish was then ladled into freshly scrubbed gallon jars or into a large crock and set in a cool place to age. After a week it could be eaten. Under refrigeration uncooked relish kept well through the winter.

Daddy's Hot Pepper Sauce

At home we raised fiery peppers that were so hot we wore rubber gloves to protect our hands when picking them. One did not touch face, mouth, or eyes for fear of burning agony. When making pepper sauce, Mother generally handled the tricky task of washing the peppers and putting them into the freshly scrubbed narrow-necked bottles. When the peppers were safely inside, she poured straight distilled white vinegar over the little scorchers and corked the bottles. In a few weeks' time, the vinegar was exceedingly hot.

My father gingerly put this sauce on his meat and Mother would add a spoonful to stew or chili. When the hot vinegar was used up, we added more vinegar, and soon it, too, was hot.

Piccalilli

This old-time relish recipe originally came from the East Indies and was brought home, no doubt, by a sailor.

Be sure to wash vegetables well, and trim bruises or other imperfections from them before chopping them.

4 cups chopped cabbage	¼ cup salt
4 cups green tomatoes, finely chopped	2 cups, packed, light brown sugar
2 red bell peppers, finely chopped	2 cups cider vinegar
3 green bell peppers, finely chopped	1½ cups water
	¼ cup mustard seed
2 cups celery, finely chopped	2 tablespoons celery seed
2 large onions, chopped	1½ teaspoons ground turmeric

Mix the cabbage, tomatoes, bell peppers, celery, and onions with the salt and let stand overnight. Next morning drain and press into a clean cloth to remove all possible excess liquid. Combine the sugar, vinegar, water, mustard, celery seed, and turmeric in a very large saucepan. (With vinegar you do not cook in cast-iron, aluminum, or chipped enamel pans. Use enamel or stainless steel, but check enamelware for a chipped surface.) Bring to a boil and boil 5 minutes. Add the drained vegetables and return to a rolling boil. Pour into sterilized and still very hot ½ pint or pint canning jars. Wipe rims well and seal with hot new lids and sterilized rings at once. Cool upright, then label and date jars. Store upright in a cool, dark, and dry place. Refrigerate after opening. *Makes 12 half pints or 6 pints.*

THE ORCHARD LANDS OF
LONG AGO

Blow back the melody that slips
In lazy laughter from the lips
That marvel much if any kiss
Is sweeter than the apple's is.
Blow back the twitter of the birds—
The lisp, the titter, and the words
Of merriment that found the shine
Of summer-time a glorious wine
That drenched the leaves that loved it so
In orchard lands of Long Ago!

O memory! alight and sing
Where rosy-bellied pippins cling,
And golden russets glint and gleam,
As, in the old Arabian dream,
The fruits of that enchanted tree
The glad Aladdin robbed for me!
And, drowsy winds, awake and fan
My blood as when it overran
A heart ripe as the apples grow
In orchard lands of Long Ago!

—James Whitcomb Riley

🌿 Apples and Cider

Early-day settlers planted apple trees as soon as the ground was cleared, sometimes before the barns or houses were built. By the turn of the century, some of those trees were a hundred years old and still bearing apples with names like Wolf River. The bounty from such trees was used for cider, pies, applesauce, and dozens of desserts, as well as jams and butters. Farm animals loved the apples, too, especially horses. Windfalls, those that dropped to the ground, were fed to cows, sheep, pigs, rabbits, and goats, which quickly realized that a farmer with a basket was bringing a treat, and they would eagerly wait for him at a particular feeding spot.

On an old hillside farm near our place, such ancient apple trees—many of the names long since forgotten—grow. Each winter the trees look dead, but the following spring there are blossoms and a crop of small, wormy apples, which, dewormed, are crisp and delicious, the flavor far surpassing today's huge shiny apples.

Apple Chutney for Christmas

By late September, giant bell peppers have turned a dark red and have become sweet and mild. They add color and flavor to this rich chutney, which usually graced the Christmas dinner table at our house.

Be sure to wash apples and vegetables well; trim any blemishes or decay from them before chopping.

2 quarts peeled, chopped tart apples
2 pounds golden raisins
4 cups, packed, light brown sugar
1 cup chopped onions (see Note)
2 large red bell peppers, chopped

2 peeled cloves garlic, minced
¼ cup mustard seed
1 tablespoon ground ginger
2 teaspoons salt
1 teaspoon ground allspice
About ¼ teaspoon ground red pepper, optional (see Note)

Note: Be sure to use good sweet storage onions, such as Yellow Sweet Spanish; *don't* use soft or moist, sweet summer onions such as Crystal White or White Bermuda.

Place all the ingredients in a fairly large canning kettle; mix thoroughly. Bring to a boil and continue boiling until mixture is thick, stirring constantly so it won't scorch. Keep the chutney hot while pouring into scrubbed and sterilized and still very hot half-pint canning jars. Wipe rims well and seal immediately using heated new lids. Cool upright, then label and date jars. Store in a cool, dark, and dry place. Refrigerate after opening. *Makes 16 to 18 half pints.*

Raw-Apple Cake

This cake is very rich in texture and flavor because it contains raw apples. It is more like a brownie or fudge than cake. Serve it in small squares, unfrosted.

2 cups sifted all-purpose flour	½ teaspoon nutmeg
1 cup sugar	1½ cups butter, melted
3 tablespoons unsweetened cocoa powder	1½ cups peeled and cored raw apple, mashed or coarsely
1 tablespoon cornstarch	pureed in a blender, in
2 teaspoons baking soda	which case leave peel on for
1 teaspoon ground cinnamon	flavor
½ teaspoon ground cloves	

Preheat oven to 350°F. Place the flour in a medium-size mixing bowl. Add the sugar, cocoa, cornstarch, baking soda, cinnamon, cloves, and nutmeg. Place the butter and apple in a large bowl and add the dry ingredients to them, stirring to blend well. Pour into a greased, lightly floured 9x5-inch baking pan and bake until done to the touch (or test with a toothpick), about 45 minutes. Cool in the pan before serving. *Makes one 9x5-inch cake.*

Oatmeal Apple Crisp

Spoon a little thick cream—perhaps lifted off the top of a crock of icy milk—over this crisp for a delicious before-bedtime snack.

4 cups peeled and sliced sweet apples	½ cup butter
¼ cup hot cider	½ cup rolled oats
¾ cup, packed, light brown sugar	Heavy cream, optional

Preheat oven to 400°F. Arrange the apples in a buttered baking dish. Pour the hot cider over them and sprinkle on ¼ *cup* of the sugar. In a small bowl, cream the butter; add the oats and the *remaining* ½ *cup* sugar, blending to form crumbs. Sprinkle over the apples. Bake until the apples are tender and the top is browned, about 40 to 45 minutes. Serve as is or topped with cream. *Makes 4 servings.*

Spicy Mulled Cider

Homemade cider is best when made with a mixture of apples, partic-ularly those with a rich, tart flavor.

1 quart apple cider	⅛ teaspoon ground ginger
2 tablespoons light-colored and flavored (clover preferred) honey	⅛ teaspoon freshly grated nutmeg
¼ teaspoon ground cinnamon	Cinnamon sticks for garnish
⅛ teaspoon ground cloves	Orange slices for garnish
	Whole cloves for garnish

In a medium-size saucepan, combine the cider, honey, ground cinnamon, ground cloves, ginger, and nutmeg. Heat over high heat until the honey is dissolved and cider is hot, then reduce heat to keep cider warm until ready to serve. To serve, pour cider into mugs and garnish with cinnamon sticks and orange slices with whole cloves stuck in the rinds. *Makes about 1 quart or 4 to 6 servings.*

❧ HARDY SOUPS AND BREADS, THE STAFF OF LIFE

On cold blustery days, I cook for the sheer pleasure of it, rustling around the kitchen, getting out pans and pots. Before long, a rich soup is simmering on the back of the woodstove and bread is rising in a warm spot. Such soup, filled with vegetables and meat, and a delicious, nourishing loaf of bread are a welcome snack to those who go out in the cold to work or play.

And since my family knows me well, my husband makes a quick trip to the house for a dipper of boiling soup, relieving the chill of working in the barn; my son drops by home, just checking to see what's cooking; my daughter remembers the good food and warmth of home and comes stamping in out of the cold; and my son-in-law, Mark, would walk a mile for the hot bread that he eats like cake without butter on it.

Cock-a-leekie

This traditional Scottish soup is made with a rooster past frying age. Such birds are butchered in the fall, since males which are not used in the flock are too costly to feed through the winter, and once past their prime would be tough and stringy if cooked.

Wash *6 large leeks;* remove the roots and about half of the tops. (Store-bought leeks have already been trimmed.) Cut leeks into 1-inch pieces. If they are strong-flavored or old, parboil them for 10 minutes, then drain.

In a deep soup pan, place *a dressed and chilled rooster* or store-bought boiling hen, and *½ teaspoon salt, ½ teaspoon ground allspice, and ⅛ teaspoon ground black pepper per pound of chicken*. Add the leeks, cover with *boiling water*, and simmer until rooster is tender, about 3 to 4 hours, occasionally skimming off any fat and other material that floats to the surface. Add additional *salt* and *pepper* to taste. Remove rooster from the broth and cut into serving pieces; place pieces in a heated tureen. Pour the leek-thickened broth over it and serve immediately. (*Note:* A dozen pitted prunes may be added during the last few minutes of cooking, or the broth may be further thickened by adding 3 or 4 tablespoons of rolled oats during the last 30 minutes of cooking.) Serve with Honey Apple Gems (page 192) and salad (such as Great-aunt Mae's Cabbage Slaw, page 192), if desired. *Makes 6 to 8 servings.*

Honey Apple Gems

At our house, cock-a-leekie soup (page 191) is usually served with these honey apple gems and cabbage slaw that is fresh from the garden, sweetened by cool weather and early rain.

1¼ cups milk
¼ cup butter or margarine
2 tablespoons light-colored
    honey
⅔ cup yellow cornmeal,
    moistened with ¼ cup cold
    water

1 egg, slightly beaten
1 cup unbleached all-purpose
    flour
2 teaspoons baking powder
1 teaspoon salt
1½ cups peeled and chopped
    Golden Delicious apples

Preheat oven to 350°F. In a medium-size saucepan, scald the milk, then add the butter and honey, stirring to blend. Remove from heat and cool slightly, then stir in the cornmeal, mixing well; take care that the cornmeal does not lump. Add the egg, flour, baking powder, and salt. Fold in the apples, blending well. Spoon batter into greased gem or muffin cups and bake until light brown on top and darker on bottom, about 25 to 30 minutes. To test, remove one gem from pan with a spatula and look at bottom surface of it. *Makes 12 to 14 gems.*

Great-aunt Mae's Cabbage Slaw

Long before mixed green salads with oil and vinegar dressing were popular, in farm homes this simple old slaw added a bit of excitement to many a supper. And when a deep glass bowl of home-canned fruit was set on the table with it, even the children knew that supper was going to be something special.

4 packed cups, white late-fall cabbage, finely minced (store-bought will do, but will not be as sweet-flavored as that made of cabbage picked just after a rain)
⅓ cup heavy sweet cream
1 tablespoon cider vinegar, more to taste

1 tablespoon sugar, more to taste
¾ teaspoon salt (old-time people often used more)
¼ teaspoon white pepper (preferred), black if you don't have it

Put cabbage in a medium-size bowl. In a small bowl combine cream, *1 tablespoon* vinegar, *1 tablespoon* sugar, and stir to blend. Add salt and pepper. Taste, add more vinegar, sugar, salt or pepper, as desired. Pour dressing over cabbage; stir to blend. *Makes 6 to 8 servings.*

Mulligatawny

This old-fashioned cold-weather soup varies, depending on the cook, from one that contains leeks, apples, and cream to a hearty soup that contains bell peppers and stewed tomatoes. We like the heartier version with leeks. It's delicious served with a piquant salad and Sturdy Brown Bread (page 194).

1 (3- to 4-pound) fryer
6 to 7 cups boiling water
About 1 teaspoon salt
About ¼ teaspoon black pepper
½ cup long grain white rice
2 cups water for cooking rice
½ cup chopped carrots
½ cup chopped celery
¼ cup chopped onions
¼ cup chopped bell peppers

1 tart apple, peeled, cored, and chopped
1 cup tomato puree, store-bought tomato puree or sauce will do nicely
¼ cup all-purpose flour
1 tablespoon chopped fresh parsley
1 teaspoon curry powder
½ teaspoon freshly grated nutmeg
4 whole cloves

Cut enough chicken meat from the bone to yield 1 cup of meat; cube the 1 cup meat and set aside. Remove all visible fat from the remaining chicken and render (melt) the fat in a skillet over moderate heat until it liquefies; measure and reserve ¼ cup (if there is not enough rendered fat, add melted butter to make up balance). Meanwhile, place the rest of the chicken (but not the cubed chicken meat) in a kettle with the 6 to 7 cups boiling water, 1 teaspoon salt, and ¼ teaspoon pepper; simmer until a good rich broth is made; remove and discard the bones and strain the broth. Measure and reserve 5 cups of broth (if there is not enough, add hot water to make up balance). The meat that cooked in the broth pot may be used for another dish or, if you wish, added to the soup. Simmer the reserved 5 cups broth, and while it simmers, boil the rice in the 2 cups water until light and flaky; drain well and set aside.

Now, in a large Dutch oven sauté the cubed chicken in the reserved ¼ cup rendered fat. When light brown, remove the chicken from the fat and set aside. In the same fat, sauté the carrots, celery, onions, bell peppers, and apple until lightly browned. Stir in the tomato sauce or puree, flour, parsley, curry powder, nutmeg, and cloves. Cover and simmer for 1 hour, stirring occasionally and adding water as needed to keep the mixture from sticking. Then you may either put the cooked sauce through a colander, saving the liquid, or leave the vegetables chunky if you like. (If you strained it, place the strained sauce back into the Dutch oven.) Add the cubed chicken, cooked rice, and boiling chicken broth; stir well, then adjust seasoning to taste. *Makes 6 servings.*

Sturdy Brown Bread

2 tablespoons dry or granulated yeast
¼ cup warm water (105°F to 115°F)
2 tablespoons blackstrap molasses
¼ cup, packed, dark brown sugar
2 cups milk, scalded, still hot

¼ cup butter, melted
2 teaspoons salt
2 eggs, beaten
1 cup raw bran
¼ cup raw wheat germ
2 cups whole-wheat flour
2 to 3 cups unbleached all-purpose flour, plus 1 cup for kneading

Dissolve the yeast in the warm water. In a large bowl, combine the molasses, sugar, milk, butter, and salt; stir until the sugar dissolves and the mixture is lukewarm. Stir in the eggs and yeast, then add the bran, wheat germ, and *1 cup each* of the whole-wheat flour and all-purpose flour; stir to make a soft dough. Cover with a dry towel and set in a warm spot to rise, about 40 minutes. When double in bulk, stir in the *remaining 1 cup* whole-wheat flour. Place *1 cup* more all-purpose flour on flat surface, spreading it about; turn the dough onto the floured surface and begin to knead it. Sprinkle on additional all-purpose flour as needed (dough will be a bit sticky), and turn the dough about in the flour on the board, until most or all of it has been mixed into the dough. When a smooth ball of medium-soft dough can be formed, cut dough in half and shape into a loaf. Place the loaves in 2 greased 4x8-inch loaf pans, inverting each loaf to grease the top. (Brush tops with more fat if needed.) Cover with the towel again and let rise until double in bulk, at least another 40 minutes. Bake in a preheated 400°F oven for 15 minutes, then reduce the oven setting to 350°F and continue baking until the loaf is well browned, sounds hollow when tapped, and has turned loose from the pan, about 45 to 50 minutes. Let the bread cool in the pans for about 10 minutes, then loosen around sides with a knife and turn onto a wire rack to cool before serving or serve slightly warm with softened butter. *Makes 2 loaves.*

Ben's Borscht

Ben, a dear friend whose singing voice has the haunting quality of the Russian soul, immigrated to these shores because his grandfather believed that God spoke to him three times, telling him to take his family and flee the Ukraine with only the clothes on their backs. They crossed the border into China, escaping the massacres that created agrarian reform in their ancestral area. Penniless, the family wandered through Asia, finding little work, knowing privation, but filled with wonder that God in his majesty had reached down to spare them.

2½ to 3 pounds boneless beef
    stew meat
1 meaty beef soup bone, 1½ to
    2 pounds
1 small onion, peeled, chopped
1 bay leaf
2 stalks celery
    Cold water
8 cups beef stock, tomato
    juice, or a combination of
    both
8 cups freshly cooked and
    cubed beets (or 8 cups
    canned cubed beets)

5 medium-size potatoes,
    peeled and cubed
2 medium-size onions, chopped
4 medium-size carrots, peeled
    and cubed
1 medium-size head of
    cabbage, cored and finely
    chopped
    Salt
    Black pepper
2 tablespoons dried parsley
    flakes

In a large soup kettle, combine the stew meat, soup bone, onion, bay leaf, and celery. Add enough water to cover all ingredients (about 12 cups); bring to a boil. Reduce heat and simmer until meat is tender and a good rich broth is made. Remove from heat and skim fat. Transfer meat to a platter, let cool long enough to handle, then cut into bite-size pieces. Remove vegetables from broth (discard vegetables). Measure broth; put 8 cups back in the washed soup kettle and freeze any extra broth, or just put all the broth back in the kettle, if you like. (Borscht should be a thin soup with the bite-size pieces of meat and vegetables floating about in the broth.) If there are not quite 8 cups broth, thin broth slightly with tomato juice, if you wish. Return the meat to the pot and add the beets, potatoes, chopped onions, carrots, and cabbage. Salt and pepper to taste. Bring to a boil, then reduce heat and simmer until vegetables are tender. Add the parsley, adjust the seasoning, if needed, and simmer about 5 minutes more. Serve immediately in large bowls, with good dark bread such as Sturdy Brown Bread (page 194) and butter on the side. *Makes 8 to 12 servings.*

WHEN THE FROST IS ON THE PUNKIN

When the frost is on the punkin and the fodder's in the shock,
And you hear the kyouck and gobble of the struttin' turkey-cock,
And the clackin' of the guineys, and the cluckin' of the hens,
And the rooster's hallylooyer as he tiptoes on the fence;
O, it's then's the times a feller is a-feelin' at his best.
With the risin' sun to greet him from a night of peaceful rest,
As he leaves the house, bare-headed, and goes out to feed the stock,
When the frost is on the punkin and the fodder's in the shock.

They's something kindo' harty-like about the atmusfere
When the heat of summer's over and the coolin' fall is here—
Of course we miss the flowers, and the blossums on the trees,
And the mumble of the hummin'-birds and buzzin' of the bees;
But the air's so appetizin'; and the landscape through the haze
Of a crisp and sunny morning of the airly autumn days
Is a pictur' that no painter has the colorin' to mock—
When the frost is on the punkin and the fodder's in the shock.

The husky, rusty russel of the tossels of the corn,
And the raspin' of the tangled leaves, as golden as the morn;
The stubble in the furries—kindo' lonesome-like, but still
A-preachin' sermuns to us of the barns they growed to fill;
The strawstack in the medder, and the reaper in the shed;
The hosses in theyr stalls below—the clover overhead!—
O, it sets my heart a-clickin' like the tickin' of a clock,
When the frost is on the punkin and the fodder's in the shock!

Then your apples all is getherd, and the ones a feller keeps
Is poured around the celler-floor in red and yeller heaps;
And your cider-makin' 's over, and your wimmern-folks is through
With their mince and apple-butter, and theyr souse and saussage, too! . . .
I don't know how to tell it—but ef sich a thing could be
As the Angels wantin' boardin', and they'd call around on *me*—
I'd want to 'commodate 'em—all the whole-indurin' flock—
When the frost is on the punkin and the fodder's in the shock!

—James Whitcomb Riley

❧ HALLOWEEN GHOST PARTY

Halloween was usually celebrated as "open house" at school with the whole community attending. Cornstalks, leaves, pumpkins, and streamers made of black and orange paper decorated the schoolyard and buildings. Parents provided cookies, cakes, candy, and other treats for the party. Children wore costumes and prizes were given for the funniest, the scariest, and the most outrageous. Special games were played, like bob for apples, fortune telling, and ghost story— the latter a terrible tale of blood, murder, and gore.

During ghost story, the storyteller sat with his audience in a pitch-black room. As the story unfolded, he passed around to his circle of listeners bits and pieces of "ick"—peeled grapes for eyeballs, shaved pieces of wood for bones, horse hair or wool for human hair. Whetted by the screams of his audience, the storyteller's fabrications grew more and more horrible, until those listening were surely afraid to go home in the dark.

Honey Pumpkin Pie

Early in the season we pick out those pumpkins from the patch that are obviously going to be giants. With a nail we write our children's names on them by scratching through the surface of the rind. As the pumpkins continue to grow, the scars that form around the scratches also grow and soon, to our children's surprise, they find Halloween pumpkins with their names etched on them.

1 unbaked Flaky Pastry pie
   shell (page 28)
1 cup steamed, pureed pumpkin
   (canned store-bought works
   nicely)

½ cup dark-colored honey
1 teaspoon ground cinnamon
¾ teaspoon salt
½ teaspoon freshly grated
   nutmeg

                                             JANE WATSON HOPPING

½ teaspoon ground ginger
¼ teaspoon ground cloves
3 eggs, beaten

1 cup heavy cream (preferred),
  light cream, or milk
Whipped cream, optional
  (page 61)

Preheat oven to 425°F. Line the pie pan with the pastry dough; refrigerate until ready to use. In a large bowl, combine the pumpkin, honey, cinnamon, salt, nutmeg, ginger, and cloves, mixing thoroughly. In a small bowl, blend together the eggs and cream. Stir the egg mixture into the pumpkin mixture. Pour two thirds of the filling into the prepared pie shell. Place the pan on the oven shelf and add the balance of the filling to the pan. Bake at 425° for 10 minutes; then reduce oven setting to 325°F and continue baking until a knife inserted into the center comes out clean, about 35 minutes more. Cool. Serve with a dollop of whipped cream if desired. *Makes one 9-inch pie.*

Toasted Squash or Pumpkin Seeds

From large winter squash or mature Halloween pumpkins, clean the seeds and remove the pulp. (Use the pulp in another recipe.) Wash the seeds; drain and dry well with paper towels. Fry seeds in a pan with a little butter until brown and heated through; salt lightly and serve immediately. (Or place seeds on a cookie sheet and roast without butter for 30 minutes at 350°F. If baking, don't brown the seeds.) To eat, crack the seeds open with your teeth; eat the kernel, discarding hulls. Those seeds cooked without butter keep very well in a covered glass jar for some length of time.

Laughlin's Persimmon Cookies

This excellent, easily made, and spicy recipe for persimmon cookies can be made with green tomato mincemeat, real mincemeat (page 205), applesauce, mashed pumpkin, or mashed sweet potato substituted for the persimmon; just bake away! The family will love any and all of these cookies.

1 cup sugar
½ cup butter
1 egg, beaten
1 cup chopped or pureed raw
  persimmon pulp
1 cup chopped walnuts

1 cup seedless golden raisins
2 cups all-purpose flour
1 tablespoon ground cinnamon
1 teaspoon baking soda

(Continued on next page)

1 teaspoon baking powder	½ teaspoon ground ginger
1 teaspoon ground cloves	¼ teaspoon salt

Preheat oven to 350°F. Cream together the sugar and butter until light. Add the egg, blending well. Add the chopped or pureed persimmons, nuts, and raisins; stir to blend. Sift the flour with the cinnamon, baking soda, baking powder, cloves, ginger, and salt and add to the sugar mixture, blending until a thick batter is formed. Drop by teaspoonfuls onto a greased cookie sheet. Bake until light brown, about 12 minutes. Remove cookies from oven; with a spatula set them on a wire rack to cool. Store in an airtight container for a short period of time, one week or slightly longer. *Makes about 4 dozen cookies.*

Taffy Apples

Before October drops its richly hued leaves, our daughter, Colleen, begins dreaming about candied apples. Her favorite is a Golden Delicious apple coated with taffy and rolled in finely chopped walnuts.

4 to 6 small Golden Delicious apples	1 cup granulated sugar
Wooden skewers for the apples	¾ cup hot water
1½ cups chopped walnuts	½ cup, packed, brown sugar
	2 tablespoons butter for buttering paper

Prepare the apples for dipping by sticking a wood skewer into the stem end of each. Place the walnuts in a shallow bowl. Have ready a large piece of waxed paper, aluminum foil, or buttered butcher paper on which to dry the finished apples. In a large, heavy saucepan heat the granulated sugar until it is melted and turns golden brown, stirring constantly and being careful not to burn it. Slowly add the water so it doesn't spatter and stir until the mixture is smooth. Stir in the brown sugar and cook until the mixture reaches the soft-ball stage (234°F to 240°F on candy thermometer), stirring constantly. Remove from heat. Promptly dip the apples in the syrup, covering completely, then roll the bottoms in the walnuts. Place on the prepared waxed or buttered kraft paper or aluminum foil to dry. *Makes 4 to 6 taffy apples.*

THE RAPTURE OF THE YEAR

Then ho! and hey! and whoop-hooray!
  Though winter clouds be looming,
Remember a November day
Is merrier than mildest May
  With all her blossoms blooming.

While birds in scattered flight are blown
  Aloft and lost in dusky mist,
And truant boys scud home alone
  'Neath skies of gold and amethyst;
While twilight falls, and Echo calls
  Across the haunted atmosphere,
With low, sweet laughs at intervals,—
  So reigns the rapture of the year.

Then ho! and hey! and whoop-hooray!
  Though winter clouds be looming,
Remember a November day
Is merrier than mildest May
  With all her blossoms blooming.

—James Whitcomb Riley

NOVEMBER

God's Gift, a Time of Plenty

Autumn lingers. Bursts of winter chill the land. Dead leaves crackle underfoot. Struck with the beauty of the month, Helen Hunt Jackson, an American novelist and poet of the 1800s, penned the following lines:

> November woods are bare and still,
> November days are clear and bright,
> Each noon burns up the morning chill,
> The morning's snow is gone by night.

For farm folk, this month is a natural rest period, broken only by the need to finish the butchering, smoking, and curing of meat before heavy snowfall or rains turn the barnyards slick with mud. At this time of year, with the harvest almost all in, thoughts of God and words of gratitude come easily to the hearts and lips of people grateful for the seasonal outpouring.

Hands cold and feet wet, family members make more trips than usual into the kitchen for hot coffee and tea. Women keep the fire up and bake a little something extra. Mincemeat simmers on the back of the stove, sending pungent, heady fragrances through the room. Some days, the kitchen table is completely covered with meat ready for brining, and soup kettles are filled with bones and odd chunks of meat being simmered into one staple or another, such as the breakfast meats panhaus and scrapple, and headcheese. Winter is close at hand.

❧ BETWIXT AND BETWEEN

Coming as it does halfway between autumn and winter, November is a betwixt and between month. Suddenly relieved of the hard, never-ceasing labor of harvest, farm people feel at a loss. It's too early to make Christmas plans and yet almost time to begin thinking about them.

Then with the lovely hazy days and the bright masses of chrysan-themums to relieve the dull landscape, and a hoary frost or even a light early winter snowfall to set the spirit going again, women begin to taste the mellowing mincemeat and put wispy plans together for Thanksgiving and Christmas. By late November the winter season is at hand, with all its social pleasures.

Old-fashioned Mincemeat

One delectably fragrant aroma that I will always associate with cool fall weather is Mother's rich mincemeat as it simmered on the back of our old wood-burning cookstove. The blend of apples, oranges, cider, and spices tempted one to peek over the edge of the pot and snitch a sample now and again. Once the heady mincemeat was done, the meat tender, and the raisins plump, Mother mixed them together and placed the mincemeat in a large crock covered with a dish towel to cool and allowed it to sit for 3 or 4 days to mellow. If pies were made, we used it then; if not, we canned it in quart jars.

Our mincemeat pies were always made of one part freshly peeled and sliced pie apples to two parts mincemeat, since Mother thought mincemeat by itself was too rich.

The recipe I've given you below yields about 12 quarts and may be canned or frozen for later use, including gift giving. To can, process the canning jars in a pressure cooker for 20 minutes at 10 pounds pressure. To freeze the mincemeat, first let it cool, then pour into washed cottage cheese cartons and place in the freezer. A general rule of thumb is to allow 1 quart of mincemeat for filling a 9-inch pie; recipes for cakes or cookies usually call for about 2 cups of mincemeat.

2½ pounds boneless boiled beef, boiled venison, or boiled elk meat

½ pound beef suet

6 pounds hard cooking apples, peeled and cored (Granny Smith works well)

4 oranges, peeled and seeded

6 cups apple cider

3 pounds large, soft seedless raisins

1 pound dried currants. Juice and grated rind from 1 lemon

2 (1-pound) boxes dark brown sugar

1 pound granulated sugar

½ cup cider vinegar

2 tablespoons ground cinnamon

2 tablespoons ground allspice

1 tablespoon ground nutmeg

1 teaspoon ground cloves

1 teaspoon ground ginger

Salt to taste

½ cup brandy, more as desired

In a food grinder (coarse disc), or by hand, finely chop the meat, suet, apples, and oranges. In a large canning kettle, combine these chopped ingredients with all the remaining ingredients except the salt and brandy and cook until mixture begins to thicken, about 45 minutes to 1 hour. Now the mincemeat is ready to can or freeze. If you wish to use a portion of it immediately, let that portion age in the refrigerator at least a day or two before using. Salt to taste. Add brandy to taste. (Some old-time mincemeat was so heavily laced it would make you tipsy if you ate it while the pie was being made!) *Makes about 12 quarts.*

Two-Egg Angel Cake with Lemon Icing

Old-time women loved inexpensive recipes that mocked more costly ones. This two-egg angel cake was a wintertime cake made when the hens weren't laying.

2 egg whites	Pinch of salt
1 cup sugar	1 cup milk
1 cup all-purpose flour	Lemon Icing (recipe follows)
1 tablespoon baking powder	

Preheat oven to 350°F. In a medium-size bowl, beat the egg whites until quite stiff. Sift together the sugar, flour, baking powder, and salt 3 times, ending with it in a large bowl. In a small saucepan, scald the milk; add the boiling milk to the dry ingredients, beating vigorously. Fold in the egg whites. Spoon batter into an ungreased 9-inch angel cake pan and bake until done, about 30 minutes. Allow to cool about 15 minutes in pan; then remove from pan. When thoroughly cooled, ice the top and sides with a thin layer of lemon icing. *Makes 1 tube cake.*

Lemon Icing

1 cup powdered sugar	1 teaspoon lemon juice (see
1 tablespoon grated lemon rind	Note)
(see Note)	2 tablespoons cold water

Note: If you like very lemony icing, double the amounts of lemon rind and lemon juice called for.

Sift the sugar into a medium-size bowl. Add the lemon rind and juice and the cold water, mixing well. *Makes enough icing to lightly ice one 10-inch tube cake.*

Rich Prune Cake

In November women baked often to keep up with drop-in company—neighborhood men who found a little time to talk crops or barter, lanky boys who drifted home from school with sons, giggling daughters who shared secrets and treats with friends. And, somehow, the whole crew seemed to end up in the kitchen to linger over milk and coffee and a bit of sweets like this rich prune cake.

1 cup butter or margarine	1 teaspoon ground allspice
1½ cups sugar	1 teaspoon ground cinnamon
4 eggs, separated	¼ teaspoon ground cloves
¾ cup dairy sour cream	¼ teaspoon ground ginger
1 teaspoon baking soda	1¼ cups cooked, pitted, and
3 cups all-purpose flour	chopped dried prunes
1 teaspoon baking powder	

Preheat oven to 350°F. In a large bowl, cream the butter and sugar until light. In a medium-size bowl, lightly beat the egg yolks. Add the sour cream and baking soda, blending well; stir into the butter and sugar mixture, then sift in the flour, baking powder, allspice, cinnamon, cloves, and ginger, beating until well blended. Fold in the prunes. Beat the egg whites until firm but not dry peaks form, then fold them into the batter. Spoon into a greased 13x9-inch baking pan. Bake until done, about 1 hour. Cool in the pan. Serve unfrosted. *Makes one cake.*

Raisin Cake with a Simple Powdered-Sugar Glaze

This old-time cake, which was very popular during the Civil War, shows up slightly modified and with different names, but it remains the well loved Poorman's Cake, the Depression Cake, the Hard Times Cake it has always been because, in spite of its simple ingredients, this cake is richly flavored, moist textured, and chock-full of sweet, plump raisins.

1 cup seedless raisins	½ teaspoon freshly grated
1½ cups water	nutmeg
2 cups all-purpose flour	½ teaspoon ground cloves
1 cup sugar	1½ teaspoons butter, melted
1 teaspoon baking soda	½ cup walnuts or pecans
1 teaspoon ground cinnamon	Flour for dusting raisins and
½ teaspoon salt	nuts

Preheat oven to 350°F. Soak or cook the raisins in the water until plump. Drain, reserving 1 cup of the liquid (if there isn't enough liquid, make up balance with more water). In a large bowl, combine the flour, sugar, baking soda, cinnamon, salt, nutmeg, and cloves. In a medium-size bowl, combine the butter with the reserved raisin juice; add to the dry ingredients, stirring until well blended. Dust the raisins and nuts, either walnuts or pecans, lightly with flour, then fold them in until distributed evenly throughout the batter. Spoon the batter into a well-greased and -floured loaf pan, 8½x4½x3 inches, or a 9-inch tube pan, and bake until the top feels firm and a toothpick inserted into the cake comes out clean, about 35 to 40 minutes. This cake need not be frosted, but it's nice to glaze it (recipe follows) while it's still hot. *Makes one loaf cake or one tube cake.*

A Simple Powdered-Sugar Glaze
Mix *1 cup of powdered sugar* with *1 tablespoon milk*, and *½ to 1 teaspoon vanilla extract*, beating until smooth. (Experiment with extracts using one that in your judgment matches the cake best; besides vanilla extract, you might want to try brandy, lemon, or orange flavoring.) Immediately brush or dribble it over the still hot cake, using it all. *Makes about ½ cup or less glaze.*

Grandpa's Cookies

Grandpa Merkins's cabin sat under a huge oak tree in our front yard, and in it were jars of shelled nuts on shelves. When my sister, Sheila, and I baked cookies as children, we went out to beg a cup of nut meats off the dear old man. He always made a ritual of it, taking them down, measuring them out. (How well we knew our part in this little family drama.) When the first batch of cookies was baked, we would run out to his cabin with a generous plateful, always to find him waiting with freshly perked coffee.

⅔ cup butter or margarine
⅔ cup, packed, light brown
   sugar
⅔ cup granulated sugar
2 eggs, well beaten
2 teaspoons vanilla extract
3 cups all-purpose flour
1½ teaspoons baking powder
½ teaspoon baking soda
½ teaspoon salt

JANE WATSON HOPPING

| ½ cup buttermilk or soured milk | 1 cup seedless raisins |
| | 1 cup chopped walnuts |

Preheat oven to 375°F. In a large bowl, cream the butter and both sugars until light. Add the eggs and vanilla, stirring to blend. Sift together the flour, baking powder, baking soda, and salt. Add the dry ingredients alternately with the buttermilk to the creamed butter mixture, mixing well. Fold in the raisins and nuts. Drop by teaspoonfuls onto a greased baking sheet about 2 to 3 inches apart. Bake until browned, about 12 to 15 minutes. *Makes about 7 dozen cookies.*

❧ CHRISTMAS BASKETS

In the old days, neighbors were more than just people who lived nearby. They were a vital part of everyday life. Country people shared trials, tribulations, pleasures, work, and the bounties of harvest.

It wasn't at all uncommon for folks to find a box of apples or a basket of vegetables sitting on the porch when they returned from church, visiting, or a trip to town. Sometimes they knew who had left the gift by the variety of fruit or produce given; sometimes they just took the sharing for granted and in turn dropped off something for a neighbor themselves.

Such openhandedness was behind the giving of farm-style Christmas baskets, usually prepared at the church or school. The women made the plans and usually knew who could use a little extra. Preparations began in early November; then weeks later folks gathered at the church or school to sing carols, and pile baskets of canned food, dressed chickens and turkeys, fresh vegetables, fruits, cakes, and pies, all carefully wrapped to keep them fresh, around a Christmas tree. After prayers and a program of sorts, the gifts were put in wagons and taken to older neighbors, widows with children, and friends who'd had illnesses or accidents during the year.

Figs Pickled in Honey

1 gallon of firm ripe figs	Juice from 4 lemons
Boiling water to cover figs	Rind from 2 lemons, grated
2 cups light-colored honey	¼ teaspoon ground ginger
⅔ cup water	

Wash the figs well and remove any blemishes or other imperfections. Trim off stems. Place in a large heatproof bowl and pour the boiling water over them; let stand until figs are room temperature. Drain. In a large stainless-steel, unchipped enamel or Pyrex saucepan bring the honey and water to a boil. Cook the figs in batches in the honey mixture until tender. As each batch is cooked, transfer figs to a large heatproof bowl, leaving the syrup behind; when all are cooked, add the lemon juice, lemon rind, and ginger to the syrup in the saucepan and boil 5 minutes longer. Pour the hot syrup over the figs, cover, and let stand overnight at room temperature. (The figs will plump up and absorb some of the syrup.) The following morning, drain the figs (reserving the syrup) and pack the figs in sterilized and still very hot half-pint canning jars up to ½ inch from the rims. Bring the syrup to a boil and pour it over them, making sure all figs are submerged.

Wipe the rims well, seal with new lids and sterilized rings, and process jars upright for 10 minutes in a boiling hot water bath. Cool jars upright, then label and date. Store upright in a cool, dark, and dry place; will be ready for use in about 1 week. *Makes about 10 to 12 half pints.*

Easy-to-Make Mock Candied Ginger

My grandmother, like other ladies of her day, thought this inexpensive, preserved imitation ginger, or the noncanned candied variation of it, served nicely whenever ginger was needed for one of her recipes. She used it in raisin bread or a sweet, fruited yeast bread.

Home-Canned Mock Ginger

1 pound large light-colored carrots, peeled
Water for parboiling carrots
1 cup water

1 pound sugar
Juice from 1 lemon
1 tablespoon ground ginger

Cut the carrots into strips or into fancy shapes, such as stars, diamonds, half moons, about ¼-inch thick. Parboil to soften slightly, but do not let carrots get tender; drain and set aside. In a medium-size stainless-steel, unchipped enamel, or Pyrex saucepan, combine the 1 cup water with the sugar, lemon juice, and ginger. Add the carrots and simmer for about 10 minutes. Remove from the heat and let sit at room temperature until mixture is cool, or overnight, whichever is more convenient.

Then with a slotted spoon, transfer carrots to unchipped glass bowl; boil the syrup again and pour it over the carrots. Let sit until mixture is cool. Then drain off syrup and boil it a third time. Meanwhile, place the carrots in sterilized and still very hot half-pint canning jars up to 1 inch from the rims. Ladle the syrup over them up to ½ inch from the rim, making sure all carrots are submerged. Wipe rims well and seal with new lids and sterilized rings as for any other preserves. Process jars upright in a boiling hot water bath for 10 minutes to guarantee a good seal. Cool, then label and date jars. Store upright in a cool, dark, and dry place. *Makes about 4 half pints.*

To Make Mock Candied Ginger

Follow the recipe for the canned mock ginger, but add *½ cup extra sugar* each time the syrup is boiled. The final syrup should be quite thick. After the last boiling, let carrots cool in the syrup. Then transfer drained carrots to a platter or place them on waxed paper and allow to dry for several days. Then roll each piece in granulated sugar to which a pinch of ground ginger has been added. Remember: ginger is a strongly flavored spice, so a little bit goes a long way. Place carrot pieces in a jar, cap tightly, and refrigerate. When well dried and stored properly, this keeps for a long time. When needed, remove lid, take only what you need, and screw lid tightly back on. *Makes 6 to 8 half pints.*

Mother's Holiday Pudding with Grandma White's Brandy Sauce

At home, Mother made this steamed dessert pudding with grated carrots and potatoes in it for Christmas, much to everyone's delight, for we all loved its tender, moist texture and rich flavor. Grandma White used a very similar recipe and served this brandy sauce over hers. (The sauce is at its best if aged for about three weeks.)

½ cup butter or margarine
1 cup, packed, light brown
   sugar
2 eggs
1 cup all-purpose flour
1 tablespoon plus 1 teaspoon
   baking powder
2 teaspoons baking soda
1 teaspoon ground cinnamon

¼ teaspoon ground cloves
1 cup seedless raisins
1 cup peeled, grated raw
   carrots
1 cup peeled, grated raw
   potatoes
1 cup chopped walnuts
   Grandma White's Brandy
   Sauce (recipe follows)

In a large bowl, cream the butter and sugar together until light. Add the eggs and beat with a spoon for 5 minutes or until the mixture is stiff and smooth. Sift in the flour, baking powder, baking soda, cinnamon, and cloves, and fold them into mixture. Then fold in the raisins, carrots, potatoes, and nuts, mixing just enough to blend. Spoon batter into 2 buttered medium-size (about 1 pint) molds. Cover with lids or aluminum or buttered kraft paper. Set molds into a deep saucepan with a wire rack at the bottom. Pour boiling water around (not in) molds to come about halfway up molds. Cover kettle and carefully bring to a boil, then simmer; steam for 2 hours, then unmold onto serving dishes. When pudding is almost cool, serve it topped with brandy sauce. *Makes 2 molds or 12 servings.*

Grandma White's Brandy Sauce
½ cup butter or margarine
1½ cups powdered sugar

1 egg yolk
3 tablespoons brandy or rum

Whip the butter and sugar together until light and fluffy. Add the egg yolk, beating until very light. Stir in the rum or brandy. Spoon into a freshly washed and sterilized glass jar, cover tightly, and age in refrigerator for about 3 weeks. To serve, spoon sauce over hot pudding, and pass the remainder at the table. *Makes 1½ cups.*

Oatmeal Christmas Cookies

This old-time recipe, a favorite at our house for thirty-five years, yields melt-in-your-mouth cookies that grace a Christmas tray.

½ cup all-purpose flour
⅔ cup sugar
½ teaspoon salt
1 cup butter or margarine, softened
2 eggs, slightly beaten

1 teaspoon vanilla extract
1 cup quick-cooking rolled oats
Candied citron, candied cherries, and/or chopped nuts (see Note)

Note: For the prettiest Christmas cookies, use a little of all three. Preheat oven to 375°F. Sift the flour, sugar, and salt into a medium-size bowl; set aside. In a large bowl, combine butter, eggs, and vanilla; beat for 2 minutes or until smooth. Stir in the flour, then the oats. Drop batter by teaspoonfuls onto a greased cookie sheet, about 2 inches apart. Flatten each cookie with side of a knife (dipping blade first in cold water keeps it from sticking to batter). Decorate tops with bits of the citron, candied cherries, and/or nuts. Bake until cookies are golden brown around the edge, about 10 to 12 minutes. Remove from cookie sheet immediately to cool on a wire rack. Store in an airtight container. *Makes about 4 dozen cookies.*

🌿 PIE SOCIAL

Although the neighborhood Christmas baskets were usually made up of home-canned or home-grown products, some of the women liked to put in a little store-bought Christmas candy or toy for the children, or a handkerchief for some dear soul. To help raise money for these extras, the church ladies organized pie socials. For this type of fundraiser, the women and girls made not one pie each, but perhaps two or three, using their very best ingredients and recipes.

Once the day arrived and all the pies were ready, folks from miles around gathered at the church. First everyone was treated to a mu-

sical program or some other homemade entertainment. Then the ladies started the auction. Pies sold for twenty-five to fifty cents each.
Single men often bid a whole dollar for a particular woman's or girl's
pie. When the men had exhausted their funds and the best of the pies
had been sold, everyone settled down for coffee and pastry. Everyone
—those who had bought pies to take home and those who had not—
dropped a few pennies or a nickel into a kitty for his slice of pie, which
gave everyone a chance to contribute to the funds for the Christmas
baskets.

After the money was counted and the amount announced to the
crowd and remarked upon, folks settled down for a little personal
visiting. Talk ranged from crops to children to weather. But since

farm doin's tended to break up early, as most people got up at dawn, people soon trailed out of the church, warmly praising the evening's work.

Cranberry Apple Double-Crust Pie

Although some women prefer this cranberry and apple mixture in their pie, others use the tart, dark-red cranberries by themselves. Those who love the sweet, pleasantly biting flavor of rhubarb pie generally don't add apples to this Cranberry Apple pie.

Double-Crust Pie Pastry (page 139)

2 cups coarsely chopped cranberries

1 cup peeled, finely chopped apples

1⅓ cups sugar

⅓ cup all-purpose flour

1 egg

Preheat oven to 425°F. Line the pie pan with the pastry dough and reserve the other half of the dough for a top crust. Refrigerate both until ready to use. In a large bowl, combine the cranberries, apples, sugar, and flour; stir until cranberries and apples are well coated. Beat the egg until frothy, pour it over the cranberry-apple mixture, and stir until well coated. Spoon into the prepared pie shell. Roll out the dough for the top crust, fit it over the pie; trim and crimp edges. Cut vents in top. Bake at 425° for 10 minutes, then reduce the oven setting to 350°F and continue baking until the filling is done and the crust is golden brown, about 35 minutes more. *Makes one 9-inch pie or 6 servings.*

Viola's Raisin Pie with Tip-top Pastry

During the Depression, raisins were cheap and women like our friend Viola made raisin bread, raisin cake, raisin tarts, mincemeat, raisin pie like this one, and endless other dishes that featured naturally sweet, dried grapes.

1 cup seedless raisins

Cold water for reconstituting raisins

Tip-top Pastry (recipe follows)

¼ cup all-purpose flour

¾ cup sugar

¼ teaspoon salt

2 cups water

1 egg, beaten

2 tablespoons cider vinegar

Preheat oven to 450°F. Wash the raisins and soak them for about 3 hours in just enough cold water to cover. (When the raisins are plump the water should be fully taken up. If it is not, reserve the raisin water to make up some of the 2 cups water you will need for the pie.)

Meanwhile, line the pie pan with the pastry dough and reserve the other half of the dough for a top crust. Refrigerate both until ready to use.

In a large saucepan, mix the flour thoroughly with the sugar and salt; set aside. In another pan or tea kettle, bring 2 cups of water (or a mixture of water and raisin water) to a boil and add to the sugar and flour mixture, stirring constantly. Place saucepan over high heat and cook until the mixture is slightly thickened, then reduce heat to low, stirring constantly. Pour 2 to 3 tablespoons of the hot mixture into the egg, stirring quickly to blend, then add the egg mixture to the saucepan with the remaining sugar and flour mixture, stirring quickly to blend. Continue cooking about 3 minutes, stirring constantly. Remove from heat and stir in the raisins and vinegar.

Roll out the dough for the top crust. Pour the hot filling into the prepared pie shell; moisten the edges of the bottom pie shell and cover filling with the dough for the top crust. Trim and crimp edges. Cut vents in top. Bake at 450°F for 10 minutes, then reduce oven setting to 350°F and continue baking until the crust is brown, about 30 minutes more. *Makes one 9-inch pie or 6 to 8 servings.*

Tip-top Pastry
This is a plain pastry used for raisin, meat, or mincemeat pie. It may also be used for a fried pie.

1½ cups all-purpose flour, plus flour for rolling out dough
1 teaspoon baking powder
½ teaspoon salt
½ cup butter or margarine
1 teaspoon lemon juice
Cold water, 2 tablespoons or more if needed

Into a large bowl, sift together the flour, baking powder, and salt. Rub the butter into the flour mixture with fingertips until the mixture is finely granulated, particles about the size of a grain of rice. Refrigerate 2 hours, then set aside ½ cup of the mixture. Add the lemon juice and just enough cold water (add it about 1 tablespoon at a time) to make a stiff dough. Turn dough onto a floured surface. Knead lightly and roll into a long narrow strip about ¼-inch thick. Next, sprinkle the rolled pastry with about half the reserved ½ cup flour mixture. Fold dough as you would a letter to make 3 layers. Turn dough half way around, then roll again into a rectangle; sprinkle on the remaining half of the reserved ½ cup flour mixture and fold in thirds again. Roll and fold twice more. Divide dough into two equal portions. Refrigerate one portion until time to roll out for the top crust. Then roll out other portion of dough and line an ungreased 9-inch pie pan with it. Fill, cover with rolled-out dough for top crust, and bake as directed in the above recipe. *Makes enough dough for one 9-inch double-crust pie.*

Butterscotch Pie

Whether women made pies for grange suppers, church doin's, or pie socials, the men folk sort of gravitated toward well-made butterscotch pies.

1 egg, separated	2 tablespoons butter
1 cup, packed, dark brown sugar	1 tablespoon vanilla extract
	¼ teaspoon salt
3 tablespoons flour	Flaky Crust (page 28)
1 cup milk	1 tablespoon powdered sugar
3 tablespoons water	

Preheat oven to 350°F. In a medium-size saucepan, combine the egg yolk with the brown sugar, flour, milk, water, butter, vanilla, and salt. Cook over high heat until mixture thickens and reaches a boil, stirring constantly. Pour the hot filling into the baked pie crust. Whip the egg white until stiff, then beat in the powdered sugar. Swirl over the top of the filling, making sure it touches the crust all the way around the edge. Bake until top is lightly browned, about 20 minutes. *Makes one 9-inch pie or 4 to 6 servings.*

Mother's Butter-Crust Quince Pie

When raw, quince fruit has a rich, delightful fragrance and a mouth-puckering flavor. Baked into a pie, it tastes hauntingly delicious. Mother loves the taste of butter in the crust of a quince pie.

Butter-Crust Pastry (recipe follows)	½ teaspoon ground nutmeg
	Pinch of salt
6 cups peeled, cored, and sliced ripe quince	1 tablespoon butter
	½ teaspoon lemon juice
1 cup sugar, plus sugar to sprinkle on pastry dough	½ cup heavy cream, plus cream to rub on top of pastry dough
1 teaspoon ground cinnamon	Flour for rolling out dough

Preheat oven to 425°F. Prepare the pastry dough and refrigerate until well chilled. Then divide dough into 2 portions, 1 slightly larger than the other. Form the smaller portion into a ball and roll out on a floured surface. Line the pie pan with the pastry dough. Arrange the quince evenly in the pie shell, mounding the fruit slightly. Combine the 1 cup sugar, cinnamon, nutmeg, and salt in a small bowl, mixing well. Sprinkle mixture over the quince and dot with butter. In a separate bowl, combine the lemon juice and the ½ cup cream and whip slightly; pour over the quince.

Moisten the edges of the bottom pie shell, roll out the remaining portion of pastry dough, and cover the filling with it. With a large, wide-tined fork, pierce the top a few times and crimp edges. With the fingertips or a pastry brush, lightly rub a few drops of cream over the top of the pastry dough, then sprinkle lightly with sugar. Bake at 425°F for 15 minutes, then reduce oven setting to 350°F and continue baking until the crust is nicely browned, about 30 to 35 minutes more. *Makes one 9-inch pie or 5 to 6 servings.*

Butter-Crust Pastry

2 cups all-purpose flour
1 teaspoon salt

¾ cup cold butter
About 2 tablespoons cold water

In a medium-size bowl, combine the flour and salt. Cut the butter in until mixture is reduced to pea-size pieces. Sprinkle on the ice water, blending with a fork just until all particles cling together, forming a ball. Refrigerate until ready to roll out. Then roll out dough and line an ungreased 9-inch pie pan with it. Fill, cover with rolled-out dough for top crust, and bake as directed in the above recipe. *Makes enough dough for one 9-inch double-crust pie.*

✽ THANKSGIVING ON THE FARM

This joyous harvest festival has always been a family day celebrated with a big dinner and heart-warming reunions. Ninety-six-year-old farmer Webster Howe's recollections of his favorite Thanksgiving is a bit poignant, but full of family warmth.

The best Thanksgiving I ever had was when me and Mother was workin' the farm in southern Missouri, south of Joplin. It was in '34 or '35. Our kids had all left home lookin' for work in California and in Kansas, takin' all the little ones with them. Draggin' the grandchildren all over the country, proba-bly to starve, Mother always put it. Those years, there wasn't no one left on the farm but me, Mother, and John, our youngest son.

In those days, there was want all across this country. Where we was you couldn't hardly make a thin dime. We milked our string of cows and couldn't sell the milk, and fed it to the pigs and couldn't sell the pigs, but Mother and me and John was blessed with food and work. That year we put up more dried and canned stuff, and put down and smoked more meat than we ever done before or since. You'd of thought we was squirrels, puttin' away nuts for a hard winter. I guess knowin' about want everywhere and thinkin' it might come to you and yours makes a person a little scared.

Anyway, it got to be the week before Thanksgivin' and we didn't hear nothin' from any of the kids, not our two youngest families livin' in southwest Kansas or the two older boys in California. Mother had writ them long letters, tellin' them she missed them and wonderin' if any of them was comin' home for the holiday.

When she didn't hear, she jest went out one mornin' and killed two big tom turkeys and dressed them. Then she set about making apple, mince, and pumpkin pies. By evenin' the bread and baked stuff began to pile up till I asked her who she was cookin' all that for, me and John? She never even answered me.

I tell you, it got to me. Mother was workin' hard and lookin' tired. I was gettin' bitter at the kids who hadn't even answered their mother's letter. John, he put in every bit of extry time he had helpin' her—when she'd let him. I could see it was botherin' him too, you know, the way she was takin' on, as if all her cookin' and wishin' would bring them other kids home.

Well, it didn't get no better and by the time we was doing chores the night before Thanksgivin' me and John was feeling low too. I still had two cows to go, when I heard a car drive up. John left the feedin' and went out to look. He come runnin' back and told me to come quick, he'd finish up later.

When I stepped out of the barn, there was my son Ken's old touring car loaded with women and kids and Jack, my son-in-law, jumpin' out of it. I jest turned around and went back into the barn. John, he come after me and told me they'd jest come down after me if I didn't come on up to the house.

At the house there was a lot of laughin' and talkin' and everyone was huggin' Mother and John and me. When we went inside, John, he poured coffee for the grownups and icy cold milk for all the children. Mother and the girls when to the pantry for somethin' to eat and we could hear them teasin' and laughin' about all the stuff she'd made.

Then with both hands full of cookies, the littlest grandchild come out to lean against my chair. She was a purty little redheaded kid. She told me that up in Kansas they didn't have no cookies like her Grandma made. I looked down at her and seen right away that she was as scrawny as a lamb whose mother didn't have enough milk to feed it. Mother and Daughter walked out of the pantry about then and seen us. Mother give a knowin' look and me and then at Daughter.

Daughter has always been the bravest of all my children, but when she looked straight at me, I saw fear in her eyes. Never sheddin' a tear, not a waver in her strong voice, she told us how they'd been broke most of the time in Kansas and how they'd sold everything—even most of their clothes—to get the money to come home. Without asking for an ounce of pity, she made me a deal to work out their keep till things picked up—as though I wouldn't a taken them in for nothin'.

My boy Ken, he never said nothin', neither did his wife, they jest let Daughter talk. Jack, our son-in-law, never said a word, jest sat there with his head kind of down and his elbows on his knees. Mother seen he was feelin' shamed for not bein' able to take care of his own, so she told him how much we was needin' help and how his comin' was a real godsend.

The next day was Thanksgivin' Day. The boys helped me with chores, then we sat awhile in the barn and talked about how we was goin' to make it. And about how bad it was in Kansas and on up north. The women spent the whole mornin' puttin' dinner together. Then about two o'clock we ate.

Sittin' there at the crowded table, covered with plates and food, the family

JANE WATSON HOPPING

all spruced up and smilin', Mother lookin' like the Spirit of God had descended on her purty face, put me to mind of my own pa and ma and my own brothers, and I remembered the old, old prayer my father said at our table.

Well, I'm ninety-six—ninety-seven my next birthday—and since then, I said that same prayer maybe fifty times over Thanksgivin' dinners, but it never give me the joy it did that first time.

From WE PLOUGH THE FIELDS

THANKSGIVING

We plough the fields and scatter
The good seed on the land,
But it is fed and watered
By God's almighty hand;
He sends the snow in winter
The warmth to swell the grain,
The breezes, and the sunshine,
And soft refreshing rain.

He only is the Maker
Of all things near and far;
He paints the wayside flower,
He lights the evening star.
The winds and waves obey Him,
By Him the birds are fed;
Much more to us, His children,
He gives our daily bread.

We thank Thee, then O Father,
For all things bright and good,
The seed-time and the harvest,
Our life, our health, our food.
Accept the gifts we offer
For all Thy love imparts,
And, what Thou most desirest,
Our humble thankful hearts.

—Matthias Claudius (1782)
music by Johanna A. P. Schultz (1900)
Translated by Jane M. Campbell (1861)

Mother's Roast Turkey with Pecan Dressing and Richly Colored Turkey Gravy

On old-time farms, Thanksgiving was a time of plenty. Women could cook at whim, stirring up anything the imagination devised. Dinner wasn't so much planned as created. And well-seasoned, moist, tender roast turkey was at the center of the festivities.

To make the turkey

Rub the turkey with *butter* and then rub salt, black pepper, and finely pulverized marjoram into it, allowing *1 teaspoon salt, ¼ teaspoon black pepper, and ¼ teaspoon finely pulverized marjoram per pound of meat.* Season the giblets and neck with the same seasonings. Refrigerate the turkey giblets and neck overnight to allow the flavors to blend. The following day, set the giblets and neck aside, and place the turkey, breast down, in a shallow roasting pan fitted with a rack. Stuff the cavity with small whole onions, whole stalks of celery, a whole, unpeeled clove of garlic, and a whole, unpeeled apple. Roast in a 350°F oven until about half done (the cooking time will vary according to size of turkey), basting with the fat that accumulates in the bottom of the pan; be sure to spoon some of the fat into the cavity to baste the breast. (If there is not enough fat, put a generous spoon of butter in the cavity, too.) Then turn the turkey breast up and continue roasting until the meat is done and the skin is golden brown, about 20 minutes per pound for birds under 12 pounds, or 15 to 18 minutes per pounds for larger birds. (*Note:* There are several ways to test for doneness: Use a meat thermometer, inserting it into the densest meat of the inner thigh near the hip bone or groin since that is the last place to be done on the bird. Be sure not to touch bone with the tip of the thermometer. When done, the temperature should read between 170°F to 180°F. If no thermometer is available, test for doneness by pressing the drumstick: If the turkey is done, the meat will feel soft and the drumstick should twist out of joint; also the meat will have shrunk up the bone so that the joint where the foot was removed will be bare.) Once done, remove from oven and let sit 15 to 20 minutes before carving, which makes for better carving.

Meanwhile, place the giblets and neck in a saucepan; add a little *salt* and *black pepper* to taste, a slice or two of *onion*, and some *celery leaves.* Cover with *water* and simmer until done. Remove meat from the pan; discard vegetables; remove neck meat from the bone and finely chop all the meat. Reserve if adding to either the dressing or the gravy. Make the dressing and gravy and serve immediately.

Pecan Dressing

I always bake the dressing in a separate pan instead of stuffing the turkey with it. (Meat cooked by itself will keep well until it can be used for leftovers, but meat that has had stuffing in the cavity is more apt to sour or take on flavors from the leftover stuffing.)

4 cups very fine dry breadcrumbs
1½ cups coarsely chopped pecans, plus pecans to garnish top (optional)
½ cup chopped celery
3 tablespoons minced fresh parsley

1½ teaspoons poultry seasoning
1 egg, well beaten
½ cup light cream
4 cups hot mashed potatoes
Salt
Black pepper
Butter for dotting top

In a large bowl, combine the breadcrumbs, pecans, celery, parsley, and poultry seasoning. In a small bowl, beat together the egg and cream, then fold into the mashed potatoes. Add salt and pepper to taste, folding until well mixed. Spoon into a greased 13x9x2-inch baking pan. Dot top with a little butter and sprinkle on a few additional pecans, if you wish. Prebake at 350°F for 45 minutes, then rewarm when you cook last-minute rolls, or bake with the turkey during the final 45 minutes of cooking time. *Makes 12 generous servings.*

Richly Colored Turkey Gravy

For country people, a thick slice of turkey goes on the plate first, and tucked in beside it is a heaping pile of mashed potatoes with clear golden gravy spooned over it.

Mother hated greasy food, so after we cooked the turkey we set the roasting pan with the pan drippings inside in a cold place; that way the fat would firm up on top of the drippings and then we spooned it off. (The broth may be cooled to lukewarm, after which ice cubes may be dropped into it. This will quickly chill the fat—it will cling to the ice cubes—and it can then be removed, along with the ice cubes.) Next, we poured the drippings into a pot large enough for making gravy, added water to taste, and adjusted the seasoning. We also sometimes added giblet and neck meat at this point. While bringing the broth to a boil, we caramelized *1 tablespoon sugar* in a small cast-iron frying pan by heating it until it bubbled and turned dark brown (we were careful not to let it burn or it would have tasted bitter.) Then we poured the caramelized sugar into the hot broth, spooning a little of the liquid into the frying pan to wash all of the sugar out. Then we thickened the gravy by stirring in *about 2 tablespoons cornstarch (moistened in cold water) for each cup of broth*. We cooked it just five minutes or so longer, tasting and adjusting seasonings. (Sometimes we also liked to add a little butter at this point for a richer flavor.)

Venison Shoulder with Sausage, Wheat and White Bread, and Cornmeal Stuffing

The Lester women, Mother's cousins, nearly always came down out of the hills with late corn, beet pickles, and wild game dishes: venison, bear, game birds, and sometimes roast varmint with sweet taters.

1 (4- to 6-pound) bone-in shoulder of venison
Melted butter
Salt
Black pepper

½ teaspoon dried marjoram or thyme leaves, more if desired
4 slices farm-style bacon
About 1 cup water
Cornmeal and Sausage Stuffing (recipe follows)

Preheat oven to 350°F. Remove shoulder bone from the venison and wipe the meat dry. Then pour the butter over all the meat, including in and around the bone cavity, rubbing it in well. Salt and pepper generously on all sides and in any pockets or folds of meat. Roll the marjoram or thyme leaves between your finger and thumb to pulverize, then sprinkle evenly over the meat. Roll the meat together and tie it tightly and evenly with strong kitchen twine to form a compact roast. Place in a roasting pan and arrange the strips of bacon over the roast. Add about 1 cup of water to the bottom of the pan. (*Note:* Venison should be cooked only until *just done;* the muscle fibers are different than those of beef and venison will toughen if overcooked. To test for doneness, pierce thickest part of meat with a long-tined fork, and wait a few seconds to see if juices run clear; if they do, the meat is done.) Remove from oven, let meat set 15 minutes before serving. Cut the string away and slice into ½-inch-thick slices. Serve with the following dressing. *Makes about 8 servings.*

Sausage, Wheat and White Bread, and Cornmeal Stuffing

3 cups cooked cornmeal mush (recipe follows)
1 (1-pound) loaf coarse-grained whole-wheat bread, crust left on, torn into small pieces
½ (1-pound) loaf white bread,

crust left on, torn into small pieces
1 pound fried (or browned) drained ground pork sausage
¼ cup butter
1 large onion, chopped

½ stalk celery, chopped
   About 4 cups Homemade
    Chicken Broth (page 11)
   Crumbled dried marjoram,
    dried thyme, and/or dried
    oregano, optional
Minced fresh garlic, optional
   About 1½ teaspoons salt
   About ½ teaspoon black
    pepper

Begin by preparing the cornmeal mush (recipe follows). Then preheat oven to 375°F. In a large bowl combine the breads. Add the cornmeal mush and drained sausage, but *don't stir*. In a frying pan, melt the butter. Add the onion and celery; sauté until vegetables are clear. Slowly add 2 cups of broth or water. Now add the marjoram, thyme, oregano, and/or garlic, if desired and salt and pepper; simmer a few seconds. Pour the vegetable mixture over the sausage mixture, stirring well. Add additional broth or water to make a moist dressing. Spoon dressing into a baking pan. Bake until the dressing is puffed and brown, about 45 minutes. *Makes 8 generous servings.*

Cornmeal Mush
1 cup cornmeal
1 cup cold water
3 cups boiling water
1 teaspoon salt

In a medium-size bowl, combine cornmeal and cold water. Bring 3 cups water to a rolling boil; add salt. Then add the cornmeal all at once, stirring constantly to prevent lumping. When the mush is thick turn the heat down very low and steam-cook until granular and puffy, about 25 minutes (watch that it does not stick and burn). Pour into a 9x5-inch loaf pan and chill until needed. *Makes 3 cups mush.*

Aunt El's Pumpkin Chiffon Pie in a Gingersnap Pie Shell

Always a conversation piece, this pie sparked a separation of the sexes; the women and girls thought this light pumpkin chiffon was delicious and elegant, but the men and boys stuck with the more traditional, richer, heavily seasoned pumpkin and sweet potato pies.

2 teaspoons unflavored gelatin
¼ cup cold water
3 eggs, separated
1¼ cups cooked and finely
   sieved pumpkin pulp (or
   canned store-bought
   pumpkin)
½ cup, packed, light brown
   sugar
½ cup milk
1 teaspoon ground cinnamon
½ teaspoon freshly grated
   nutmeg

(Continued on next page)

¼ teaspoon ground ginger
  Pinch of salt
⅓ cup sugar to beat into egg
  whites
1 unbaked Gingersnap Pie
  Shell (recipe follows)

Whipped cream (page 61)
  spiced with ½ teaspoon
  cinnamon and a sprinkling
  of freshly grated nutmeg

In a small bowl, soften the gelatin in the water for 3 to 5 minutes. Meanwhile, beat the egg yolks and place in a medium-size saucepan. Add the pumpkin, sugar, milk, cinnamon, nutmeg, ginger, and salt; stir to blend. Place over low heat and cook until mixture begins to thicken, stirring constantly. Remove from heat. Stir in the gelatin. Beat the egg whites until soft peaks form; beat in the sugar, 1 tablespoon at a time. Fold egg whites into the pumpkin mixture. Pour the filling into the prepared pie shell and chill until firm. Whip the cream just until soft peaks form, then spoon it evenly over the filling. Serve immediately. *Makes one 9-inch pie.*

Gingersnap Pie Shell

1½ cups finely crushed
  gingersnap cookies
6 tablespoons butter
¼ cup powdered sugar

½ teaspoon ground cinnamon
½ teaspoon freshly grated
  nutmeg

In a medium-size bowl, combine all the ingredients, blending well. Pat the crumbs firmly into the bottom and sides of a 9-inch pie pan. *Makes one 9-inch pie shell.*

THE SCHOOLBOY'S FAVORITE

Over the river and through the wood,
    Now Grandmother's cap I spy!
Hurrah for the fun! Is the pudding done?
    Hurrah for the pumpkin-pie!

                  —Old School Reader

    Fer any boy 'at's little as me,
        Er any little girl,
    That-un's the goodest poetry-piece
        In any book in the worl'!
    An' ef grown-peoples wuz little ag'in
        I bet they'd say so, too,
    Ef *they'd* go see *their* ole Gran'ma
        Like our Pa lets *us* do!

                  —James Whitcomb Riley

DECEMBER

Goodwill, Treats, and Trifles

On the farms of the past, frosty, icy December was actually the warmest of the winter months. Even so, all birds but English sparrows and chickadees went south to warmer climates. Groundhogs and bears hibernated; muskrats built domed homes of ice in frozen streams and ponds. Only fur-bearing animals—mink, beaver, fox—were active, warm in their sleek winter coats, chasing rabbits through the snow.

Country people settled in for the long winter ahead. Wood piles were as tall as men, silos were full of grain, and hay in the barn was stacked to the rafters, promising plenty for cattle and sheep. The farm and the family were ready, stored in against the ancient "time of want." Everyone had chores to do—milking, feeding hens, throwing out hay to the cattle and sheep, stoking the fire—but for the most part, days were spent joyfully preparing for the coming holiday season. After the rush and hard work of the harvest, a little time for just resting and talking was welcome. Women cooked now for sheer pleasure. Meals tended to be long, visity, sit-down dinners instead of the hurried meals of summer and fall.

From SETTING THE TABLE
IN VERMONT

About as soft a scene, I swan!
As my old eye remember,
Is sisters getting supper on
Along in dark December;
The lamplight glazed the linen cloth,
The shadowed floor grew sable—
How I'd love to see again
My sister set the table.

—*Daniel L. Cady*

WHEN SISTER SET THE TABLE

Farm girls were taught to be good homemakers. They learned not only how to milk cows, make butter, and cook, but also how to set a proper table. There was a place for everything and everything was put in its place. The castor* sat in the center of the table, the platter

---

* A castor was a very decorative stand—silver or silverplated—that held condiments like oil, vinegar, mustard, salt, pepper, and a container of cayenne.

of meat and carving tools before the father or head of the house, the soup at the opposite end of the table before the mother. Bread, butter, jelly, vegetables, and other foods were all placed neatly around the table in assigned spots. Usually only a knife and fork were put beside the plate; a spoon was considered unnecessary unless there was a soup or dessert.

Cabbage, Carrot, and Celery Perfection Salad with Sour Cream Dressing

In spring, women sometimes substituted fresh green peas—blanched for five minutes—for the cabbage in this salad. Make this salad a day before serving.

1 tablespoon unflavored gelatin	½ cup finely shredded green or white cabbage
½ cup cold water	½ cup grated carrots
¾ cup boiling water	½ cup chopped celery
2 tablespoons lemon juice or cider vinegar	1½ cups cottage cheese
1 tablespoon sugar	Large lettuce leaves or other leaves from fall edible greens
Pinch of salt	
Pinch of black pepper	Sour Cream Dressing (recipe follows), optional

Because this is a layered salad, divide gelatin into 2 equal portions; soften each portion in ¼ cup of the cold water for 3 to 5 minutes. In a large bowl, combine the ¾ cup boiling water with the first portion of the softened gelatin, stirring until dissolved. Place the bowl on ice or in the freezer so it will chill quickly. When it begins to cool and thicken, stir in the lemon juice, sugar, salt, and pepper and continue cooling until it has the consistency of unbeaten egg whites. Fold in the cabbage, carrots, and celery. Pour the mixture into a large fancy mold or into 6 individual molds, which have been dipped in cold water, filling mold or molds only half full. Refrigerate until firm. Then place the second portion of softened gelatin in a double boiler over a pan of hot water and stir until dissolved. Remove from heat and add to the cottage cheese; stir well to blend. Add salt and pepper, mixing well. Leave the cottage cheese in curds or, if desired, whip it smooth. Cool slightly, then pour the cottage cheese mixture over the jellied vegetables. Refrigerate overnight. When ready to serve, unmold and serve on a bed of lettuce or other edible greens. Garnish with dollops of sour cream dressing, if you wish. *Makes 6 servings.*

Sour Cream Dressing

1 cup dairy sour cream

3 tablespoons cider vinegar, or
   2 of vinegar and 1 of lemon
   juice

1 teaspoon salt

1 tablespoon sugar
   Dash paprika or, if you prefer,
   cayenne

In a small bowl, combine all the ingredients; stir well to blend. *Makes about 1 cup.*

Jellied Roast Beef Loaf

The day before the beef loaf is needed, place *one* (4- to 5-pound) *bone-in beef roast* in a roasting pan. Season with *salt, black pepper*, and *chopped celery and parsley*, and a few minced, relatively mild herbs, such as *marjoram* and *sweet basil* (don't use a strong herb such as sage). Cover pan and roast at 350°F until well done, about 2 hours. Test with a meat thermometer; should read 165°F to 170°F. Transfer roast to a platter and cover to keep it warm. Skim as much fat as you can from the drippings in the pan. Soften *3 tablespoons unflavored gelatin* in ½ cup cold water. Dilute the meat drippings with just enough water to have 1½ cups. (Don't add water if you have 1½ cups drippings.) Heat drippings to the boiling point and add the gelatin, stirring until the gelatin is completely dissolved. Let cool. Next remove the bone from the roast, discarding bone. Trim excess fat. Separate the larger, straight-grained pieces of meat from the small and not-as-tender pieces; keep the large straight-grained pieces warm until you are ready to use them (they will be packed whole). Grind the smaller and not-as-tender pieces and mix them into the hot drippings and gelatin mixture; the mixture should be somewhat watery. Place enough of the mixture into a 2-quart deep casserole dish, about 1 inch deep. Lay the reserved larger pieces of meat on top of the ground meat mixture with the grain straight from end-to-end so that the larger pieces of meat will be sliced across the grain when the jellied loaf is cut. Pour the remaining ground meat mixture in around the larger pieces of meat, settling it in with a fork so there will be no air pockets in the loaf. (If the jellied stock does not cover the top of the meat, mix more gelatin with hot water, using *1 tablespoon gelatin* to *½ cup water*, and add this to the mold or pan.) Weight the loaf down, perhaps using a smaller pan with something heavy placed inside it or a smooth board wrapped in plastic or aluminum foil. Chill overnight before unmolding. Serve immediately on large lettuce leaves. *Makes 8 to 10 servings.*

Scotch Eggs: Boiled, Coated with Meat, and Deep-fried

We prefer this dish made with lean ground beef; however, it can be made with finely chopped cooked ham, veal, or ground lamb. Serve the eggs plain or with Spicy Meat Sauce. (If using the sauce, make it well ahead and reheat just before serving.)

Vegetable oil for deep-frying
6 hard-cooked eggs
½ cup milk
½ cup very fine dry white breadcrumbs
1 cup very lean ground beef

1 raw egg, beaten
1 teaspoon dried sweet basil, finely pulverized
½ teaspoon salt
¼ teaspoon black pepper
Spicy Meat Sauce, optional (recipe follows)

In a deep fryer or deep pan, heat the oil to 365°F or until hot enough to brown a crust of bread. Remove fat from heat while you prepare the eggs.

In a large saucepan, heat the milk until hot. Add the breadcrumbs, stirring together to make a paste. Remove from heat and add the ground beef, the raw egg, and the basil, salt, and pepper; mix well. Coat each hard-cooked egg with the mixture.

Reheat oil to 365°F or until it will brown a crust of bread in a couple of minutes. Gently lower the coated eggs into the hot oil and fry until crust is golden brown, about 3 to 5 minutes. Remove the eggs from the hot fat with a slotted spoon and drain on kraft paper (a brown grocery bag). Serve while still hot, with heated spicy meat sauce spooned over them if desired. *Makes 3 to 4 servings.*

Spicy Meat Sauce

2 tablespoons butter or margarine
¼ cup minced onions
3 minced fresh sweet basil leaves
1 large sprig fresh parsley, minced

1 small clove garlic, peeled
1 quart canned tomatoes, drained
½ teaspoon red pepper (cayenne preferred)
Salt
Black pepper

In a medium-size skillet, melt the butter. Add the onions, basil, parsley, and garlic and sauté until the vegetables are tender, but not browned. Add the tomatoes and pepper; simmer until a thick sauce is made. Salt and pepper to taste. *Makes about 3 cups.*

Old-fashioned Duchess Potatoes

Always a treat, this old-style potato dish can be plain or fancy depending on the cook and the need. If you wish, dress it up with a dusting of poppy, caraway, or sesame seed, or add parsley or chives, or herbs like savory, or sweet marjoram to the potatoes when you add the salt, pepper, and nutmeg.

2 pounds potatoes, peeled	Black pepper
3 egg yolks	Scant ¼ teaspoon freshly
2 tablespoons butter or	grated nutmeg
margarine	Flour
1 tablespoon heavy cream	1 egg, beaten
Salt	

Preheat oven to 400°F. Boil the potatoes; drain and then dry off excess moisture in the oven. (Leave oven at 400°F.) Then rub them through a sieve or put them through a ricer. Add the egg yolks, butter, cream, salt and pepper to taste, and the nutmeg, mixing well. Turn onto a floured surface and divide mixture into 8 to 10 equal portions. Shape each piece into a square about 1 inch thick. With a spatula, transfer each piece to a greased baking pan and brush tops with the beaten egg. Bake until well browned, about 20 minutes. Serve immediately. *Makes 8 to 10 servings.*

Grandmother Sitha Jane's Trifle

Farm people of English descent often served a trifle, which is a dessert made of sponge cake or stale, unfrosted cake soaked in wine or fruit juice, covered with fresh fruit, such as raspberries or peaches, or cooked, sweetened, and slightly thickened fruit such as sweet cherries, or with jams or marmalades, then covered with a rich custard and topped with whipped cream. Such desserts are lovely when garnished with toasted almonds.

While the recipe that follows is fairly precise, I would urge you to experiment with your own ingredients. For example, use a larger or smaller proportion of cake to custard (depending on how much stale cake you wish to use up), use whatever berries are in season—strawberries in summer are delicious in trifle—or spread fresh blackberry jam on the cake, cover with custard, and spoon on very ripe, sweet, freshly picked wild blackberries.

Enough unfrosted stale cake to line a medium-size, deep dessert bowl with about 1½ inches of cake

Apricot, quince, strawberry, or raspberry jam, or marmalades, about ¼ to ½ cup

¼ to ½ cup sherry, brandy, or cordial

Soft Custard, thoroughly chilled (recipe follows)

½ cup heavy cream, whipped

Garnish, such as jam, toasted almonds, candied cherries, or Candied Violets (page 71)

Slice the cake into pieces about 1½ inches thick and spread pieces generously with the jam on one side only, as you would toast. Line a dessert bowl with them, jam side up. Pour the sherry, brandy, or cordial evenly over the cake and let stand at room temperature until liquid has been absorbed, about 5 minutes or slightly more. Then pour soft custard over the top. Refrigerate until the cake has partially absorbed the custard, about 10 minutes, then serve immediately. Swirl the whipped cream on top and garnish if you wish with almonds, jam, candied cherries, or candied flowers, or any favorite dessert garnish. *Makes about 6 servings.*

Soft Custard

This delicately flavored custard may be eaten as is or spooned into serving dishes and sprinkled with sweetened toasted coconut or one of the other garnishes.

⅔ cup sugar
¼ cup cornstarch
½ teaspoon salt
2 cups milk

3 egg yolks, slightly beaten
1 tablespoon butter or margarine
1 tablespoon vanilla extract

In a saucepan, stir the sugar, cornstarch, and salt together. Add the milk and egg yolks, stirring until well blended. Cook over medium heat until the mixture thickens and boils, stirring constantly. Then boil 1 minute, stirring constantly. Remove from heat and blend in the butter and vanilla. Pour into a bowl, cool slightly, and refrigerate until well chilled. *Makes about 3 cups.*

December drops no weak, relenting tear,
By our fond summer sympathies ensnared,
Nor from the perfect circle of the year
Can even winter's crystal gems be spared.

—C. P. Cranch

❧ A TRIP TO THE WOODS

When our children were small, each year we went up to the woods for a Christmas tree. For this trip—less than a mile from the house —Raymond and I stuffed our children into boots, coats, hats, mittens, wrapped them up in scarves and took a blanket, just in case. Raymond hitched a trailer to our little John Deere tractor and off we went in search of a perfect Christmas tree, a few sprigs of mistletoe, and some red berries and pine cones.

Our children's voices piped "Jingle Bells!" and the rattle of the bumping and sliding tractor sang delightfully back. Now and again, Raymond would break out into song, interrupting the carol and forcing the rest of us to follow his off-key tenor rendition of some other joyous song.

Then, when a likely tree was spotted, we would all hop out and, with children in tow, continue our search for the "best of everything for a special Christmas." When the tree had been cut, more than enough other bounty gathered, and the children were freezing, we bundled up in the blanket and bumped and slid our way back down the hill, through the pasture (still amazing the cattle with our songfest), and back to the house for a quick meal and hot chocolate.

Everyday Beef Stew

During the winter months, the soup and stew pot did yeoman's service for one-dish meals. This everyday beef stew was a favorite.

1½ pounds stew meat	1 quart whole canned
2 tablespoons butter	tomatoes, heated to boiling
½ cup chopped onions	Boiling beef stock or water
1 clove garlic, peeled	1½ cups peeled and cubed
Salt	potatoes
Black pepper	1 cup peeled and cubed carrots

½ cup chopped celery	1 teaspoon fresh minced
½ to 1 cup of any other	thyme
vegetable desired, such as	½ teaspoon fresh minced
fresh young lima beans,	oregano
fresh peas, or young corn	⅛ teaspoon cumin seed

Trim the excess fat from the stew meat; set aside. Melt the butter in a large Dutch oven. Add the onions and garlic and sauté until tender but not brown. With a slotted spoon, transfer onions and garlic to a plate. Sear the meat in the same butter used for sautéing the vegetables until brown on all sides. Salt and pepper meat lightly. Return onions and garlic to the pot. Add the heated tomatoes and enough boiling stock or water to cover the meat. Simmer for about 1 hour or until the meat is almost tender. Then add the potatoes, carrots, celery, another vegetable of your choice, and the thyme, oregano, and cumin seed. Adjust salt and pepper if needed. Continue simmering until the vegetables are tender and the gravy is thick, about 20 minutes. *Makes 4 to 6 servings.*

Upside-down Sausage and Onion Corn Bread

This is scrumptious with soups or stews of any ilk. We especially like it with Everyday Beef Stew (page 236) and Mulligatawny soup (page 193).

2 medium-size sweet onions,	1 cup yellow cornmeal
chopped	1 cup all-purpose flour
½ pound ground fresh pork	2 tablespoons sugar
sausage, crumbled	2 teaspoons baking powder
⅓ cup plus 3 tablespoons butter	1 teaspoon salt
or margarine	½ teaspoon baking soda
½ cup minced field (meadow)	1 egg
mushrooms, optional	1 cup buttermilk

Preheat oven to 350°F. In a 9-inch or 10-inch skillet, sauté the onions and sausage in *3 tablespoons* of the butter until the pork is done. Remove from heat and drain off excess fat, leaving just enough to grease the skillet, about 1 tablespoonful. Add the mushrooms if using. Set aside. In a medium-size bowl, combine the cornmeal, flour, sugar, baking powder, salt, and baking soda; mix well. With a pastry blender, cut the *remaining ⅓ cup* butter into the dry ingredients. Beat the egg and buttermilk together and add to the dry ingredients, mixing just enough to blend; do not overbeat. Pour batter evenly over sausage mixture in the frying pan. Bake until light golden brown on top and firm to the touch, about 25 to 30 minutes. Immediately turn onto a serving plate; cut into wedges and serve while piping hot. *Makes 8 servings.*

Taffy Tapioca Cream

This rich but delicate pudding is easy to make and a natural around farms where milk and eggs are in constant supply.

2 egg yolks, lightly beaten
½ teaspoon salt
2 tablespoons butter
1 cup, packed, light brown sugar

2 cups milk
2 tablespoons quick-cooking tapioca
2 egg whites
1 teaspoon vanilla extract

In a small bowl beat together the egg yolks and salt; set aside. In a heavy saucepan, cook the butter and ¾ *cup* of the sugar over low heat until the mixture bubbles, about 1 minute, stirring constantly. Add the milk and tapioca. Cook until the tapioca is clear, then remove from heat and very slowly add the egg yolks, stirring briskly. Then continue cooking until mixture is thick enough to heavily coat a spoon, stirring occasionally. Remove from heat. Beat the egg whites and the *remaining ¼ cup* sugar together until stiff. Fold into tapioca mixture. Let cool slightly, then fold in the vanilla. Spoon into a large serving bowl or 4 individual dessert dishes. Chill well before serving. *Makes 4 servings.*

THE STORK AND
THE HOLY BABE

The stork, she rose on Christmas Eve
And said unto her brood:
"I now must fare to Bethlehem
To see the Son of God."

She gave to each his dole of meat
And tucked them safely in,
And fair she flew and fast she flew
And came to Bethlehem.

"Now where is He of David's line?"
She asked at house and hall.
"He is not here," they softly spoke,
"But in the manger stall."

She found Him in the manger stall
With Mary, Holy Maid;
The gentle stork, she wept to see
The Babe so lowly laid.

Then from her snowy breast she plucked
The feathers white and warm
And strewed them on the manger crib
To keep the Babe from harm.

"Now blessèd be the gentle stork
Forever more," said He,
"For that she saw my lowly bed
And comfort gave to me.

"Full welcome shall she ever be
In hamlet and in hall
And called henceforth the blessèd bird,
The friend of babies all."

—*A Christmas ballad originally found
on the fly leaf of a king's prayer book
dated 1549; a popular children's poem,
1900*

❧ Choir Practice

In a small-town church I once visited, this ballad, "The Stork and the Holy Babe," originally found on the fly leaf of a king's prayer book dated 1549 and popular in the 1900s as a children's poem, was traditionally sung by the children's choir to the music of the carol "It Came Upon a Midnight Clear." At times it was accompanied by a budding violinist and was nearly always followed by a rendition of "Away in a Manger" by the littlest members of the chior.

Once the small children had practiced their songs and other bits of Christmas pageantry, the older folks settled down to the very serious work of the Christmas cantata, which varied in complexity according to the musical talents of the congregation. When everyone was positive that the year's Christmas program would be the best ever, we adjourned with much laughing and talking to a table set with steaming hot coffee and tea, and treats made especially for the occasion by the women of the church.

Chocolate Angel Food Cake

Farm women whose favorite party cakes were those called angel food liked to surprise everyone with this light, delicious melt-in-your-

mouth version. All of the ladies knew that angel food cakes should be mixed as quickly as possible so as not to lose the volume created by the air captured in the stiffly beaten egg whites.

¾ cup sifted cake flour
¼ cup unsweetened cocoa powder
1¼ cups egg whites (about 10 to 12 egg whites)
¼ teaspoon salt

1 teaspoon cream of tartar
1¼ cups granulated sugar, sifted
1 teaspoon vanilla extract
Whipped cream or Chocolate Glaze (recipe follows), optional

Preheat oven to 350°F. Sift the flour and cocoa together 5 times, ending with it in a medium-size bowl. In a large bowl, whip the egg whites until frothy. Add the salt and cream of tartar and whip until mixture is stiff but not dry. Gradually add the sifted sugar, folding in 1 tablespoon at a time. Fold in the vanilla. Sift about ¼ cup of the flour and cocoa mixture over the cake batter and fold it in thoroughly, using a quick, light hand; repeat sifting and folding in some of the flour and cocoa mixture until all has been mixed in. Spoon batter into an ungreased 9-inch tube pan. Run a knife around the edge of the pan to break any air bubbles. Bake until the cake springs back when touched, about 45 minutes to 1 hour. Remove from the oven; invert pan and let cool on a wire rack for 1½ hours. Then turn pan right side up and run a knife blade between the cake and the pan to loosen it slightly, being careful not to gouge the cake. (Be sure to also loosen the cake from the center tube.) Then turn cake out, upside down, onto a cake platter.

Serve unfrosted with a swirl of whipped cream or glaze it with a chocolate glaze. *Note:* Don't make glaze until cake is thoroughly cool. For a special treat glaze cake, then serve with a swirl of whipped cream. *Makes one 9-inch tube cake.*

Chocolate Glaze

⅓ cup butter or margarine
2 cups powdered sugar
2 ounces unsweetened chocolate, melted and cooled

1½ teaspoons vanilla extract
2 to 4 tablespoons hot water

Melt the butter in a saucepan; remove from heat. Add the sugar, chocolate, and vanilla and stir to blend. Stir in enough hot water to make glaze smooth and of spreading consistency. Immediately spread on cake. *Makes enough to glaze 1 tube cake.*

Heavenly Pies

For those whose hearts and minds are turned toward the stars, toward that which is spirit, these wispy pies are a nice surprise.

4 egg whites
1 teaspoon vanilla
½ teaspoon vinegar
¼ teaspoon salt
1 cup sugar
½ cup raw, quick-cooking rolled oats
2 cups heavy cream, whipped

⅓ cup sugar
1 teaspoon vanilla
2 cups peeled and cubed ripe winter pears, sweetened with ¼ cup sugar
¼ cup candied cherries
¼ cup slivered almonds

Note: Peel, cube, and sweeten pears just before assembling pies. Preheat oven to 275°F. In a medium-size bowl, combine the egg whites, vanilla, vinegar, and salt and beat with a wire whisk or electric mixer until frothy. Very gradually add the sugar, about a tablespoon at a time, beating well after each addition, until mixture is stiff and glossy. Fold in the oats (fold lightly so as not to lose the volume of the egg whites).

Divide the mixture into 8 equal portions and mound on a layer of greased, heavy, unglazed paper (kraft paper or an open brown grocery bag will do); place on a baking sheet. Hollow out the center of each mound with the back of a spoon and shape to resemble a pie shell. Bake until light tan in color and firm when touched lightly, about 45 minutes to 1 hour. Cool thoroughly before filling with sweetened (⅓ cup sugar) and flavored (1 teaspoon vanilla) whipped cream into which the pears, cherries, and almonds have been folded. *Makes 8 servings.*

Nun's Sighs

As delicate as a good sister's exhalation of breath, these fragile little treats will disappear in a moment.

1 egg, well beaten
2 tablespoons heavy cream
  Butter the size of a walnut, melted (2 scant tablespoonsful)

1 cup all-purpose flour, plus flour for rolling out dough
Vegetable oil for deep-frying
Granulated or powdered sugar for dusting tops

In a small bowl, combine the egg and cream, mixing well. Add the butter and stir to blend. Place the flour in a medium-size bowl and hollow out to make a well in the flour. Pour the liquid ingredients into the cavity and stir to form a medium dough (one that is firm enough to roll out rather easily without being sticky). On a floured surface, roll out dough very thin, like pie crust. Cut dough into 8 to 10 circles, each the size of a saucer. Fry circles in hot oil until light-golden on each side. Drain on paper towels and sprinkle with sugar. Serve warm. *Makes 8 to 10 servings.*

A CHRISTMAS CAROL

God bless you all this Christmas Day
And drive the cares and griefs away.
Oh, may the shining Bethlehem star
Which led the wise men from afar
Upon your heads, good sirs, still glow
To light the path that ye should go.

As God once blessed the stable grim
And made it radiant for Him;
As it was fit to shield His Son,
May thy roof be a holy one;
May all who come this house to share
Rest sweetly in His gracious care.

Within thy walls may peace abide,
The peace for which the Savior died.
Though humble be the rafters here,
Above them may the stars shine clear,
And in this home thou lovest well
May excellence of spirit dwell.

God bless you all this Christmas Day;
May Bethlehem's star still light thy way
And guide thee to the perfect peace
When every fear and doubt shall cease.
And may thy home such glory know
As did the stable long ago.

—*Edgar A. Guest*

❧ CHRISTMAS DAY

On cold winter nights just before Christmas, Mother told us stories about farm life when she was a little girl. Our favorite was about Christmas Day, 1911. It always started the same way.

Early in the morning before daylight, booted and bundled up in heavy coats and scarves, we took lanterns to the barns and corrals to water and feed the livestock. We younger children carried Christmas treats—apples and carrots —from the family pantry to the milk cows, horses, and pet sheep. Mother would also let us take scraps of meat from the upcoming feast for barn cats that usually lived on milk and the mice and rats they could catch raiding the grain bins.

Our old barn, lit only by lantern light, was hauntingly beautiful. As we moved about, there were the familiar sounds of horses blowing and the stanchions opening and closing as Dad brought in one cow to milk and let another out to feed. There was something comforting and warm about putting hay in the mangers, ladling out grain, brushing against each other in the close quarters. It was as though a truce had been called for a few hours.

We little girls could hear the boys complain softly about cold feet and hands and yearning for the warmth of Mother's kitchen, while we hugged bottle-fed calves and whispered "Merry Christmas" against their warm sleek necks. Now and again Dad rumbled at us, urging us to get on with the work. Finally, stamping and laughing, we burst into the kitchen, ready for hot chocolate and a few swiped Christmas cookies. Boots were quickly lined up and coats hung on pegs to dry.

Mother, hair combed neatly back, was always waiting for us in the parlor with the family Bible on her knees. We settled near her, and Dad sat nearby waiting for the littlest ones to find a cozy spot. Then she began to read:

> "And it came to pass in those days, that there went out a decree from
> Caesar Augustus, that all the world should be taxed . . . "

And we all sat enraptured, once again, at the account of the baby Jesus being born in a manger not so different from those in our barn, and about the sheep and shepherds and wise men who came to see him.

When Mother carefully closed the old Bible, we knew that it was time for presents. Many would be homemade, for who could afford store-bought gifts for six children?

Each year a different child handed out gifts. There were wooden rocking horses, several wagons in assorted sizes, a rifle for one of the boys who had won the right to go hunting with the men, new hooks and fishing poles all around, even for the girls. A heritage quilt or two to be put in our older sister's hope chest, which held dreams of a home of her own. Made of small bits of scrap cloth, stitched with a million tiny stitches, each quilt signified our mother's love for a daughter who one day would move away.

There were scarves and homemade shirts—warmer and better made, Mother always said, than any at the mercantile. Out of simple wrapping paper came piles of socks, home knitted and store-bought. New linen handkerchiefs for girls, and red and blue bandana handkerchiefs for men and boys. Those who needed them most got new boots and all got a little bag of hard candy. Mother got a lovely blue fabric for a new Sunday dress and Dad's biggest present was a tall can of pipe tobacco.

Looking back, I suppose we were just poor farm people, but we didn't know it. The piles of gifts, made and saved for months, were a wonder to each one of us, beautiful things to circle and touch, to marvel at.

That year, I turned to tell Mother something. I saw Dad looking at her in a gentle way that embarrassed me. Even so, I secretly watched as she put their gifts aside. Years later, after I had children of my own, I could not forget that look or her act of love. I understood then that she did not want a single one of us children to notice that their presents were always few, made up mostly of childlike cards and childish treasures, and that little money ever went into their presents.

At church, the pastor reminded us all that Christ's message to us was about a New Kingdom where people lived in harmony, where the lion laid down with the lamb, and where men pounded their swords into plowshares. I can still see Mother looking down the long row of us at our scrubbed faces and clean hair, and hear her praying for peace and telling God about her fear that her sons might someday have to go to war.

Dad, out of his overalls, uncomfortable in his Sunday best, whispered to her that he had doubts that man would ever be able to curb his lusts and cruelties and live so noble a life, but then he told her sternly that all things are possible with God's help. And I wondered whether he spoke that way to her or to himself.

After church, we all gathered for dinner. It was a great feast; no woman or girl would be outdone for such an occasion.

Unlike now, none of us was distressed because Aunt Maggie and her father, Grandpa, were feuding and wouldn't sit at the table with each other, not even in the same room. We children would run back and forth from Aunt Maggie to Grandpa, gathering bits of news which we shared with the other. We took them coffee and kisses, cookies and messages.

The adults, all relatives, visited back and forth from kitchen to parlor, making sure they learned all the family news. I'm sure that someone tried to get Aunt Maggie and Grandpa to patch things up, but I don't think it worked . . . not in 1911.

When dinner was ready, one of the women fixed each of them a plate and took it to them. It was amazing to me that his anger at his daughter never stopped Grandpa from eating her snowy mountain cake.

In time, the inspiring, wonderful day was over. We had chores to do and the littlest children needed to go to bed. But everyone agreed then (and still agrees now) that those wonderful Christmas days refreshed the spirit and mind, and more than one person has admitted that they felt stronger, better able to lift life's burdens and carry on after feasting and filling up at the family well.

Vada's Braised Elk Roast

Our cousin Vada's family were the best hunters in the entire family. When they came down to the flatland farms for a doin's, they brought Grandma and Grandpa Hodge, twelve children of all ages, their three grown children's own babies, and enough food to last a week. We loved to see them come (Vada was Mother's favorite cousin), and we all ran out to help them unload the wagons. We little children jumped for joy to see the instruments they carried in, knowing there would be singing and dancing before the day was out.

We loved Vada's elk roast. Besides all the ingredients listed below, Cousin Vada always added a few wild herbs, but she would never tell us what they were! Nevertheless, this recipe makes a delicious roast just as written.

½ cup butter, melted
1 (9-pound) bone-in elk shoulder roast
About 1½ tablespoons salt
About 2 teaspoons black pepper
1 tablespoon dried thyme, pulverized
1 tablespoon dried marjoram, pulverized
5 or 6 strips bacon or about ¼ pound salt pork, sliced thin

3 cups water
1 large onion, quartered
½ cup dried celery
¼ cup chopped parsley
5 pounds carrots, scraped and halved lengthwise
7 to 8 pounds red potatoes, peeled and halved
Boiling water
Salt
Black pepper

Preheat oven to 375°F. Rub the butter over all surfaces of the meat. Sprinkle generously and evenly with salt, pepper, and herbs. Arrange several strips of bacon or salt pork over the roast and place it in a large roasting pan. Add the 3 cups water to the bottom of the pan. Add the onion, celery, and parsley to the water. Cover and roast until done, about 3½ to 4 hours. (*Note:* Check every hour and add more water if needed if liquid is evaporating; baste with pan drippings if the roast looks dry.) When the meat is almost done, arrange the carrots in the broth around the roast, then the potatoes, which can rest on top of the carrots to steam-cook. Add enough boiling water to about half cover meat and vegetables. Salt and pepper lightly. Continue baking, covered, until the vegetables are tender but not overcooked. *Makes 18 to 20 servings.*

Old-fashioned Baked Sweet Potatoes

Allow one medium to small sweet potato per serving. Rub each scrubbed and dried potato with butter and bake in an open pan for 35–45 minutes in a moderate (350°F) oven until each feels tender or soft when squeezed between thumb and fingers (be careful not to burn yourself), or test by sticking each with a fork; when done the fork should come out easily. Serve with the jackets on; at the table let

JANE WATSON HOPPING

each person cut his or her potato lengthwise and season it with fresh *butter*, *salt*, and *pepper* to taste.

Vera's Pear Pudding with Cream or Whipped Cream

Vera Kamping, a dear old friend, could in her prime ride the tractor all day in the field, planting or harvesting, hop off it late in the afternoon, and set this lovely pear pudding on the table at six o'clock with supper.

For this pudding she used fresh or home-canned pears. When she was a girl at home, the fruit was spooned out of a heavy glass jar that had been sealed with a rubber ring bound down with lined zinc lids.

4 eggs	1½ cups chopped nuts, walnuts
2½ cups sugar	(preferred) or pecans
1 teaspoon vanilla extract	1½ cups all-purpose flour
2 teaspoons lemon juice	1 tablespoon baking powder
2¼ cups chopped peeled fresh	½ teaspoon salt
pears or canned pears	Whipped cream (page 61)

Preheat oven to 375°F. In a large bowl beat the eggs until frothy; gradually add the sugar and vanilla, stirring well. In a medium-size bowl, combine the lemon juice with the pears. Fold the pears and walnuts or pecans into the sugar mixture. Sift in the flour, baking powder, and salt, stirring to blend. Spoon mixture into a greased 9x13x2-inch baking pan. Bake till browned and firm to the touch, about 35 to 40 minutes. Top with a dollop of whipped cream or a tablespoon of heavy cream as desired. *Makes 8 to 10 servings.*

Snowy Mountain Cake with Snowy Mountain Frosting

In 1911, when vegetable shortening became commonly available on the market, Aunt Maggie made a pure white cake that was light and moist and delicious. Mother thinks it was called something different, but Great Grandpa fell in love with it and said it should be called a snowy mountain cake because its texture was as light as a snowflake and the frosting had a crunch like crusted-over snow.

½ cup vegetable shortening	1 tablespoon baking powder
1½ cups sugar	¼ teaspoon salt
1 teaspoon vanilla extract	4 egg whites
1 cup milk	Snowy Mountain Frosting
2½ cups sifted cake flour	(recipe follows)

Preheat oven to 350°F. Cream the shortening in a large bowl. Gradually add *½ cup plus 2 tablespoons* of the sugar, creaming the mixture until light. Add the vanilla to the milk. Sift together the flour, baking powder, and salt, and add mixture alternately with the milk to the shortening mixture, blending well. Beat the egg whites until soft peaks form; gradually add *the remaining ½ cup plus 2 tablespoons* sugar and beat until peaks round over gently. Fold egg whites into the batter. Pour into two 9-inch cake pans that are greased and lined with waxed paper that is also greased. Bake until done, about 25 to 30 minutes. (Test doneness with a toothpick.) Remove from oven, let pans sit on a wire rack about 10 minutes, then remove cake layers from pans to the rack to cool. When thoroughly cool, frost with snowy mountain frosting. *Makes one 2-layer cake.*

Snowy Mountain Frosting

1 cup sugar
⅓ cup water
1 tablespoon light corn syrup

1 egg white
1 or 2 drops vanilla extract, optional

In a saucepan combine the sugar, water, and corn syrup, mixing well. Cook until mixture reaches the soft-ball stage (240°F on candy thermometer). Remove from heat and let cool. Meanwhile, beat the egg white until stiff but not dry. Pour the cooled syrup over the egg white in a thin, steady stream, beating constantly; continue beating until the frosting is thick enough to spread. Mix in 1 or 2 drops of vanilla if desired. *Makes enough frosting for one 2-layer cake.*

OLD YEARS AND NEW

Old years and new years, all blended into
one,
The best of what there is to be, the best of what
is gone—
Let's bury all the failures in the dim and dusty
past
And keep the smiles of friendship and laughter
to the last.

Old years and new years, life's in the making
still;
We haven't come to glory yet, but there's the
hope we will;
The dead old year was twelve months long, but
now from it we're free,
And what's one year of good or bad to all the
years to be?

Old years and new years, we need them one
  and all
To reach the dome of character and build its
  sheltering wall;
Past failures tried the souls of us, but if their
  tests we stood,
The sum of what we are to be may yet be counted
  good.

Old years and new years, with all their pain and
  strife,
Are but the bricks and steel and stone with which
  we fashion life;
So put the sin and shame away, and keep the fine
  and true,
And on the glory of the past let's build the better
  new.

—*Edgar A. Guest*

JANUARY

*Soups, Warm Fires,
Hot Chocolate, and Rest*

January is the coldest month of the year. Old-timers say, "As the days get longer the cold gets stronger," and with the bitter cold come the predators, such as wolves or coyotes, entering pastures in search of food. All natural activity slows or ceases. Birds travel about less; groundhogs and their ilk are burrowed in the ground or in dens hidden away from the cold.

During January, country folk visit and work at indoor crafts. Weather permitting, neighbors drop in for coffee and a chat. Baking and cooking are constant and people eat way too much. Food is brought out of storage as there are few fresh vegetables, fruits, or meats on hand. Except for doing their everyday chores, men sit idle or play with the children.

In times past, quilting frames were hung on hooks from the kitchen ceiling. This was a chance to gossip, as women gathered around the frame to work on the quilt or sat in the kitchen knitting, their needles clicking loudly. In some kitchens, wool that had been cleaned and carded during the summer was brought out for spinning.

251

Sewing was constant, as the quiet months brought free time for checking over the family's wardrobe, for clothes in need of mending and for making quilts.

From A TALE OF THE AIRLY
DAYS

Tell me a tale of the timber-lands—
    Of the old-time pioneers;
Somepin' a pore man understands
    With his feelins 's well as ears.
Tell of the old log house,—about
    The loft, and the puncheon flore—
The fi-er-place, with the crane swung out,
    And the latch-string thrugh the door.

Tell of the things jest as they was—
    They don't need no excuse!—
Don't tech 'em up like the poets does,
    Tel theyr all too fine fer use!—

Say they was 'leven in the fambily—
    Two beds, and the chist, below,
And the trundle-beds that each helt three,
    And the clock and the old bureau.

Then blow the horn at the old back-door
    Tel the echoes all halloo,
And the childern gethers home one't more,
    Jest as they ust to do.

                     —*James Whitcomb Riley*

COMPANY'S COMIN'

Dark January days were fine days for visiting, sitting by the fire, telling the true and tall tales country folk love. At first the menfolk talked about crops, past and present, and especially about word-of-mouth reports on high-yielding new varieties that they loved to think about but didn't really believe existed. Boys talked about rabbit hunting and about chopping wood. Women and girls talked recipes, giving each other secret methods that they thought improved the product, and they shared old family quilting patterns.

But after a while, someone stoked the fire and everyone's stories turned to tales about mysterious sights seen in the woods or fields: a fight between a big king snake and a rattlesnake near a ditch in the garden, how the king snake whipped that old rattler and swallowed him whole; or how a rat in the hay barn tried to raid a gray squirrel's hoard of walnuts, and how that old gray got up on its hind legs and nearly bit an ear off the rascally rat. Then someone always reminisced about a gem rock or old arrowheads and Indian stuff dug up while plowing.

Sometimes the talk turned to nonsense about "haunts," and folks would recall stories about a woman who in the face of danger had seen her mother's image outside the window—though her mother had been dead for years—frightening her and bringing a warning to her. Or men would tell of plowing alone in fields where no human could hide but hearing voices call out. One favorite topic along such lines was about "seein's" and folks who could tell something was going to happen before it did.

Often women got a little edgy about such conversation with children listening and changed the subject to something more everyday, like food. Men and boys always seemed ready to go along with the change of topic and sat waiting for the woman of the house to do the invitin', "You folks have got to stay and eat with us. We wouldn't hear of nothin' else." The meal, planned for early afternoon, was simple but nourishing and delicious.

By two-thirty, men were getting restless to leave the table, since chore time came early in January.

Wild Rabbit Stew

2 medium-sized onions, chopped
1 clove garlic, peeled and left whole
¼ cup butter
2- to 3-pound young rabbit, about 1½ pounds boned meat, cut into bite-size pieces
¾ cup all-purpose flour

2 teaspoons salt
½ teaspoon black pepper
3 cups boiling water
2 large potatoes, peeled and chopped
2 large carrots, sliced
1 cup chopped celery
¼ cup chopped fresh parsley
½ cup cold water

In a large Dutch oven, brown the onions and garlic in the butter. Remove vegetables with a slotted spoon, leaving the butter behind. Dredge the rabbit meat in a mixture of ½ *cup* of the flour and the salt and pepper; brown the meat in the Dutch oven. Return the onions and garlic to the pot. Add the 3 cups boiling water and simmer for 30 minutes (or for 1 hour if the rabbit is not very young). Add the potatoes, carrots, celery, and parsley and cook until the vegetables are tender, about 20 minutes. Blend the *remaining ¼ cup* flour with ½ cup of the cold water until smooth; gradually stir into the stew and continue cooking until the flour taste is gone, about 5 to 10 minutes more. Serve immediately. *Makes 6 to 8 servings.*

Mother's Old-fashioned Winter Succotash

When corn was in season, Mother blanched it, cut it off the cob, and dried it on trays on the roof of our house. Several days later, it was dry, hard, tan, and nutty in flavor. She then stored it in a clean cloth flour sack, which she hung in the pantry. Such corn was cooked like dry beans, which were harvested later and threshed in the barn on dry, windy, wintery days.

On such a day Grandpa would beat the beans out of the crisp pods and vines that had been drying in the bed of his wagon, then throw beans, broken pods, and vines all together into the air with a scoop shovel, so that the heavy beans fell back into the wagon bed and the chaff, which was lighter, blew away.

Note: To oven-dry, set the oven temperature at 225°F to 250°F. Dry until hard, tan, and nutty flavored, about 2 hours, perhaps more. If moisture remains in corn it will spoil.

Soak *1 cup dried corn* and *1 cup dried lima beans* overnight in separate pots. The following morning, drain the water off the beans, add *a slice of salt pork* which has been pan-fried long enough to render out a bit of the fat. Cover beans and salt pork with water and simmer until the beans are tender, which will take an hour or more.

Simmer the corn separately in the same water it was soaked in. When the beans are tender, remove the salt pork from the pot and chop it; return it to the pot and season the beans with a little *salt* and *black pepper*. Season the corn with salt and pepper, too, and mix the corn with the beans. Add only enough cooking juice from each pot to make the dish moist. Use as a main dish or as a vegetable side dish. Serve with cooked, smoked meat and a salad, such as Merkins's Family Apple and Carrot Salad (page 282).

Fitzgerald's Colcannon

Traditionally, colcannon is eaten by the Irish communally from the same dish, instead of each having a plate or a bowl. Each person takes a piece of bacon and then a bite of the potatoes and cabbage.

2 pounds potatoes, peeled and quartered	1¼ cups milk
Water for boiling the potatoes	¼ cup heavy cream
	6 green onions, finely chopped
2 teaspoons salt	1 tablespoon finely chopped fresh parsley
2 cups shredded cabbage	Black pepper
Water for cooking the cabbage	8 slices bacon, fried and drained
½ cup butter or margarine	

In a saucepan, cover the potaoes with water. Add *1 teaspoon* of the salt; cover and cook until tender. While the potatoes are cooking, place the cabbage in another pan; add just enough water to keep it from sticking, about ¼ cup water and the *remaining 1 teaspoon* salt; cook covered for about 5 minutes. Drain the cabbage, then cover to keep warm. When the potatoes are done, drain off water and place pan with potatoes in it over low heat; shake the pan until the moisture has evaporated. Remove from heat. Mash and whip potatoes until light. Gradually beat in ¼ *cup* of the butter and the milk and cream. Stir in the reserved cabbage and the green onions, parsley, and add pepper to taste. Warm over low heat until steaming hot. Mound in a heated serving dish; hollow out a well in the top and place the *remaining ¼ cup* butter into the cavity. Break the bacon into bite-size pieces and arrange pieces around the edge of the dish. *Makes about 6 servings.*

Caramel Bread Pudding

Mother often browned a little granulated sugar to obtain the color and flavor of caramel.

¼ cup butter	1 cup sugar
3 cups fine very dry	2 eggs, well beaten
breadcrumbs	1 teaspoon lemon extract
½ teaspoon salt	Freshly grated nutmeg
1 quart hot milk	Whipped cream, optional
	(page 61)

Preheat oven to 350°F. Place the butter, breadcrumbs, and salt in a large bowl. Add the milk and soak 10 minutes. Meanwhile, melt and brown the sugar in a small heavy saucepan over medium heat until the sugar is light brown, stirring constantly. Add it to the breadcrumbs, stirring to blend. Add the eggs and lemon extract, and nutmeg to taste. Pour into a greased 13x9x2-inch pan and bake until firm, about 45 minutes. Serve hot or cold, as is or topped with whipped cream. *Makes 6 or more servings.*

The Fitzgeralds' Tea and Milk

The old country folks loved their hot black tea and milk, first pouring the tea into the cup and then adding the milk, and then blowing on it to cool it enough to drink. And no matter how tight money was, there was always a bit for good tea—Indian, Darjeeling, or Pekoe to be exact.

Grandma Fitzgerald made tea this way. She poured boiling water into the teapot, then set the pot aside momentarily while she put the tea leaves into a tea ball, allowing 1 teaspoon per cup (more or less). Then she emptied the pot and placed the ball inside and poured more boiling water into the pot (she never measured it). Next, she covered the pot with a hand-crocheted cosy, which kept the tea hot while she steeped it for 3 to 5 minutes. Then she served it immediately. It was a beautifully rich, dark color and tasted fruity.

She had sugar for those who wanted it, and everyone took milk from a small pitcher. Usually there was a bit of sweet, fruited bread like barmbrack (page 26) to go with it.

THE QUILTING PARTY

In the sky the bright stars glittered,
On the bank the pale moon shone;
And 'twas from Aunt Dinah's quilting party
I was seeing Nellie home.

On my arm a soft hand rested,
Rested light as ocean foam;
And 'twas from Aunt Dinah's quilting party
I was seeing Nellie home.

—Poet unknown

THE PIONEER LADY'S COUNTRY KITCHEN   257

✍ QUILTING PARTY

When Mother was young, people often made play out of work. A quilting bee or party was just such an event. Women and girls—neighbors, friends, family—would gather at a friend's home and completely stitch a patchwork quilt in one afternoon. While the women and girls worked, the small children played about them or had projects of their own; little girls sometimes stitched quilt blocks, the squares that would make up a quilt, using large-size needles, or they might make pomander balls out of cloves and oranges. Then when evening came, husbands and older children joined them for supper and for singing or dancing afterward.

Old-time women were quite creative in their quiltmaking. Emma Smith once sent to a ribbon factory to answer an advertisement which offered a large box of ribbons for a dollar or so. When the order arrived, it was a huge box of mill ends in every conceivable width and color. The ribbon quilt Emma made from them was never entered in a contest, but had it been, it would have taken every prize.

Piece quilts tended to follow favorite patterns. These geometric designs often had more than one name, depending on whether Pennsylvania Dutch women quilted them or whether the patterns had been handed down from generation to generation by early day English, Scottish, or Irish settlers in the hills of Missouri.

Some designs like pine tree, sunburst, wedding ring, rose of Sharon, or the various "star" patterns have survived in heirloom quilts that were carefully laid away in wooden trunks. One of my favorites is the friendship quilt. It is made from a simple block pattern, each piece made by a friend who embroiders her name and the date in the corner of her finished block. When all blocks are completed, the women gather to set the pieces together and stitch them into a quilt.

Pomander Balls

Farm mothers usually worked (even in the fields, hoeing and pulling weeds, or harvesting produce) with their children—especially the small ones—about them. The children would sail toy boats in trickling irrigation ditches, make toys out of overgrown vegetables, or inside, they could stand on boxes at their mothers' elbows, rolling dough and tasting goodies or clipping designs out of scraps of fabric as the mothers sewed. About Christmastime, when oranges were available, they might have made pomander balls.

To make a pomander ball, use a *small orange* or *tangerine.* Thread a piece of string through the eye of a large, long needle; insert the needle in the blossom end of the fruit, sticking it completely through the fruit and drawing it out the stem end. Tie the string into a loop big enough so that the pomander ball may be hung up. Then insert as many *whole cloves* as possible into the orange and hang it in a cool, dry place. Let the orange shrivel and dry up. When the orange is thoroughly dried out and hard, remove the string and thread a very narrow ribbon through the string hole, leaving another loop to hang it from. Then, using another wider ribbon, tie a decorative bow on top, fastening it to the ribbon that acts as a hanger. If you wish, fasten silk or satin roses or other small artificial flowers (found in sewing centers) into the bow.

When pomander balls are hung in a closet or in a chest, they perfume the contents and yield up a marvelously clean fragrance when the closet or chest is opened. Make extras and give as gifts.

Hot Slaw

Grandpa stored cabbage for winter use, tucking the cabbage plant's roots into a trench in the ground, covering the heads with boards or feed sacks to protect them from freezing; or he hung whole cabbage plants upside down in an insulated shed or cellar. Then Mother, as late in winter as January, could make a hot slaw like this one.

1 onion, chopped	1 tablespoon sugar
3 tablespoons butter	½ teaspoon salt
4 cups shredded cabbage	⅛ teaspoon black pepper
3 tablespoons cider vinegar	1 cup dairy sour cream

In a large skillet, sauté the onion in the butter until tender but still a bit crisp and not yet brown. Add the cabbage, vinegar, sugar, salt, and pepper. Cook just until cabbage is heated through; remove from heat and stir in the sour cream. (The cabbage should not be cooked, just heated. Once the slaw is made, don't reheat it or the cream will curdle.) Serve warm. *Makes 4 servings.*

Roast Pork and Sauerkraut with Fried Apples

When we lived on the Hubbard place, Mother put down a great wooden barrel of kraut for winter use. She packed layers of finely shredded cabbage, grape leaves, apples, and cucumbers to ferment in a crock. The top was completely covered with clean grape leaves, and after fermenting, the result was mouth-puckering, delicious fermented apple and cucumber pickles, and piles of sauerkraut for use in dishes like this one.

1 (5-pound) bone-in pork roast (any cut will do)
1 tablespoon salt
1 teaspoon black pepper
1 onion, chopped
1 cup boiling water

1 quart Prizewinning Sauerkraut in a Jar (page 144) or 1 quart store-bought sauerkraut
¼ teaspoon caraway seed
Cold water
Fried Apples (recipe follows)

Preheat oven to 350°F. Season the roast evenly with the salt and pepper. Place the roast in a roasting pan, cover, and bake until some of the fat has rendered out, about 45 minutes. Dip out 2 tablespoons of the rendered fat and place them in a heavy skillet. (Recover the roasting pan and continue baking the meat.) Sauté the onion in the fat until the onion is tender; set aside. After the meat has cooked about 30 minutes longer, drain off all the fat that has accumulated in the bottom of the roasting pan. Pour the boiling water around the base of the meat, recover the pan, and continue baking until the roast is done (until a meat thermometer inserted in the densest part of the meat reads between 160°F and 170°F). Drain the sauerkraut and add it and the caraway seed to the reserved skillet containing the onion; add just enough cold water (start with 1 to 2 tablespoons) to keep the sauerkraut from sticking; simmer the kraut for 15 minutes. Slice the roast pork and serve it immediately with the heated sauerkraut and fried apples. *Makes 8 to 10 servings.*

Fried Apples
Approximately 20 minutes before the pork roast is done, peel and cut 8 to 10 green apples into about ½-inch slices. In a heavy skillet (cast-iron preferred) heat 1 tablespoon fat (drain hot fat off the roast or use butter). When fat is hot, fry the apple slices in it until tender, stirring frequently. Serve immediately. *Makes 8 to 10 servings.*

Smothered Chicken with Mushroom Gravy

This mouth-watering dish was usually made with dried morels, since they reconstitute well and taste almost like fresh mushrooms.

About 1 cup dried mushrooms (preferably morels)
Hot water for reconstituting
Salt
Black pepper
2 (2- to 2½-pound) fryers or 1 (3½- to 4-pound) fryer, cut up into serving-size pieces
2 teaspoons dried sweet marjoram
1 clove garlic, peeled
¼ cup butter or chicken fat
½ cup boiling Homemade Chicken Broth (page 11)
About 1 tablespoon chopped fresh parsley
3 tablespoons flour

Preheat oven to 350°F. Place the dried mushrooms in a medium-size bowl, and cover with hot water; set aside for about 30 minutes to reconstitute them (mushrooms will continue to reconstitute while cooking). Salt and pepper the chicken pieces, then roll sweet marjoram leaves between your thumb and forefinger and sprinkle evenly over both sides of the chicken.

In a large skillet, sauté the garlic clove in the butter *or chicken fat* over medium heat, then remove garlic from the fat. Add the chicken pieces to the skillet, skin side down, and fry until pieces begin to brown. *Note:* Just brown the pieces on one side. Remove the chicken from the frying pan and arrange pieces in a single layer in a roasting pan, flesh side down (browned side up). Pour the butter or chicken fat from the skillet over the meat. Add *½ cup* of the boiling broth to the bottom of the pan, not over the top of the chicken. Cover the pan and bake until done, about 1 hour. Then transfer the chicken pieces to a heated platter, sprinkle the parsley over it, and make a gravy with the drippings in the roasting pan; add *remaining* broth to the drippings to make about 3 cups of gravy (drain the mushrooms and use the liquid to make up some of the 3 or 3½ cups, if you wish). Add the mushrooms and simmer the mixture on top of the stove until mushrooms are tender.

To make gravy, bring broth to a boil. Meanwhile measure into a small bowl *2 tablespoons* of flour for each cup of broth; moisten with enough water to form a very thin batter; beat thoroughly to prevent the flour from lumping in the gravy. When the broth is boiling, pour the flour mixture all at once into the broth; stir constantly. Simmer about 5 minutes until the flour taste is gone, continually stirring. Serve immediately with the gravy spooned over the chicken. *Makes 6 or 8 servings.*

Note: You may heat the platter and keep the chicken warm by setting them in a 225°F warming oven, or over the hot oven in which the chicken was cooked.

Celeriac with Cheese Sauce

This old-fashioned multipurpose root vegetable is not in use as much today as it once was. Even so, when creamed, served with a cheese sauce as it is here, or when added to salads or stews, it proves to be delicious.

3 celeriacs (root celery)
  Boiling water for cooking
   celeriacs
  Salt
  Black pepper
1 tablespoon minced green
  onions

1 tablespoon butter
  Cheese Sauce (recipe follows)
  Toasted sesame seed, or sweet
   paprika and minced fresh
   parsley, for garnish

Peel the celeriacs, cutting out spots; chop into pieces as you would a potato for boiling. Place in a large saucepan, cover with boiling water, lightly salt the water. Simmer until tender, then drain and set aside. In a large skillet, sauté the green onions in the butter just until tender. Add the drained celeriac and stir until all pieces are well coated. Salt and pepper to taste and continue cooking just until the celeriac is heated through. Top with cheese sauce, garnish with sesame seed, or with paprika and parsley, and serve immediately. *Makes 4 to 6 servings.*

Cheese Sauce
For a richer sauce mix milk and half-and-half.

2 tablespoons butter
2 tablespoons flour
1 cup milk or milk and half-and-
  half

½ cup grated cheese (Cheddar
  or Swiss preferred)
  Salt and pepper, to taste
¼ teaspoon Worcestershire
  sauce, optional

In a small heavy saucepan, melt the butter over low heat; stir the flour into it; blend well. Add the milk (or milk and half-and-half), blend with a wire whisk to keep the sauce smooth as it thickens, stir continually. Bring to a boil; reduce heat and cook about 2 minutes, stirring constantly. Add grated cheese and stir until cheese melts. Season with salt, pepper, and Worcestershire sauce, if you wish.

Walnut Pudding with Lemon Whipped Cream Sauce

This old-fashioned steamed pudding is delicious.

2 cups all-purpose flour
½ cup sugar
2 teaspoons baking powder
½ teaspoon salt
2 eggs, well beaten
1 cup chopped English walnuts

1 cup milk
¼ cup butter or margarine,
  melted
1 teaspoon vanilla extract
  Lemon Whipped Cream
  Sauce (recipe follows)

In a large bowl, combine the flour, sugar, baking powder, and salt, mixing well. Add the eggs, walnuts, milk, butter, and vanilla, blending well. Divide batter into 10 greased individual ½-cup molds or custard cups, cover with lids, greased brown kraft paper, or aluminum foil, and steam steadily (see "To Steam the Pudding," below) until done, about 45 minutes. Turn out immediately, and serve on dessert plates topped with the whipped cream sauce. *Makes 9 or 10 servings.*

To Steam the Pudding
Set the covered molds or custard cups in a steamer or on a rack fitted into a large Dutch oven or a soup kettle. Pour boiling water around (not on) the molds up to the level of the rack. Cover steamer or pot and steam steadily until done, about 45 minutes. Keep the water boiling while steaming the pudding. *Note:* If additional water must be added, work quickly to lift the lid and carefully add more boiling water to bottom of pan, taking care not to spill any on the tops of the molds. To test for doneness, insert a toothpick in the center of one of the puddings; if done, the toothpick will come out clean.

Lemon Whipped Cream Sauce
3 egg yolks, well beaten
1 cup sugar
½ cup water

1 cup heavy cream
½ cup lemon extract

Place the egg yolks in a large bowl and set aside. In a medium-size saucepan dissolve the sugar in the water and boil until the syrup spins a thread (230°F to 234°F on a candy thermometer). Pour the hot syrup in a thin steady stream over the egg yolks, beating quickly and vigorously until smooth and light. Let cool, stirring occasionally. Just before serving, whip the cream. Then stir the lemon extract into the sauce and fold in the whipped cream. *Makes enough to top 10 servings of pudding, about 3 cups.*

The Old Sexton

THE FIRST SNOWFALL

The snow had begun in the gloaming,
　And busily all the night
Had been heaping field and highway
　With a silence deep and white.

Every pine and fir and hemlock
　Wore ermine too dear for an earl,
And the poorest twig on the elm tree
　Was ridged inch-deep with pearl.

From sheds new-roofed with Carrara
　Came Chanticleer's muffled crow,
The stiff rails were softened to swan's-down,
　And still fluttered down the snow.

I stood and watched by the window
　The noiseless work of the sky,
And the sudden flurries of snowbirds,
　Like brown leaves whirling by.

　　　　　　　　　—*James Russell Lowell*

SNOW PARTY

Our west pasture is a gently rolling hillside that slopes south toward the winter sun. When the snow is on the ground, it is a perfect place for young children to slide downhill on inner tubes and sleds. At the lower end of the field, a fence long overgrown with berries and bushes acts as a barrier so that high-riding daredevils never overshoot onto the country road.

That old field many times has hosted a flock of mittened snow-birds, laughing and squealing, ringing every ounce of joy out of a lovely winter day. And when they were chilled, the whole flock of children flew into my kitchen where fresh hot doughnuts waited. And once they warmed up, everyone ran outside again to scoop up some clean snow for ice cream.

Snow Ice Cream

One of the greatest treats in life is to sit by a warm fire and eat snow ice cream. All you need to remember is to brush the top layer off clean snow and dip out the clean center, never dipping the cup deep enough to pick up dirt from the ground or off old boards or buildings.

To make snow ice cream, whip *1 cup of heavy cream.* Then fold in *sugar* and *vanilla extract* to taste. Take a large bowl outside and scoop up about *one quart (4 cups) of perfectly clean snow.* While the snow is still frozen, fold it into the cream mixture, and adjust the sugar and vanilla to taste. Eat immediately or pack the bowl in a snowbank (well covered to protect the ice cream from wild or domes-ticated animals) and let it chill until the ice cream has hardened. *Makes about 6 servings.*

Mama's Snow Party Doughnuts

Nothing warms cold children who have been playing in the snow more than hot chocolate along with Mama's doughnuts that are still warm from the frying kettle.

1 tablespoon dry or granulated yeast	1 tablespoon baking powder
½ cup warm water	About 4 cups all-purpose flour
⅓ cup plus 1 tablespoon sugar	3 to 4 cups shortening or vegetable oil for deep-frying
1⅓ cups milk	
⅓ cup butter or margarine	
1 teaspoon salt	Granulated or powdered sugar

In a small bowl, combine the yeast and water; add *1 tablespoon* of the sugar and set aside to proof. In a saucepan, combine the milk, butter, salt, and the *remaining ⅓ cup* sugar. Heat until the milk is scalded and the butter melts, stirring constantly; set aside to cool. Sift together the baking powder and *3 cups* of the flour. When the milk mixture is lukewarm place it in a large bread bowl and add the yeast. Stir in the sifted flour mixture to make a medium-soft to soft dough, adding more sifted flour if necessary. Turn onto a floured surface and knead; don't work too much flour into it; dough should be pliable but not sticky. Pat or roll out dough ¼ to ½ inch thick. Using a large and small cutter, cut into circles with holes in them. (Old-fashioned cooks used their thimbles as small cutters.) Or use a knife to cut dough into bars.

Cover with a clean, dry dish towel and let the dough rise until almost double in bulk. Then heat the fat or oil until hot enough to smoke a little and quickly brown a crust of bread. Fry the doughnuts in the hot fat in batches until golden brown on both sides, turning once. Drain on paper towels, then roll while still hot in granulated or powdered sugar. Serve immediately to cold, hungry children, after which there is no need for storage! *Or* put in an airtight container and eat within a week; may also be frozen for later use. *Makes about 4 dozen doughnuts, depending on size of cutter.*

OLD MAN'S
NURSERY RHYME

In the jolly winters
　Of the dead-and-gone,
Bub was warm as summer,
　With his red mitts on,—
Just in his little waist-
　And-pants all together,
Who ever heard him growl
　About cold weather?

—*James Whitcomb Riley*

✒ Potluck Supper with Neighbors

January is the month for renewing friendships and a great month for potluck suppers. The snow and ice have freed men and boys from the rigid demands of seasonal work and given them time to wander the fields, tramping through the snow together as they talk and hunt for a little fresh meat. The women have stores of pickles, jams, fruits, and vegetables in the pantries and cellars. All that is needed is a feast to turn country kitchens into social centers.

Folks come in, the women with their small children wrapped in robes, eager to visit after the isolation of summer work. Men tuck mud-caked boots under plain wooden tables and hunch over steaming cups of coffee, dunking freshly baked cookies. Talk is loud and vigorous as men complain about the price of cattle and seed, or laugh about some old boy they know who has a no-good hunting dog. Children giggle and tease friends whom they've rarely seen during the previous months. Women pass new babies—born while the mothers were apart—from hand to hand in the old ritual of acceptance.

Soon the table is set. Women pull spicy cinnamon-flavored pies out of baskets and give recipes for their fried pies filled with golden nuggets of dried apricot. The smell of onions and a waft of garlic escape as meat and other dishes are set out. It is impossible to keep teenage boys from circling the table.

Old-Time Rabbit Cutlets

When I was a child, Grandpa lived with us and raised rabbits to supplement the never-ending flow of beef and pork over our supper table. When he butchered, it meant that there would be not just one rabbit for the skillet, but large buckets and bowlsful of the tender light-colored rabbit meat, and that Mother would very likely have rabbit cutlets for the night meal or fix them for a potluck supper.

4	back legs, boned, and 4 tenderloins from 2 young (2- to 2½-pound) rabbits	½	teaspoon dried sweet basil, pulverized
1½	teaspoons salt	½	cup heavy cream
½	teaspoon black pepper	1	cup very fine dry breadcrumbs
½	cup all-purpose flour		About 6 tablespoons butter
¼	teaspoon dried thyme, pulverized	2	cloves garlic, peeled

Pound the pieces of rabbit very thin and salt and pepper them. Combine the flour, thyme, and basil in a large bowl; rub mixture with your fingertips to evenly distribute the herbs throughout the flour. Place the cream in a separate bowl, and the breadcrumbs in a third bowl. Heat about 3 tablespoons of butter in each of two large heavy skillets over medium heat until hot, but don't let butter smoke (it burns easily). Sauté *1 clove* of the garlic in each skillet of butter in order to flavor the butter, removing garlic as soon as it begins to brown. Meanwhile, dredge rabbit in the flour, then soak in cream and dredge in the breadcrumbs. Carefully add the rabbit pieces to the skillets and fry until the coating has taken on a nice golden-brown color on both sides. Transfer to a heated platter and serve while still hot. *Makes 6 to 8 servings.*

Oven-Cooked Round Steak

This old-fashioned method for cooking steaks that are less than tender is a good one. In this recipe the meat becomes tender and delicious, and flanked with baked red-skinned potatoes and a hearty vegetable such as Carrot Salad with Cream Dressing (page 21), buttered corn or string beans, one couldn't ask for more.

½ cup all-purpose flour
1½ teaspoons salt
½ teaspoon black pepper
1 (1½-pound) round steak,
   about ¾ inch thick
2 tablespoons margarine

2 cloves garlic, peeled and
   minced
2 cups milk
1 teaspoon dried sweet basil
   or dried thyme
About ½ cup dried onions,
   optional

Preheat oven to 350°F. Combine the flour, salt, and pepper. Dredge the steak in the flour and pound in as much of the flour as the meat will hold. Heat the margarine in a large ovenproof skillet. Sauté the garlic in the margarine just until golden, then move the garlic to one side of the skillet (transfer it to a plate if it's browning too much) and brown the meat on both sides in the garlic-flavored margarine. Pour the milk over the meat and sprinkle on basil or thyme (a few dried onions over the top is a nice addition). Place the skillet in the oven and bake until the meat is quite tender and the milk has formed a gravy over it, about 45 minutes. (The gravy will bubble and when done will brown lightly.) Remove skillet from the oven and serve immediately. *Makes 6 servings.*

Squirrel Pot Pie with Buttermilk Biscuit Dumplings

Even the poorest family could usually provide meat for themselves. Men and boys took their squirrel rifles out and came back with enough squirrels for the stew pot or a pot pie like this one.

3 gray or fox squirrels, about 3 pounds, dressed, cut into serving-size pieces.
½ cup all-purpose flour, plus 1 tablespoon
3 tablespoons butter

4 cups Homemade Chicken Broth (page 11) or water
1 onion, chopped
1 teaspoon salt
¼ teaspoon black pepper
Buttermilk Biscuit Dumplings (recipe follows)

Dredge meat in *½ cup* of the flour. Melt *2 tablespoons* of the butter in a large Dutch oven and sauté the squirrel pieces until brown. Add the stock or water and the onions, salt, and pepper. Cover tightly and simmer over low heat until the squirrel meat is tender, about 1 hour. Meanwhile, make the dumpling dough, roll it out, and cut out rounds. After the squirrel meat is tender, remove lid and lay biscuit rounds over the squirrel. Cover again and boil for 15 minutes. Transfer dumplings and meat to a heated platter and set in a warm place. Melt the *remaining 1 tablespoon* butter and blend it with the *remaining 1 tablespoon* flour. Add to the liquid in the Dutch oven, blending well to make a gravy; cook about 5 minutes more. Pour gravy over meat and dumplings. *Makes 6 to 8 servings.*

Buttermilk Biscuit Dumplings

2 cups all-purpose flour, plus flour for rolling out dough
2 teaspoons baking powder
1 teaspoon salt

½ teaspoon baking soda
¼ cup pork lard or butter
1 cup cold buttermilk or sour (blinky) milk

Mix together the flour, baking powder, salt and baking soda. Cut in the lard with a fork or pastry blender or rub it in with your hands until the mixture is fine grained and well blended. Stir in the buttermilk, just until well blended; do not overmix. Turn the dough onto a floured surface and knead lightly and quickly. Then roll out about ¼ inch thick and cut into rounds with a biscuit cutter. Cook as directed in the above recipe. *Makes enough dumplings for 1 pot pie.*

Mashed Potatoes and Turnips

Peel and quarter *2 large turnips* and *2 large potatoes*. Simmer together in the same pot until tender; drain. Mash together, adding *salt, black pepper, and butter to taste*. Fry *2 strips of bacon* crisp; drain, then crumble over the top of the dish. *Or* grate a little *Cheddar cheese* over the turnips and potatoes. *Makes 6 servings.*

Swiss Apple Pudding

1½ cups very fine dry breadcrumbs
 1 pound, about 4 good cooking
   apples, peeled and thinly
   sliced (Jonathan, Northern
   Spy, or Winesap preferred)

¼ cup, packed, light brown
   sugar
   Rind from 1 lemon, grated
 2 tablespoons butter or
   margarine
   Sugar
   Heavy cream

Preheat oven to 350°F. Grease a quart pudding mold or ovenproof dish. Place ⅔ cup breadcrumbs on the bottom, pressing them against the sides of the dish. Arrange a layer of apple slices on top, then some sugar, a little of the grated lemon rind or any other flavoring preferred (vanilla perhaps), then continue with the layers, ending with breadcrumbs for the top layer. (Pile the mixture up a bit, as it shrinks while cooking.) Dot top with butter. Bake until apples are quite tender and the pudding is browned on top and bottom, about 40 minutes. Remove from oven; let pudding set about 10 minutes, then turn out onto a serving plate and sprinkle granulated sugar over the top. Serve the pudding hot or cold with thick, cold, heavy cream. *Makes about 4 servings.*

From OLD WINTERS ON THE
FARM

I have jest about decided
    It 'ud keep a *town-boy* hoppin'
    Fer to work all winter, choppin'
Fer a' old fireplace, like *I* did!
Lawz! them old times wuz contrairy!—
    Blame' backbone o' winter, 'peared-like,
    Wouldn't break!—and I wuz skeerd-like
Clean on into *Feb'uary!*
    Nothin' ever made me madder
Than fer Pap to stomp in, layin'
In a' extra forestick, sayin'
    "Groun'-hog's out and seed his shadder!"

            —*James Whitcomb Riley*

FEBRUARY

Thin Winter Sunshine, Valentines, and Newly Butchered Pork

Even though February promises the heaviest snowfall of the year, it also brings a few warmer days, a little thin winter sunshine, and crisp clear air.

With the change in the weather, country people—at heart creatures of the outdoors—begin to stir about. Weather permitting, men might butcher a 150-pound September-born pig for a bit of fresh meat, or if rain showers are light, they might spend days at farm auctions standing around in the misting rain looking for needed machinery. On good days they haul fertilizer onto fields, and if the ground dries out enough they might plow a little. Women, tired of indoor work, leave household chores undone and escape into the yards, gardens, and fields to prune the roses and table grapes.

Seed catalogs come in the mail and during long February evenings families pores over the pages, making plans for new crops. Farmers dream of seeding new fields to pasture, women make long lists of vegetables and flower seeds, and children love to order the "penny packages" of seed for giant pumpkins, popcorn, and watermelons.

⟿ FEBRUARY WANT

By midwinter, country folks were good and tired of salted and cured meat. They hungered for fresh lamb chops, fresh beef steaks and roasts, and fresh pork sausage. Their supply of lard was low, having been used liberally throughout the cold months for cooking, as an ointment into which powdered medicines were stirred to produce a healing salve, for a lubricant (axle grease) for wagon wheels, for softening leather, and even for lamp oil.

When the menfolk put off butchering September-born pigs to relieve the situation, they might have found honed sticking knives and bell scrapers on their empty breakfast plates. Soon platters of fresh pork along with the stored food were set on the table, providing a late February feast.

Fresh Pork Sausage

Good country sausage is made of one-third fat pork and two-thirds lean pork. When too much fat meat or poor-quality trimmings are added to the sausage, too much fat melts out in cooking, leaving the sausage greasy. Conversely, if the mixture is too lean, the cooked meat will be dry or hard. One old-fashioned method for evening up the fat and lean is to add a pork shoulder to the pile of meat for sausage making.

1 (12-pound) ground pork
   shoulder
4 tablespoons salt
1 tablespoon rubbed sage, more
   if desired (but too much sage
   will leave a soaplike taste)
2 teaspoons black pepper, more
   if desired

1 teaspoon ground red pepper,
   optional
2 teaspoons dried sweet
   marjoram, pulverized
2 teaspoons freshly grated
   nutmeg, optional

Spread the meat out in a very large pan or in a freshly scrubbed sink. Sprinkle the salt and spices over the meat; mix and knead with your hands, using a little cold water if necessary to aid in the mixing and binding. Divide into 1-pound or 2-pound portions and package immediately for the freezer. Each package makes from 4 to 8 servings, depending on the weight of the package. *Makes 12 pounds.*

Frenched Pork Tenderloin

In the old days, people often saved the tenderloin, a tender little muscle that lies under the short ribs, for babies and for old folks with poor teeth. The older children and less fragile adults ate the boned-out loin itself. Either way, the following recipe yields up a tender steak that can't be beaten for flavor.

1 (1½- to 2-pound) pork tenderloin	2 cups reconstituted dried morels, drained
Salt	1 tablespoon dried parsley, pulverized
Black pepper	¼ teaspoon dried sweet basil
Flour for dredging	About 1 tablespoon apple cider or water
2 tablespoons butter	
1 clove garlic, peeled	

To "French" the tenderloin, first cut it crosswise into 2-inch slices. Stand the slices on end cut side up and flatten them with the broad side of a cleaver. Salt and pepper the meat and dredge it in flour. Melt the butter in a heavy skillet. Add the garlic clove and sauté until the butter tastes garlic flavored; remove and discard the garlic. Brown the pork slices in the garlic butter on both sides, waiting for the blood to come to the surface before turning the meat. Sprinkle the mushrooms, parsley, and basil over the meat and cover pan. Simmer very slowly just until the pork is cooked through; do not overcook or undercook it. (*Note:* Should the skillet seem too dry, add about 1 tablespoon apple cider (preferred) or water. *Makes 4 to 6 servings.*

Old-fashioned Pork Pie

When my grandmother cooked for her large family, she often used a huge pan that would just fit in her oven, with little room to spare. While she would never have used a recipe for this old-time dish—she would be cooking by instinct—had she glanced at this one, she would have immediately doubled or tripled it, knowing that hard-working farm men and boys could wipe out this little pork pie in minutes.

Pork Pie Pastry (recipe
follows)
2 cups potatoes, peeled and
thinly sliced
½ cup onions, chopped
1½ pounds lean raw pork, cut
into bite-size pieces
1½ to 2 teaspoons salt

¼ teaspoon black pepper
½ teaspoon dried marjoram,
pulverized
2 tablespoons minced fresh
parsley
Homemade Chicken Broth
Gravy (recipe follows)

Note: Make Pork Pie Pastry and Homemade Chicken Broth Gravy
before assembling the pie.

Preheat oven to 350°F. Line the sides of an ungreased, deep 2-quart
casserole dish with about half the pastry. Arrange potato slices
evenly in the bottom of the dish, then do the same with the onions,
then the pork. (The drippings from the meat should drain down
through the gravy and vegetables to season the potatoes at the bottom of the casserole where, when well covered with gravy, they become moist and tender.) Season with salt and pepper and with
marjoram and parsley to taste. Pour the gravy over the top. Cover
with rolled-out dough for the top crust; trim, crimp edges, and cut
decorative slits in top to allow steam to escape while cooking. Bake
until the meat is well done, approximately 1½ hours. *Makes 6 or more
servings.*

Pork Pie Pastry
2⅔ cups all-purpose flour, plus
flour for rolling out dough
1 teaspoon salt

¾ cup cold pork lard (rendered
pork fat)
About ½ cup cold water

Note: This pastry is rolled thicker than a pastry for a pie; think of it
more as a biscuit-type recipe than a crispy pie dough.

In a medium-size bowl, mix together the flour and salt. With a pastry
blender, cut in the lard until mixture has a granular texture, working
quickly so lard softens as little as possible. Add just enough ice water
to the mixture to make the dough hold together, stirring well. Turn
onto a floured surface and form into a ball. Cover and chill for at least
30 minutes before using. *Makes enough dough for 1 pork pie.*

Homemade Chicken Broth Gravy
2 cups Homemade Chicken
Broth (page 11)
2 tablespoons cornstarch or

4 tablespoons flour, for
thickening
½ cup cold water

Bring chicken broth to a rolling boil. Meanwhile, stir the cornstarch or flour into the cold water; blend thoroughly or the gravy will have lumps in it. When the broth is boiling, pour the cornstarch (or flour) mixture into it all at once, stirring immediately and constantly until gravy thickens and is clear. Set aside. *Makes about 2 cups gravy.*

VALENTINE'S DAY FROLIC

In the old days, city folks might have given each other fancy valentines, but in the country it wasn't the custom, if for no other reason than that the cost was prohibitive. Country people were accustomed to "making their own fun."

Viola May Bradford tells about Valentine's Day when she was young:

When we was young, you never did see no real fancy valentines, mostly they were homemade. At that time you didn't see no smart aleck ones like you seen later that said rude things to people. Ours was jest a little red heart or somethin' and on it was written a little verse. Folks was partial to "Roses are red; Violets are blue; Sugar is sweet; and so are you."

Whenever we girls saw some bit of lace or wrappin' paper that we thought was purty, we'd save it to make valentines for our mothers or aunts with. We didn't give fancy valentines to the boys, though. If we give them somethin' it was a little paper that said "Happy Valentine's Day" or "To a Real Pal." For us girls a boy might cut out a red heart and write something on it like "You're purty!" or if he felt bolder, "I got a crush on you!" but then he probably signed it "An Admirer" 'stead of puttin' his name on it.

On Valentine's Day or on a Saturday close before or after the fourteenth, we would all get together at someone's house for cookies and other treats. Sometimes we'd make popcorn and pull taffy. If anyone could play some music we'd sing or maybe dance if the house was big enough or if there was enough lamps to see by.

Young folks did a lot of teasin' and makin' eyes at each other, and stealin' a kiss, but we younger ones wasn't as forward as today. And too, we was married at sixteen, and an old maid at eighteen.

—Viola May Bradford, *an oral historian*

Molasses Candy

Place *2 cups* of *light molasses* in a heavy kettle and bring to a boil. Continue boiling (to 270°F to 290°F) for about 30 minutes, stirring constantly and being careful not to let it burn. When a drop of the hot syrup becomes brittle when dropped in *a cup of ice water*, add *½ teaspoon baking soda* (it will boil up as you stir it, so be careful not to burn yourself), mixing quickly. Pour the hot syrup onto a buttered heatproof platter. Rub your hands generously with *butter* and pull the molasses to the desired light-golden tan shade. Or let it harden on the platter as is. *Makes about 1 pound.*

Peanut Fudge

On farms in warm climates, peanuts are grown in the gardens or as field crops. The raw peanut, which is the seed, is planted in rows; when ready for harvest, it is pulled or dug much like potatoes are. These old-time goober nuts (African in origin, said to be Congo nguba) were a staple food in many parts of this country.

1 cup milk	¼ teaspoon salt
2 cups, packed, light or dark brown sugar	1 cup chopped peanuts
2 tablespoons butter or margarine	1 teaspoon vanilla extract

Combine the milk, sugar, butter, and salt in a saucepan, mixing well. Bring to a boil without stirring and cook until mixture reaches the soft-ball stage (240°F on candy thermometer or when tested in cold water). Remove from heat, add the peanuts and vanilla and beat until creamy. Pour into greased 8x8-inch cake pans, and let cool thoroughly before cutting into squares. Store in an airtight container with waxed paper between layers. *Makes about sixty-four 1-inch squares.*

My dreams at night are all of you,
Your face and form divine,
And if dreams come true
As they sometimes do,
You 'll be my Valentine.

Bachelor's Buttons

Because of this cookie's crunchy outside rim and soft tender inside, some witty lass may have thought of a particular crusty old bachelor when she named it.

¼ cup cold butter
1⅓ cups all-purpose flour
5 ounces sugar, plus sugar to sprinkle on "buttons"

1 egg
Pinch of salt
Pinch of freshly grated nutmeg

Preheat oven to 350°F. In a large bowl, rub the butter into the flour. In a small bowl, beat the egg with half of the sugar; add the egg mixture and the remaining sugar to the butter and flour mixture. Add the salt and nutmeg and mix well. Roll the dough between the palms of your hands to form 18 pieces the size of a walnut; moisten your hands or flour them for rolling the dough. Sprinkle dough pieces lightly with sugar and place 2 to 3 inches apart on a cookie sheet lined with buttered kraft paper. Bake until very lightly browned around the edges and on the bottoms, about 8 minutes. (The tops should be done, but not browned.) Remove from oven; transfer to wire rack. Cool completely, then store in an airtight container. *Makes about 18 cookies.*

From A SONG OF LONG
AGO

And the low of cows that call
Through the pasture-bars when all
The landscape fades away at evenfall.

—*James Whitcomb Riley*

Late in February, the God-given promise of a new planting and harvesting year makes itself apparent. Even though thick mist and a chill night turn woven-wire pasture fences into delicate lacework, fall-planted grain covers the earth with a mantle of green, promising that spring is on its way. Close to buildings, crocus spread bright blooms over the cold earth. Newborn lambs, fragile and gangling, delight children who are kept busy feeding the bummers—those lambs abandoned by their mothers.

Women dig through the stores and share carrots and apples left over in abundance with the children, who feed them to their horses as end-of-winter treats. Potatoes and onions are sprouting and will soon be planted again. Men dig through last year's garden—when the ground isn't frozen—for last year's root vegetables, such as parsnips and carrots. Volunteer Swiss chard is putting on leaves that will soon be large enough to eat. Chickens begin to lay a few eggs.

Everyone begins to look forward to March and April.

Mother's Mustard-and-Horseradish-Glazed Pork Shoulder Roast

This old-time method of my mother's for cooking a pork roast will give you a moist, flavorful one that isn't greasy. First the roast is simmered in a pot until done, then it's cooled so most of the fat from the meat and broth can be easily removed; finally, it's glazed and reheated in the oven, which gives the meat a delicious, delicately roasted flavor.

1 (6- to 8-pound) pork blade
    shoulder roast
    Boiling water to cover roast
    About 2 tablespoons salt
1 teaspoon pepper
1 onion, quartered
2 stalks celery
1 sprig of fresh parsley
1 sprig of sweet marjoram or
    ¼ teaspoon dried marjoram
    leaves

A few sage leaves or
    ¼ teaspoon ground sage
    Brown sugar
    Prepared mustard or prepared
      horseradish mustard
    Mustard Horseradish Glaze
      (recipe follows)
    Sesame seed, optional

Place roast in a large pot and cover it with boiling water. Lightly salt and pepper the water. Add the onion, celery, parsley, marjoram, and sage. Cover and simmer until the meat is done, about 3 to 4 hours. Remove from heat and set the pot in a cool place, uncovered, until the broth has cooled. Transfer roast and liquid to a large container suitable for refrigerating; cover and refrigerate overnight (preferably) or at least until the fat has risen to the surface, forming a solidified cake on the surface of the broth.

Preheat oven to 350°F. Remove the cake of fat from the top of the broth and reserve the fat for other cooking needs. Transfer roast from the broth to a large baking pan. Trim off excess fat and score the top of the roast. For a glaze, mix equal parts of brown sugar and prepared mustard (or horseradish mustard) together and spoon over the top of the roast before baking or use our favorite Mustard Horseradish Glaze (recipe follows). Sprinkle top of roast with sesame seed if you like. Bake until the meat is hot and the glaze has set. *Makes 12 to 16 servings.*

Mustard Horseradish Glaze

¼ cup honey
¼ cup water
2 tablespoons butter
1 tablespoon prepared mustard, natural stone ground (preferred)

1 tablespoon prepared horseradish
Dusting of freshly grated nutmeg, optional

In a small saucepan, heat honey, water, and butter until honey is dissolved. Stir in mustard and horseradish. Spoon over meat, several times, until glazing forms and meat is hot clear through. Remove meat from oven and if you wish dust lightly with freshly ground nutmeg. *Makes about ¾ cup.*

Merkins's Family Apple and Carrot Salad

When we lived on the farm in Missouri, we either used a simple homemade dressing like the one given below, or Mother occasionally made mayonnaise from scratch.

2 cups, firmly packed, grated carrots
1 large sweet apple, peeled and chopped
½ cup seedless raisins

Salt
Black pepper
½ cup heavy cream
2 tablespoons vinegar
1 tablespoon sugar

In a medium-size salad bowl, combine the carrots, apple, and raisins. Salt and pepper lightly. Dress with a mixture of the cream, vinegar, and sugar. Serve immediately. *Makes 4 to 6 servings.*

Scalloped Cauliflower with Cottage Cheese

A hundred years ago, cauliflower—a member of the cabbage family —came in many varieties and colors; some types, for example, were purple, others bright green. Even today, a colored variety such as Park's Purple Cap can be found in seed catalogs for home gardeners.

1 medium-size head cauliflower	2 cups cottage cheese
Salt	Cream Sauce (recipe follows)
Water	Minced fresh parsley or
Black pepper	sesame seed, for garnish,
2 cups very fine dry	optional
breadcrumbs, toasted	Sweet paprika

Turn the cauliflower head upside down and trim out most of the core, leaving just enough to hold the flowerets together; remove the leaves. Submerge the cauliflower head, upside down, in salt water (use 1 teaspoon salt to each quart of water) and let stand for 30 minutes; drain, then rinse well and drain again. Break or cut the head up into small flowerets. Place flowerets in a medium-size saucepan and add enough water to have about 2 inches of liquid in the pan. Season lightly with salt and pepper if you wish. Cover the pan and simmer until the flowerets are tender but still crisp. Drain.

Preheat oven to 350°F. Grease a large flat 2-quart casserole dish. Starting with the breadcrumbs (reserve 1 to 2 tablespoons to sprinkle on top, if desired), layer the breadcrumbs, cauliflower, and cottage cheese in the dish, adding salt and pepper to the cauliflower if needed. Make the cream sauce and pour it over the cauliflower mixture. Sprinkle top with the reserved breadcrumbs, or with parsley or sesame seed, then dust top with paprika. Bake until the top is bubbling and lightly browned, about 30 minutes. Serve immediately. *Makes 6 to 8 servings.*

Cream Sauce

¼ cup butter	¼ teaspoon white pepper
¼ cup flour	(black if you don't have
2½ cups milk	white)
½ teaspoon salt	

In a heavy saucepan, over medium heat, melt the butter and stir in the flour. When bubbling, add the milk, immediately begin to stir, and continue stirring until sauce has thickened. Add salt and pepper, as desired. *Makes about 2½ cups cream sauce.*

Red Velvet Cake with Ermine Frosting

Old-fashioned women iced this cake with a boiled frosting we call Ermine Frosting, so named for its light, fluffy texture.

½ cup butter or margarine
1½ cups sugar
2 teaspoons vanilla extract
3 eggs, well beaten
2 cups sifted cake flour
1½ teaspoons baking powder
1 teaspoon baking soda

½ teaspoon salt
1 teaspoon vinegar
1 cup buttermilk
½ cup unsweetened cocoa
1 tablespoon red food coloring
About 2 tablespoons boiling water

Preheat oven to 375°F. Cream the butter in a large bowl. Gradually add the sugar, creaming the mixture until light and fluffy. Add the vanilla, stiring to blend. Add the eggs, beating well. Sift together the flour, baking powder, baking soda, and salt. Add the vinegar to the buttermilk. Alternately add the buttermilk and flour mixture to the creamed butter mixture, stirring well after each addition. In a small bowl, combine the cocoa, food coloring, and just enough boiling water to make a thick paste; cool slightly, then add to the cake batter, beating well. Spoon the batter into 2 well-greased and -floured 9-inch cake pans, or 1 greased and floured 11x8-inch baking pan. Bake until done, about 25 to 30 minutes for the cake pans, or 35 to 40 minutes for the rectangular pan. Remove from the oven and if using layer cake pans turn out cake onto a wire rack. (Leave rectangular cake in the pan to cool.) Let cool thoroughly, then brush off crumbs and ice. *Makes one 2-layer round cake or one 11x8-inch single-layer cake.*

Ermine Frosting
½ cup light corn syrup
¼ cup sugar
2 tablespoons water

2 egg whites
Pinch of salt
1 teaspoon vanilla extract

In a heavy saucepan, bring the corn syrup, sugar, and water to a boil, then remove from heat. In a large bowl, whip the egg whites until stiff but not dry. Add the salt and slowly pour the hot syrup over the egg whites, beating constantly. Continue beating until frosting is light and fluffy and hangs in peaks. Fold in the vanilla. *Makes enough to frost one 2-layer cake or one 11x8-inch cake.*

Scottish Ginger Wine

This old-time homemade wine tastes more like mead, an ancient honey wine, or a hard liquor than wine. Country people often served it alone or in tea as a warming drink when someone had a cold or when the weather was bad and people were chilled from outdoor work.

½ cup sugar, caramelized to light or dark brown (recipe follows)

3 pounds sugar

3 heaping tablespoons ground ginger

1 tablespoon cream of tartar

¼ teaspoon dry yeast (or wine yeast, if you have it)

Juice from 4 lemons

Caramelize the ½ cup sugar and set aside. Pour a gallon of boiling water into a freshly scrubbed 2-gallon crock. Add the 3 pounds sugar and the ginger, cream of tartar, yeast, lemon juice, and the caramelized sugar. Stir until sugar dissolves. Cover with a clean dish towel and let wine ferment for about two weeks in a warm spot, until all fermentation (bubbling) has ceased, then rack off —pour the wine off the dregs and into freshly scrubbed jugs or bottles—and cork. Stored in a cool, dry place, ginger wine will last for years. Serve over ice or at room temperature. *Makes about 1 gallon.*

To Caramelize Sugar
When stirred into the wine, the caramelized sugar will turn the wine a light to dark straw color. If you prefer a light-colored wine, make the caramelized sugar fairly light-colored. Cook the sugar darker for a darker-colored wine. Place *½ cup sugar* in a heavy pan and cook until the sugar has liquefied and turned light to dark brown, as desired, about 8 to 10 minutes, stirring constantly. If not used immediately, add *1 tablespoon water* to caramelized sugar, then use this mixture in recipe. *Makes about ¼ cup.*

AND A LITTLE BIT MORE

Notes from the Author

I hope you have enjoyed this book about old-time farms and country cooking. As to the addenda, I've included here at the back of the book some things I thought you might enjoy: detailed information and hints for making candy at home; baking breads and pies from scratch by using simple old-time methods; and a little bit more.

Nowadays, of course, we cook mostly from recipes that are in cookbooks, but in the old days, farm women—and men, too—cooked from memory, or from recipes they inherited from their friends and family. The basics I've included here, which most of us don't need to know today in order to cook well, were the cooking skills every cook would learn at a very early age. Reading about them might enrich your own cooking, but I think it will also give you an even greater appreciation for the delicious foods that were created by those old-fashioned cooks in their country kitchens.

❧❀ HOMEMADE CANDY: DOWN-HOME LORE

When Mother was a little girl, the family did not use as much sugar as we do today. Sweeteners meant a beehive's being robbed, dried fruit, a little maple syrup, some molasses, sorghum, or brown or white sugar. These were valued possessions. Therefore, candy and confections made at home with store-bought sweeteners were special-occasion treats.

We all grew up tresuring and collecting recipes for the usual kinds of candies—three classes in all. Some women seemed expert at making *plain and pulled candies* such as taffy, stick candies, and crystallized creams. Some women, such as Aunt Lula, had a gifted hand with the *whipped candies* that were made with egg white, gelatin, or pectin. (Aunt Lula's divinity was called "angel's down" or something like that.) My cousin Joan loved to make the kinds of *candies that contained other special ingredients*, like nuts, in addition to sugar. Her fudge was rich and creamy, made with acids—lemon juice, cream of tartar or vinegar—before the advent of corn syrup.

Then and now, all candies must contain a combination of sugar and acid to have a good texture. In my youth, candy recipes—those containing only white sugar—always called for vinegar, lemon juice, or cream of tartar as sources of acid. Acid was an important ingredient, because without adequate acid, large crystals would form, making candy grainy and rough textured. When brown sugar, sorghum, molasses, sour cream, and the like were used, the natural acid in them was adequate, so no vinegar, lemon juice, or cream of tartar was also called for. Old-time women called these "never-fail candies." The brown sugar-butter-cream combinations that are used to coat candied popcorn are examples of such natural acid at work.

Today you will still see candies made with brown sugar and other high-acid foods. However, controlling the action of acids has always been difficult, and results are often varied. Therefore, modern recipes are more often made with corn syrup, which coats the sugar molecules with a film, thus preventing the formation of crystals and giving an excellent texture. The use of corn syrup also aids in retention of moisture and prolongs the freshness of candy. The use of corn syrup in candy making was perfected during the Second World War. Prior to then, candy sent to the troops was a sad affair—it kept poorly and was grainy. Then professional candy makers developed the bar candies using corn syrup—which improved the government-issue chocolate bar, making it smoother and, through the addition of para wax (an edible canning wax), more stable and less apt to melt. This provided hundreds of tons of candy, which yielded quick energy to soldiers on the battlefield.

The rules for acid in candy are as follows:

If you have an older recipe that calls for cream of tartar, lemon juice, or vinegar (instead of corn syrup), you will notice that for each 2 cups of sugar the recipe will call for ⅛ teaspoon cream of tartar or ¼ teaspoon lemon juice or vinegar.

Those recipes that call for corn syrup usually call for 1 part corn syrup to 4 parts sugar, which will make a good candy that is not as sweet as one made entirely of sugar and seldom becomes grainy. Such candy is beaten longer than those that call for cream of tartar, lemon juice, or vinegar.

Brown sugar, sorghum, molasses, and sour cream contain natural acid; therefore, cream of tartar, lemon juice, vinegar, or corn syrup are not needed or used with them. Sometimes, when natural acids such as brown sugar are used in candy making with cream or milk, the acid in them will curdle the milk.

Old-time cooks learned to spin a thread, test for a "soft ball" by dropping a small amount of the candy into a cup of ice water, and to count off seconds or minutes of cooking time in order to determine when the candy syrup finished cooking. Such methods are still very much in use (see traditional testing methods below). However, today most candies are cooked to a specific temperature and tested with a candy thermometer. Keeping track of the temperature is very important, since if the temperature is off by several degrees, the recipe may fail.

Besides a candy thermometer, for candy making you need a heavy-bottomed pan that is large enough so the syrup won't boil over, a clean cloth for wipe-ups, a long-handled wooden spoon, and a heavy stoneware platter or marble slab on which to cool the candy. A lightweight food platter may be used, but a stoneware platter or marble slab (preferred) holds the heat, letting the candy cool more evenly.

Choose a cool dry day for candy making; on humid days candy making requires a cook to make some tricky judgments, including using a longer cooking time and hotter temperatures. Before you start, test your candy thermometer, especially if it is a new one: Boil water, then put the thermometer into it; the thermometer should read 212°F.

When testing the temperature of candy syrup with a candy thermometer, the boiling syrup often sticks to the glass of the thermometer. To relieve this problem, bring three to four cups of water to a boil, pour the boiling water into a quart-size canning jar (or a quart-size mayonnaise jar), and between dips to check the candy syrup's temperature, keep the thermometer upright in the jar of boiling hot water. The candy will melt off, leaving a clean thermometer for the next testing. Since the boiling candy syrup is very hot, keeping the thermometer in hot water also helps reduce the danger of the thermometer's breaking as you go back repeatedly to test the syrup.

Below are the traditional methods for testing the stage (temperature) of syrup needed to produce a certain type of candy. Along with the accepted temperature readings as taken with a modern candy thermometer are the old-time "sight and touch" methods.

Soft Ball: 234°F to 240°F (fudge and fondant). Drop ¼ teaspoon hot syrup into a cup of ice water. The soft ball formed will hold its shape in the water, but when removed will flatten.

Firm Ball: 242°F to 248°F (caramels and nougats). Drop ¼ teaspoon hot syrup into a cup of ice water. The firm ball formed holds its shape when taken out of the ice water and does not flatten unless pressed with the fingers.

Hard Ball: 250°F to 268°F (molasses taffy and soft-pulled candies). Drop ¼ teaspoon hot syrup into a cup of ice water. The syrup separates into hard threads when it hits the water, but can thereafter be shaped into a hard ball with the fingers, one that will roll about on a chilled buttered salad plate.

Soft Crack: 270°F to 290°F (toffee, butterscotch, and hard-pulled candies). Drop ¼ teaspoon hot syrup into a cup of ice water. The syrup separates into hard threads that, when removed from the ice water, will bend but not be brittle.

Hard Crack: 300°F to 310°F (clear, brittle candies). Drop ¼ teaspoon hot syrup into a cup of ice water. The syrup separates into hard threads that, when removed from the ice water, remain brittle and break easily.

Should the syrup stick to the bottom of the pan while cooking, gently draw the wooden spoon across the bottom a couple of times, but don't stir; stirring some candies makes them grainy.

It's best to lightly grease the sides of a candy kettle with unsalted butter or shortening to avoid the formation of crystals. If crystals form anyway, cover the pan for 2 or 3 minutes, which will wash the sides clean with the steam being formed, or wrap a long-handled wooden spoon handle with a slightly damp cloth and gently wipe the sides of the pan with the spoon handle, which will leave the crystals on the cloth, not in the pot. *Never* stir the crystals down from the sides of the pan, since those crystals which drop into the cooking syrup form clusters of larger crystals, giving the finished product a grainy texture. (Beating fudge while hot also causes crystals to form.)

While cooking candy syrups made primarily of sugar, if the temperature goes above the desired level, quickly remove from heat and add a little cold water to cool them (start with about a tablespoon), then raise the temperature again—this should be an emergency measure only. When the temperature has gotten too far out of hand, it is better to cook the syrup to a hard-crack stage (290°F to 320°F), then pour it onto a heatproof platter, which will make a hard candy. Then, if you wish, start your recipe again, watching the temperature more carefully. Watch the temperature extra closely with soft candies such as fudge, because with the larger number of ingredients these recipes usually contain, the syrup can't be cooked off to a hard-crack stage. Often the batch is just ruined. Throw it away and try again.

Candy is perishable and should be stored well covered in a box or covered candy dish. During warm weather, soft or chocolate candies need to be refrigerated. When serving candy that has been refrigerated, let it return to room temperature before unwrapping it. Fudge, fondant, taffy, and caramels will keep for a week if they are first wrapped in waxed paper, then in a clear plastic wrap, and stored in an airtight container. Fudge, nougat, and marshmallows may be frozen if they are first wrapped in aluminum foil, then in a plastic wrap to keep moisture out. When thawing, leave the candy wrapped until it reaches room temperature.

✺ BAKING FROM SCRATCH: KNOW YOUR INGREDIENTS AND HOW TO USE THEM

Old-time farm women did all their own baking and they did it with wood-burning cookstoves. Armed with sacks of flour, cornmeal, oatmeal, a little salt, sugar, and honey, and blessed with the milk of a good cow and the eggs of a few prolific hens, it was "woman's work" to see that the family didn't go without.

All of which was not so hard to do. Recipes were seldom written down, but the women had "pattern" recipes in mind, learned by memory in childhood, and they knew well the ingredients on hand.

FLOUR
There are many different kinds of flour but all have some things in common. For example all flours take up odors and should not be stored in a cupboard or pantry with sour liquids, gasoline, kerosine, soap, or perfumed products. Any supermarket flour will keep for a long time if it's stored in a tightly closed can, but "health food" flours or natural whole grain which has been ground whole (which means they contain bran and germ) must be stored in small (5 pound) quan-

tities, in the original wrapping, placed in a plastic bag sealed with a wire twist, in the refrigerator or in larger amounts in the freezer.

Government regulations stipulate how much moisture flour may contain at the time it is packaged, but flour takes on moisture under humid conditions. This is why when you follow recipes containing flour, the amount of liquid at times just doesn't seem to be right for the amount of flour called for. One must learn to give or take a little by looking at the dough and making an educated guess. Many recipes you'll see in cookbooks include tips on how to decide when a bread dough or pastry has enough flour. It's important to pay attention to those guidelines, rather than just measuring the flour precisely and going ahead. You'll get a better-tasting product if you learn to gauge the proper amount of flour to use in your baking, *each* time you bake.

None of the coarser flours or meals are sifted, but all of the light or fine flours are sifted to obtain even a lighter texture. When used for bread and rolls, flour is usually sifted once; for cakes, cookies, and pies it is sifted two or three times, depending on the lightness desired.

All-Purpose Flour: Since this flour is used for bread, pastry, cakes, cookies, and as a thickening agent, it is a good blend of good-quality soft and hard wheat. All-purpose flour is enriched, which means the manufacturer has attempted to replace some of the nutrients that were lost in the milling process. To improve the nutritional quality of all-purpose flour, replace 3 tablespoons of each cup of all-purpose flour with 1 tablespoon *each* of soya flour, nonfat dry milk, and wheat germ. This will not change the flour's behavior when it bakes.

Unbleached all-purpose is a flour that has not been chemically bleached and therefore is a light buff color. It may be used in any recipe that calls for (bleached) all-purpose flour.

Bread Flour: This is a true hard-wheat flour, and it is high in gluten content. Gluten causes dough to be expansive and elastic, trapping the gas the yeast has produced, thus making the texture of the baked bread light. Bread flour is also granular and a little gritty to the touch. Often it absorbs more liquid than does all-purpose flour. It is difficult to find good hard-wheat flour on the market, except in health food stores and farmers' markets.

Cake Flour: This flour is made from selected soft wheat and therefore has a fine texture. Because of its low gluten content, it expands less, giving cakes a delicate, more crumbly texture. Generally sift this flour before using.

Presifted White Flour: Appearing to be almost pulverized, this white flour has a very fine grain that works well in yeast and quick bread, pie crust, and cookie recipes. But since it contains a large

JANE WATSON HOPPING

percentage of hard wheat, the gluten content is almost too high for making airy, light-textured cakes. (High gluten content tends to toughen cakes.)

Dark Wheat Flours: Dark flours are usually added to a recipe to improve flavor and texture or to increase nutritional value. Whole wheat, stone ground, and graham (unsifted whole wheat) flours may or may not be used alone. Most often they are used with a little pure gluten flour when making a sponge for bread, or with white or unbleached flour (as a substitute for up to one half of the total amount of flour called for in the recipe).

Additives: Since the nutritious layer of bran and the wheat germ are removed from so many wheat flours during the milling process, they have become popular additives to baked products.

Bran, ground or flaked, is the outer layer of the wheat kernel. When used alone, it makes a product that is too dry and hard, so it is combined with other flours in a ratio of one-third bran to two-thirds flour.

Wheat germ, the center of the wheat kernel, is a powdered or flaked product that is added to other flour. The germ is only about 2 percent of the entire wheat berry, but it contains the highest grade protein and all of the fat. There are recipes that call for using 100 percent wheat germ in place of any flour, but for better results substitute ⅓ cup wheat germ and ⅔ cup flour for each cup of flour called for in the recipe. Or use only 1 cup wheat germ to a bread recipe that calls for 5 or 6 cups flour. To do this, use 4 cups flour in the dough, plus 1 cup wheat germ and use remaining 1 cup flour for kneading.

Note: If you want to add both bran and wheat germ to the bread, limit their use to about 1½ cups (1 cup bran and ½ cup wheat germ) to 5 or 6 cups of flour.

Variety Flours and Cornmeal: Besides the common wheat flours, there are many other grain flours, the most important being those made of rye, barley, and oats, and meals, with cornmeal leading all others. While variety flours may be used alone, they are generally combined with each other or with white or unbleached wheat flour.

Rye Flour: When rye flour is used alone, the baked product is very solid and moist, since there is little gluten in the flour. For a lighter product, half rye flour and half white flour is used, or sometimes a mixture composed of one third each of rye, bleached or unbleached wheat, and whole-wheat flours is used.

Barley and Oat Flours: These finely ground flours are always used in combination with wheat flour, using about one-third part barley or oat flour to two-thirds part wheat flour. Rolled oats (raw oatmeal) can be used in cookie and bread doughs. When used in bread, oatmeal is sometimes heated with the liquid called for in the recipe before it is added, since this cooked oatmeal creates a smoother texture.

Rice Flour: Such flour is often used in wheat-free diets. Made into cookies and cakes, it gives a very fine and delicate texture. When coarsely ground, it may be used like cornmeal, of if very finely ground, like cornstarch.

Cornmeal or Indian Meal: This meal is made from both white and yellow corn and is grainy in texture. When the germ is removed during the grinding process, as it usually is, the meal will keep in storage for a long time. However, when it is water ground (which gives it a superior flavor), it retains the germ and therefore will not keep as long when stored. Cornmeal should be either refrigerated in small amounts or frozen in large amounts. Cornmeal may be combined with wheat flours or used alone to make mush, puddings, and yeast or non-breads. When its natural graininess is objectionable, cornmeal may be cooked in the liquid called for in a given recipe, thus the flavor remains but the graininess is gone.

Corn flour in its starchy, rather than its granular, form is most often called cornstarch and is used only for thickening sauces, gravies, puddings, and pie fillings. However, it may be combined with bleached or unbleached wheat flour to make a homemade cake flour, which gives a cake a more delicate crumb. Substitute from two tablespoons to one-fourth cup cornstarch for flour in each cup of bleached or unbleached wheat flour called for in a given recipe. Sift the cornstarch and wheat flour together a couple of times to blend them well. In its granular form it is used to coat fish for frying. (At home, Mother fried fish in a homemade seasoned mixture of half wheat flour and half cornmeal.)

LEAVENING AGENTS

For the most part, the light breads, cakes, and other products we are accustomed to are the results of a lift that comes from the action of yeast as it produces gas, or the action of alkaline in combination with acid as baking powder or baking soda produces carbon dioxide gas, or from the formation of gas caused either by fermentation of sourdough or salt-rising bread starters.

Such leavening agents are very effective when conditions are right: The oven should be preheated before baking, the fat and sugar should be well creamed, the batters and dough ought to be mixed as recommended, and the eggs should be beaten, whipped, separated, or otherwise prepared and added in correctly.

Yeast: Yeast is a living plant form, a fungus, wild spores of which float in the air almost everywhere. When yeast is mixed with dough to ferment, enzymes from the yeast cells attack the starch in the flour and change it to sugar. This sugar is in turn changed to carbon dioxide gas, the leavening agent, which bubbles up through the bread mixture, creating a light porous mass.

Yeast cultures today are available in dry, granular, and cake form. (Dry yeast and granular are virtually the same, except dry yeast has a finer texture.) All are perishable and should be refrigerated. Cake yeast lasts for a while under refrigeration before it molds, but dry yeast and granular yeast are much more stable, lasting as long as a year in refrigeration, and for several months in the kitchen cupboard. Seal in an airtight container.

One yeast cake equals 1 package of dry or granulated yeast, both dry and granulated yeast packages both equal 1 tablespoon. This amount will raise as much as 8 cups of flour, but for quicker rising use 1 yeast cake (or 1 package dry yeast or 1 tablespoon granular yeast) to 3 cups of flour. Always soften yeast (using about 2 tablespoons hot water and 1 teaspoon sugar for a cake of yeast, or ¼ cup warm water and 1 tablespoon sugar for 1 package dry or granulated yeast) before adding it to the other ingredients. Use caution: Too much sugar will kill the yeast. Cake yeast is more easily damaged by heat than dry or granulated yeast, so warm water added to it should not be hotter than 90°F. Dry yeast can tolerate temperatures as high as 105°F to 115°F. Excessive salt as well can kill yeast.

To test yeast for freshness and life, make a sponge of 1 tablespoon yeast cake (or the equivalent), 1 tablespoon sugar, 1 tablespoon all-purpose flour, and ½ cup water. Set in a warm spot for 30 minutes. Then, if it is lively, this sponge may be used in baking, and the rest of the yeast in the package will be lively as well.

Old-time yeast cultures were sporadic—sometimes they worked and sometimes they didn't; even so, light bread was worth the effort and highly prized. Here is an old-time yeast recipe. Experimenting with this unreliable bread leavener gives one insight into the skills needed in the old days.

Emma's Everlasting Yeast

1 large potato
1 tablespoon dry yeast or granular yeast or 1 yeast cake

¼ cup sugar

Cook the potato in at least a pint of water until it is mushy. Mash it into the water until there are no lumps. Then pour it into a quart jar, filling the jar about ⅔ full. Add the yeast and sugar. Set the starter out at room temperature until it is bubbling and lively, then cover loosely with a piece of cheese cloth fastened with a rubber band and refrigerate. (Don't use a metal lid and ring because the yeast may form enough gas to blow up the bottle.) When needed, remove the jar from the refrigerator and pour out a pint of the liquid yeast. (To replace the yeast that has been taken, add more potato, water, and sugar to the jar, and let it stand at room temperature to grow more yeast cells, then refrigerate again.) Use the pint (2 cups) of liquid yeast to start a sponge for bread making.

One pint of starter is about the equivalent of 2 tablespoons of dry yeast. Reduce the liquid in the recipe by half a cup.

Baking Soda and Baking Powders: Both depend on a reaction of alkaline with acid to form carbon dioxide gas.

Baking Soda (Bicarbonate of Soda): Baking soda is alkaline and has no acid to make it work. Therefore, in any recipe requiring soda alone, some acid must be introduced, usually applesauce, sour milk, molasses, honey, and spices. Baking powders, on the other hand, are made up of both alkaline and acid materials, which react on the introduction of heat and moisture. Powders are used in sweet milk recipes.

Double-Acting Baking Powders: This baking powder reacts very slowly, releasing some of its carbon dioxide at room temperature and the rest when it is heated. On the side of the can there is usually a list which reads something like baking soda, sodium aluminum sulphate, cornstarch, calcium sulphate, calcium acid phosphate, and calcium silicate. (I like to use this type of baking powder.)

Tartarate Baking Powder: Anything to be made with this type of powder should not be allowed to stand long before it is baked, since this quick-acting powder gives off gas the moment liquid is introduced. It is generally a combination of baking soda and tartaric acid.

In a yellowed newspaper clipping, tucked between the pages of an 1887 "for man and beast doctor book" I found the following:

Since the alarming adulterations of almost everything used in cooking, a chemist, unnamed, suggests the following to be used for Baking Powder which will be cheaper and purer than that which you now can buy. Sift together 6 ounces of corn starch, 6 ounces of bi-carbonate of soda, 4 ounces of cream of tartar or tartaric acid from the drug store, several times. The main thing is to sift it enough times. Keep it in a closed jar.

Phosphate Baking Powder: This type of baking powder gives up about two thirds of its carbon dioxide gas in the cold dough and the rest when heat is introduced. It is a slow reactor like double-acting baking powder.

When in doubt about the freshness of any baking powder, add 1 teaspoonful of it in about ¼ cup water. If the powder is good, it will bubble in a lively manner.

Sourdough: Sourdough is a flour and milk mixture that ferments, creating gas that gives bread, pancakes, and the like "a lift." When making and keeping a sourdough starter, don't cap the jar—it might explode. During the winter starter can be left in a crock on the kitchen counter, but during summer when room temperatures are warmer, it should be refrigerated. Sourdough starter may be frozen for one or two months without losing its strength.

Salt Rising: This leavening agent depends on the fermentation of a bacteria in cornmeal (water ground) or potatoes, which are salt tolerant. This starter smells of fermentation and must be kept warm.

SALT

Table salt is used in most recipes. It is a finely ground mixture of sodium chloride, about 40 percent, and a carrying agent, frequently a dehydrator. (This salt is not good for making pickles because of the carrying agent). Salt preserves, flavors, and stabilizes fermentation in baking. To much salt in bread making inhibits gluten formation and kills the yeast and yet, in salt-rising bread salt kills the undesirable bacteria and allows those to survive that give the bread its characteristic flavor. (For baking, 1 teaspoon of salt is usually used with each 2 cups of flour. When making yeast bread, often 1 teaspoon is used for each cup of liquid.)

FATS

Fats add flavor and texture to baked goods. When mixed with flour, they envelop the gluten strands and "shorten" them into a more tender structure. A half cup of fat weighs a quarter of a pound. Those fats that are not liquid are generally set out to warm up to room temperature before being used for baking—except fat used for pie crust and biscuits, which should be chilled.

Butter: This fat gives a very delicate flavor to cakes and cookies, and it makes bread and pastry brown nicely. When substituting butter for vegetable shortenings, use cup for cup, as the water in the butter, which will evaporate during baking, is about equal to the air in the shortening.

Cream: Cream, which contains a considerable amount of butterfat, has long been a staple on farms and in cities. Women of the past, particularly in rural areas, used cream because it could be taken directly off the top of the milk and stirred into breads or cakes, while butter had to be churned before it could be used. Thick—whipping—cream is substituted for both the fat and liquid in a recipe: 1½ cups thick cream equaling ½ cup butterfat and 1 cup milk. Thin cream—like half-and-half or coffee cream—is used primarily to add a richer flavor to different products.

Lard: For centuries, lard was an indispensable fat in cooking. Recently, however, it has fallen into disfavor because of the cholesterol scare. Even so, in many rural areas it remains one of the two most available and serviceable fats. Because of its crystalline structure, it cuts into the flour, giving a crisper and flakier texture to biscuits and pie crusts. Lard may also be used in sweet breads or any heavy product, but it is not good for fancy cakes.

Lard made from the fat around the kidneys, called the leaf lard, is high quality and should be saved as a substitute for butter in baking when necessary. Use 20 to 25 percent less lard than butter or vegetable shortenings.

To render lard, old-time cooks put all excess back fat, or leaf lard, in a large kettle on top of the stove or in a large roast pan in the oven and cooked it until the fat liquefied. When it became clear, and the fibers—cracklings—turned light tan, which was a good indication that the moisture had evaporated out of the cooking fat, it would keep in a crock, covered but unsealed, over the winter.

Vegetable Shortenings and Margarines: These are modern, highly refined products made from vegetable oils. Those that are not low-fat products may be substituted cup for cup with butter. Those that are low-fat should not be used for baking.

Oil: Most oils are made from vegetables and seeds that are pressed, refined, bleached, deodorized, and further treated to remove cloudiness until there is no flavor. Nut oils break down under high heat and so are better for salads. Once opened, they should not be held at room temperature, but stored in the refrigerator.

Olive oil and other natural oils are not as indestructible as the commercial products. They have more flavor and are more healthful. Like lard, vegetable oil is 100 percent fat and should be reduced by about 20 percent when substituted for butter. (In my experience oil, especially olive oil, should be used only in certain recipes and not substituted willy-nilly for other fats. If flavor didn't prohibit such use, cost would.)

Chicken, Turkey, Duck, and Goose Fat: When properly cared for, poultry fat need not be strong or unpalatable. Such fat may be used to good advantage in pastry for meat pies, biscuits, or corn breads. When substituting, use ¾ cup poultry fat for 1 cup of butter.

Drippings: Bacon drippings and fat rendered (cooked so as to liquefy the fat and free it from the lean meat) in cooking meat may be strained through a cheese cloth, then refrigerated or frozen for later use. Such fats may be used in biscuits, other breads, and crusts for meat pies. (Drippings are excellent for making soap or for a fire starter—¼ cup spooned over wood will make a great blaze.) Beef tallow is usually used for frying meat, not for baking, but pork fat is quite acceptable for baking, especially when used in drop biscuits or corn bread. Decrease the amount of fat used by 20 to 25 percent.

SWEETENERS

Besides helping to brown the crust, sugars give tenderness and flavor to dough. While there are several such sweeteners, they are not exchanged cup for cup in recipes.

White Granulated Sugar: This is an all-purpose sugar used for almost any baking need. By measure, 2 cups equal 1 pound. White powdered sugar, sometimes called berry sugar, is a finer grind than granulated sugar but is not the icing sugar. Substitute powdered sugar cup for cup with granulated sugar. Confectioner's sugar is the icing or frosting sugar. It is very finely ground and contains cornstarch to keep it from lumping. (If it does lump, put it through the flour sifter.) To remove the uncooked flavor of the cornstarch, which some people object to, heat the sugar over water in the top of a double boiler for about 10 minutes—don't overheat.

Brown Sugar: This sugar, both light and dark, sometimes called Barbados sugar, is a beet or cane sugar with molasses added for flavor. It is moister than white granulated sugar and is strongly flavored, the dark being more richly flavored than the light. This sugar is used in spiced baked products. Brown sugar lumps easily and must be tightly sealed to keep it from drying out (if it should lump, a slice of bread or a firm whole apple laid in the container will often impart enough moisture to soften it again). When substituting brown sugar for white, pack the brown sugar firmly, allowing cup for cup.

Honey: Honey is sweeter than sugar. Products made with honey brown more readily than those made with sugar. When baking with this sweetener, temperatures should be reduced and baking time watched carefully. Such products remain soft and moist longer than those made with either white or brown sugar. To substitute honey in recipes that call for sugar, use ¾ cup honey to replace 1 cup sugar and remove 3⅓ tablespoons of milk or liquid. Since honey is acid, if sweet milk is used, a pinch to half teaspoon of baking soda will have to be used to neutralize the acid—strongly flavored, dark honey is more acid than mild, light-colored honey.

When a chocolate cake is being made with honey, or one in which there are raisins, dates, nuts, or mixed fruit, none of the liquid should be removed. For other cakes, like a white cake, the best results are obtained when only one third to one half of the sugar is replaced with honey. In pie fillings and custards, honey may be substituted up to 100 percent as long as you keep in mind that honey is sweeter than sugar.

When honey is stored at room temperature, it often crystallizes.

It can be reliquefied by placing the jar in a very hot water bath—but don't boil it or let the temperature rise above 150°F to 160°F, since too much heat ruins the flavor. Old-timers thought honey, which is named according to the type of blossom from which it is made, was at its best when it aged like wine for at least a year.

Corn Syrup and Maple Syrup: Liquid sugars such as light and dark corn syrup and maple syrup are usually used in baking to add flavor or for novelty's sake. Corn syrup is difficult to substitute because 1 cup of sugar equals 2 cups corn syrup and the liquid in the recipe must be reduced accordingly. Substituting maple syrup is easier: ¾ cup syrup is substituted for 1 cup sugar and the liquid in the recipe is reduced by about 3 tablespoonsful.

Molasses: There are three main types of molasses: unsulphured, which is made from the juice of sugar cane; sulphured, which is a by-product of sugar making; and blackstrap, which is a waste product. Usually, molasses is used half and half with brown sugar, sometimes with white. When a substitution must be made, use 1 cup molasses for each cup of sugar called for and add ½ teaspoon soda for each cup of molasses; also omit the baking powder or cut the amount in half, and reduce the liquid by ¼ cup for each cup of molasses used.

EGGS

Eggs add flavor, color, delicacy of crumb, and texture. Though freshness is vital to the quality of a good egg, one less than three days old should not be used to bake with, because it will not beat up to proper volume. Old-time women used to test farm eggs by putting them in a kettle of cold water: If the egg rose on its tip only slightly, they knew it was only a few days old; if it stood straight up, they used it immediately; if it floated, they threw it out or fed it to the animals.

One large chicken egg weighs 2 ounces. When using off-sized chicken eggs or eggs from some other fowl, measure or weigh them —three medium eggs weigh the same as two large ones. Turkey eggs are often large enough to weigh twice as much as a chicken egg; often it takes four small Bantam or pullet eggs to weigh as much as two large eggs. For best results, don't substitute one egg for another unless you weigh it or use the rule of thumb above.

The color of the shell has nothing to do with the flavor or any other quality of a chicken egg. The texture, thickness of the yolk, richness of the yolk of both duck and turkey eggs does make a difference, though, as it affects the moisture and fat content. Such eggs, however, yield an excellent product (I like to use both in sponge or angel cakes).

When using whole eggs and the recipe reads "well beaten," it means to whip them until they turn light and creamy in texture.

If separated eggs are called for, the eggs must be cracked (pulled in half) and the yolks put in one bowl, the whites in another. To separate eggs, have clean, dry, fat-free hands and two clean bowls, hold the egg around its middle, and tap one side of it against the rim of one of the bowls. Pull the egg open carefully, tipping it back and forth until the white can be poured out, leaving the yolk still in the shell. Put the white in one bowl and the yolk in another. When separating several eggs for one recipe, break each egg over a small extra bowl, just in case the yolk breaks and runs into the white—egg whites with yolk in them will not beat up to full volume. Sometimes the break is small and the yolk can be removed—use a piece of the shell or the tip of a spoon. If eggs are in short supply, use such eggs; if not, set them aside for other purposes.

Once separated, the yolks and whites may be beaten to full volume. Eggs should be whipped at room temperature. When only the whites are used, put the yolks in a jar that has a tight lid, pour water over them to cover, and seal. Use them promptly in a jelly roll, sponge cake, or add them to whole eggs and scramble.

Cream of tartar is often called for in a recipe to stabilize egg whites. Since it reacts on metal and sometimes on plastics, egg whites with cream of tartar added should be beaten in glass bowls. (Always fold beaten egg whites into other ingredients, never beat or stir.)

LIQUIDS

Milk, water, potato water, and sometimes applesauce and the like are added to recipes as liquid.

Milk is most nutritious, it browns the crust to a darker color, and the product lasts longer in storage. Raw milk—straight from the cow —is often scalded before baking bread to kill all yeasts and bacteria in it so the added yeast can work alone. Pasteurized milk, powdered milk, and canned milk can be used without heating. Sweet milk is used with baking powder and yeast; sour milk is used with baking soda, sometimes in combination with baking powder.

When a recipe calls for sour cream and none is at hand, a good substitute can be made by allowing a pint of heavy cream mixed with 5 tablespoons of commercial buttermilk to stand in a warm spot for twenty-four hours and then in the refrigerator for another twenty-four. For instant results, 2 tablespoons of vinegar (or lemon juice) will thicken 1 cup of cream, which then may be used instead of sour cream. Either method will also sour milk. (If it isn't thick enough in 10 minutes, add 1 more tablespoon vinegar.) Always use baking soda with sour milk or acid ingredients.

Water makes the crust crispier and gives bread an earthy taste. Potato water, made by cooking one medium potato in about 2 cups of water, gives bread a coarser crumb and sometimes makes a loaf larger. One seldom sees water in a recipe for cake (except chocolate) or a quick bread (except gingerbread), but in a pinch it can be used.

For breads made with yeast, usually 1 cup of liquid is used to 3 or 4 cups of flour, but in quick breads and cake the proportions are more like 1 cup milk to 2 or 2½ cups flour. (Of corse, pour batters contain more liquid.)

When using applesauce, pumpkin, and the like in a recipe as the liquid ingredient, go by the recipe, but 1 cup of mashed or sauced fruit is usually the correct amount to use with 1¾ cups of flour.

❧ HOMEMADE YEAST BREADS: A SIMPLE OLD TIME BREAD-MIXING PATTERN

I've noticed that the young women I teach to make bread often seem intimidated by the process, somehow thinking of it as a difficult job requiring special knowledge and skills, muscled forearms, and precise directions. Nothing is further from the truth. Most breads can be made following a simple bread-mixing pattern, even those that contain eggs, extra sugar, candied fruit, raisins, and the like.

This simple old pattern is the one I like to use, and the one that Mama used to bake the week's bread for a family of nine—Grandmother, Mother, Father, and six children.

Set out a large bread pan. Put the yeast—called for in the recipe—in the bowl and add half a cup of warm water (the water should not be hotter than 90°F for cake yeast and 105°F to 115°F for dry or granulated yeast). Add 2 tablespoons sugar—to feed the yeast, which is alive—and at times (if a recipe calls for it) a little mashed potato or potato water for the same purpose. Let this starter stand for ten minutes or more until it bubbles up, is quite puffed on top, and nearly double in bulk.

While the yeast is softening and getting started, in a saucepan warm the liquid—the amount given in the recipe—and add the fat and sugar. Heat until the fat melts and the sugar dissolves, but do not boil. (If the milk is raw, heat it until it forms a scum on the surface.) Let the hot milk or liquid cool until lukewarm. When the liquid has cooled, add all of the ingredients except the flour and stir them together. Some recipes call for beaten eggs or baking powder to be added at this point. Using a measuring cup, add half of the white flour called for and stir it in to make a batter that is about as thick as hotcake batter or a little thicker.

This batter is called a *sponge*. Set the sponge aside in a warm place for an hour or until it has doubled in bulk (a lively sponge will often be ready in half an hour). Without heat, yeast doughs do not rise, so it is important that the sponge (and the dough and the loaves of unbaked bread) be set in a warm spot. If the weather is cold, put the sponge in the oven over a pilot light, or turn the oven on and set the bowl on top of the stove over the oven heat (too much heat will kill the yeast).

When the sponge is ready, add the remaining flour and turn the dough out onto a floured breadboard to knead—any smooth surface which is large enough may be used for a breadboard. Kneading is a simple procedure designed to develop the elasticity of the bread so that it will expand and trap gas formed by the yeast.

Using care not to add too much, sprinkle the dough with extra flour and turn it about, working it until it can be handled without sticking. (Often, I pour the last cup of flour in the recipe onto the breadboard and knead it in instead of stirring it into the dough.) Knead the flour into the dough with the sides and heels of the hands, pushing it down again, and so on. Some women knead by pulling the back side of the dough forward and pressing it down, then turning it and folding toward the front again; others knead around and around, always folding toward the back and kneading as they turn the dough clockwise. Either way works just fine.

When the dough is smooth—elastic on the surface and has a sheen to it—the kneading is finished. The dough should then be placed in a greased bowl and set in a warm spot to rise, covered with a clean cloth. Usually it takes an hour, but heavy breads may take two hours for the dough to double in bulk. To test, stick the tip of your forefinger into the dough: A hole left in the dough means it has doubled in bulk. If it closes, it has not risen enough.

When the dough has risen sufficiently, punch it down—but not too hard. Pinch the dough apart to shape it into loaves or rolls and set to rise again. When double in bulk, bake. I put rolls in a hot oven (425°F) for the first 15 minutes of the baking time, then turn the heat down to 375°F and finish baking until golden brown, about 10 to 15 minutes more. You can always tell if the rolls are done, because they will be nicely browned on the bottom.

When baking loaves, I set the pans in a hot oven (425°F) and bake for 15 minutes, then turn the temperature down to 350°F or 375°F and continue baking for 45 minutes to an hour. Loaves of bread will be nicely colored on top and bottom and will sound hollow when tapped with the knuckles. When in doubt as to whether they are done, let them bake an extra 10 minutes.

🌿 PASTRY AND PIES: VARIOUS CRUSTS, TECHNIQUES, AND TIPS

Since men who work hard in the fields require well-prepared food to supply the needed energy, farm women have always been judged by whether or not they could "set a good table." A woman who could make excellent pies and pastries soon found she had a husband who had many drop-in friends. Women took pride in their apple, mince, or lemon pies, making them for church socials or grange dinners—or just to please the men.

For a novice, making a pastry is the big bug-a-boo in pie making, and it needn't be. A good pastry is a simple thing made of flour, fat, salt, and water—sometimes sugar, vinegar, and lemon juice. The most important ingredient is the fat—the more fat used, the flakier or crumblier and lighter the crust. (Bear fat makes a crust that will lift out of the pan.)

Here's my basic pastry-mixing pattern:

Basic Pastry-Mixing Pattern

Once you learn this pattern, you can mix all sorts of crusts and put in your own secret ingredients. Note that any ingredient added to the basic pastry ingredients (flour, salt, fat, and water) are logically added, dry to dry, liquid to liquid, otherwise all crusts are made in the same manner (except graham cracker crusts).

Sift the flour and salt together into a large mixing bowl, cut the fat into it, using a pastry blender or two dinner knives (or rub it lightly into the flour with the hands) until the pieces are the size of small peas. Gradually sprinkle the water over the flour mixture, mixing lightly with a fork after each addition and adding only enough cold water to hold the pastry together. Turn out onto a floured surface and shape into a soft ball. (Sometimes the dough is chilled at this point, especially in hot weather.) Divide as needed, according to the type of pie being made (single crust or double crust). This recipe will make two or three single crusts and one double crust. Roll out and shape to the pie tin (for more detailed instructions for rolling and handling see material above). When fitting into the pie tins, do not stretch the dough as it will shrink when baked.

When making any pastry it is necessary to have a light touch, since excessive handling toughens the dough. Flakiness in pastry is caused by many particles of fat, each surrounded and separated by flour. During the baking, each fat particle melts and forms a delicate flake. The object, then, is not to press the flour too firmly into the fat, either by excess working of the dough or by handling the dough so much that the fat melts from the warmth generated by the hands of the cook and combines with the flour to make a solid mass of dough. Such dough, when baked, becomes tough instead of flaky. Starting with well-chilled ingredients, which slow the melting of the fat until the pastry can be put together, prevents such problems.

Once the fat has been worked into the flour, water is added at the rate of 2 to 4 tablespoons water for each cup of flour. The amount of water needed is not uniform, because flour may pick up moisture, and different fats work into the flour in a variety of ways. Too much water will cause a hard, brittle crust; too little causes a dry crust that cracks when rolled or when baked. The water should be sprinkled over the fat-flour mixture a little at a time, as the fat-flour mixture is tossed lightly together using a pair of forks, lifting from the bottom. (Liquid added to pastry dough is not stirred in heavily as it is in cake batters.) More water is added and combined until the dough is sufficiently damp so that it will not crumble when pressed with the fingers.

Sticky dough will not roll. If too much water has been added, do not add extra flour to take up the extra water, which would change the balance of fat and flour, perhaps not leaving enough fat to make a good, flaky pastry. Instead, mix a little fat and flour together in a different bowl until it is mealy—pieces the size of small peas—and use this to take up the extra water.

When making any pie crust, choose a pastry that complements the filling. Most pastry recipes are developed to make enough dough for a double-crust pie, so when making a single-crust pie either plan to make two pies or half the ingredients called for in the pastry recipe. Always dust the breadboard (either a separate board or any smooth surface that is large enough, smooth, and easily cleaned) with flour and use chilled ingredients, especially fat. If the weather is warm, start with very cold ingredients *and equipment* (a chilled bowl can save a pie crust on a hot day) and work fast. Mix the pastry and shape it into a ball, divide roughly in half—equal portions for two single-crust pies; one ball a little larger for a double-crust pie. Turn the pieces of dough with your hands, a gentle shaping action to form smooth balls. Never overhand pie dough. Now, with a patting, rolling motion, flatten one ball. Pat in all directions from the center to keep the dough in as near a perfect circle as possible. If you're making a double-crust pie, put one ball in the refrigerator while you work with the first.

Working from the center, roll the dough in all directions toward the edges, lifting the rolling pin as the edge is reached to avoid splitting or cracking the dough. Occasionally, give the dough a quarter turn. If it is sticking, dust both the breadboard and the rolling pin very lightly with flour. Don't turn the dough over. Work quickly, shaping the dough (with as little handling as possible). Continue the rolling, until the dough is about ⅛ inch thick. It should be about 4 inches bigger than the top of the pie pan. Fold the dough in quarters, lay the point in the center of the ungreased pie tin. Unfold the pastry and let it stand for about 5 minutes. With the fingers, press it gently into the tin so that it fits snugly. Again, handle only enough to put in place.

For a single-crust pie, finish the shell by fluting. Cut the excess pastry dough off the pan, leaving about 1½ inches overhang. Fold the extra dough under, tucking it between pan and dough. Straighten this fold so it stands up, and with the thumbs and index finger sharply crease or pinch the dough at about ½-inch intervals until it has sharp and distinct flutes. Sometimes the edge is left flat and is firmed against the ridge of the pan with the tines of a fork.

The bottoms of single-crust pies are often brushed with an egg wash made of a whole egg or more often egg white, which is thought to keep the crust from getting soggy after it is filled. Since such pies are so often filled with liquid fillings like custard or pumpkin custard, a soggy bottom crust is a problem. Another way to firm the crust so that it remains crisp is to bake the crust for about 5 or 10 minutes in a very hot oven before filling.

To make a double-crust pie, line the tin with the smaller ball of dough; fill the shell as the recipe directs. Take the larger half of the dough out of the refrigerator (if you chilled it) and roll out the second half of the pastry. Fold it in quarters and with a very sharp knife cut small slits at the edges of the folds to form air vents. (It is easier for an inexperienced pie maker to put the top crust on without cutting it and then stick it with the point of a sharp knife or prick it with the tines of a fork to form air vents.)

Moisten the rim of the bottom crust with cold water. Lay the folded top pastry over the filling, the point marking the center of the pie, and unfold. Press the edges down against the rim. Trim the top crust with a knife, leaving about a ½-inch overhang. Fold the over-hanging dough under the edges of the bottom crust. Flute with your fingers or press the edge of the crust against the rim of the pan with the tines of a wide fork or the tip of a spoon.

The top of the pie will brown nicely if it is brushed with milk, cream, or beaten egg white. Sugar may also be sprinkled on top for a delicious-looking crust.

Other decorative tops are possible. To make a lattice top, place seven ½-inch pastry strips of equal length across the filling. Make eight more strips for the weaving. Start in the center by laying a strip across, then lifting the first strips alternately to create a basket weave. Work other cross strips over the first seven, lifting every other strip to create the weave. When finished, fold the bottom crust, at least ½ an inch of dough, over the woven top. Flute or press with a fork or scallop with a teaspoon around the edge. Using thinner or fewer strips in the weave allows the filling to show through; a tight weave looks like a pastry basket.

Another top may be made by cutting the dough into ¾-inch strips. Pinch the edges of the strips together so that one long rope of dough is formed. Twist the dough into an even spiral, beginning at the center of the pie and swirling the dough into circles, working out to the edges of the pie. You can leave spaces between parts of the spiral or place it so the strip touches. For this pie, leave the bottom crust at least 1½ inches bigger than the pan, so it can be turned back to form its own rim. Flute the rim.

Filled Single-Crust Pie: Some single-crust pies are baked, then the filling is put into the pie shell after it has cooled. The shells for this type of pie are either baked on the back side of the pie pan with the pan placed upside down in the oven or they are baked right side up after being pricked full of holes so that they will not puff up and distort the shape of the shell, or they are filled with dry beans before they are baked. I've had the best luck with pricking.

Such shells are baked at 400°F until crisp and light brown.

Baked Single-Crust Pie: Other pies like pumpkin and custard pies are baked in a raw-dough shell. (In some pies, such as slipped custard pie, the filling is baked separately, then slipped into a crisp shell.)

Tarts: These small, open-faced pies may be filled with the same fillings as larger pies or with a mixture that tastes better in small servings. Any of the pastry doughs may be used for tarts, depending on the filling used. Shape tarts to small pans, or shape over the backs (or insides of) cupcake or muffin tins. Prick them so that the air escapes and does not distort the shells. Bake at 400°F.

Deep-Dish Pies: These pies are single-crust pies in reverse, having only a top crust. Baked in casserole dishes, such pies are filled with fruit. The sweetened, sometimes spiced, fruit is thickened with cornstarch or tapioca (usually about 2 tablespoons or slightly more), butter is dotted over the top, and a single top crust is cut to fit the top of the dish, leaving 1½ to 2 inches of crust as an overhang, which is then fluted. Deep-dish pies are generally baked at 425°F for about 45 minutes or until the crust is nicely browned. Included among these pies are meat pies. A bit of leftover stew or hash can be tucked into a small casserole dish (1 quart) and a crust baked on top, which makes a quick and frugal meal.

Mincemeat Pies: These pies are filled with already prepared mincemeat. Sometimes apples are added because mincemeat alone is often very rich. The top crust may be solid with vent holes cut in it or it may be woven into a lattice or basket design.

Meat Pies: Such pies may be tarts, turnovers, fried pies, deep-dish, single-crust, or double-crust pies. The crust is a plain pastry and, therefore, not too rich. The filling may be either a thick one all of meat, or one that is a combination of meat and vegetables, or one that is simply a cream sauce with bits of meat in it. The meat may be precooked (intentionally or as a leftover), or it may be raw. Generally, such pies are well seasoned, served as the main part of a meal, and eaten hot.

Turnovers: Turnovers are small individual pies. The filling is generally thicker and less juicy than a regular fruit pie. Mincemeat, apples, softened dried fruit, and meat all make good turnovers. The pastry is rolled as for a pie crust and cut into 4-inch squares or into circles (as for pasties) that are about 4 inches across. The filling is laid on half, and the other half is folded over. The edge is moistened with cold water and pressed together with the tines of a fork or it is fluted. Turnovers are baked on a cookie sheet at 450°F for 20 to 25 minutes or until the crust is nicely browned.

Fried Pies: These little pastries are made like turnovers. A thick fruit filling is sealed inside the dough, and the pie is deep-fried. Dried fruit that is moistened but still quite thick works well in these pies. The filling must not be too juicy or it will spill out into the hot fat— the seal *must* be good.

While cooks love to experiment with the variety pie crusts—those containing "secret" ingredients like eggs, baking powder, or vinegar, which they sometimes feel set their pies off from the usual—a few basic pastry recipes, a little "crust know-how," and a sure hand can win all the praise one can stand. I like to put my secret ingredients into the filling: a bit (1 teaspoon) of vanilla in a Golden Delicious apple pie, or light brown sugar, cinnamon, and a dash of nutmeg into the pie when winter apples have lost some of their flavor. (Substitute brown sugar for white, add 1 teaspoon cinnamon, and ¼ teaspoon nutmeg when apples have been stored and lost some of their flavor.)

To give yourself a little extra crust know-how, notice the amount of fat required in relation to the flour used in the following pastry patterns:

Plain Crust

This type of pastry, or a variation on it, is used for meat pies, fried pies, and often fruit pies or deep-dish pies. Many cooks prefer to use it with mincemeat and raisin pies as it is not overly rich. I use it in my double-crust (page 215) cranberry apple pie. The recipe will make two or three single crusts or one double crust.

3 cups sifted flour	⅓ to ½ cup cold water, moisture
1 teaspoon salt	needed being determined by
1 cup butter, margarine,	the dryness of the flour
shortening, or ⅔ cup lard	

Flaky Crust

This rich pastry is excellent for use when making tart shells or turnovers. The texture is very nice, complementing the smooth light texture of pudding or creamy fillings in cream pies, or those like my

Butterscotch (page 217) or the old-time Slipped Custard pie (page 27). Use it with pumpkin, lemon, even fruit pies.

2 cups all-purpose flour
1 teaspoon salt

1 cup butter, margarine, shortening, or ⅔ cup lard
¼ cup cold water

Graham Crust

This type of whole-wheat crust is excellent when used with meat or fruit pies. You could use it for any meat or fruit pie in this book. It makes delicious cases or tart shells for use with creamed fish or some meat filling. Notice that cinnamon has been added to the combined flours and salt, and that honey has been added to the water—those are secret ingredients. For meat pies or a quiche, herbs could be substituted for the cinnamon, using about the same amount (thyme, chives, onion bits, and such).

1 cup unbleached all-purpose flour
1 cup whole-wheat flour
1 teaspoon salt
1 teaspoon cinnamon

1 cup butter, margarine, shortening, or ⅔ cup lard
3 tablespoons honey
⅓ cup cold water

Blend the unbleached and whole-wheat flours with the salt and cinnamon. Cut the butter into the flour, or rub it in lightly with the hands, until the mixture is granular. Don't overwork the dough. (Notice that this mixing pattern is fundamentally the same as for plain and flaky crusts.) Add the honey to 3 tablespoons water, stir to dissolve, then sprinkle over the flour-fat mixture and blend with a fork until the mixture holds together, adding a little additional water if needed. Turn the dough out onto a floured surface and knead three or four times, just enough to make a soft ball of dough. Roll out to fit pie pans. (For more detailed instructions about rolling and handling, see basic pastry-making instructions above). Do not stretch the dough when fitting the pans, as it will shrink when baked. And do not flute this type of dough into high ridges—the pie should be as flat on top as possible, since the higher surfaces brown too much before the rest is baked (due to the addition of honey, which browns more quickly than sugar).

Graham Cracker Crust

Gingersnaps, lemon, and vanilla wafers may be used in this recipe, which is a very nice crust for pies and fresh fruit tarts. This is a perfect crust for summer, since warm weather sometimes makes other pastries a challenge—and often the fillings for graham cracker crusts don't require any cooking, either, so both cook and kitchen stay cool.

⅓ cup butter
2 tablespoons light brown
   sugar

1¼ cups graham cracker crumbs

Stir the butter and sugar together in a saucepan over low heat until butter is melted. Blend in the cracker crumbs. Press evenly into a pie tin or into tart pans. Chill before filling.

✻ STORING BAKED GOODS: FREEZING AND SUCH

On cold days when outside work is impossible, I set aside a baking day, one during which I make yeast breads (loaves and rolls), quick breads, cakes, cookies, and pies for the freezer. I have found that while the oven is hot it takes very little longer to make several items than it does to bake one. These products, cooked, uncooked and partially cooked, are then stored away in the freezer for later use.

Yeast Bread: As for all frozen products, take care to wrap tightly so as to exclude air and moisture. Uncooked bread dough can be stored for about three weeks—wrap it and freeze it before it rises, or let it rise once, punch it down, shape it into a loaf, then freeze it. When the dough thaws, let it rise in a warm place and bake as for fresh bread.

Rolls can be partially baked, until they are done but not brown, removed from the oven, cooled, and frozen. They should be thawed and browned just before the meal is ready.

I freeze most of my bread already baked and browned and thaw it in its freezer wrap. Rolls that have been baked, wrapped in foil, then frozen can be heated in that foil. Breads baked prior to freezing have a better freezer life than those frozen raw or partially cooked—they will remain in good condition for two or three months but do lose quality rapidly after that period.

Quick Breads: Biscuits, muffins, doughnuts, cornbread, nutbread, waffles all freeze well, but they must be cooked before they are frozen. Cool before wrapping. Such products will remain in good condition for about three months. Once removed, thaw and heat wrapped in foil, or do as my mother did to warm leftover biscuits—rub the tops lightly with water before heating, so they don't dry out.

Cakes: Simple cakes, sponge and angel cakes may be baked and frozen for bases for desserts such as fruit shortcake or trifle, which is cake broken in pieces and layered in a bowl with pudding. Usually stale cake is used for such desserts, but a fresh one-egg cake layered with bananas and vanilla pudding makes a delicious dessert, as do many other combinations of fruit and cake, pudding and cake, ice cream and cake, whipped cream and cake, and so forth.

Cakes should be wrapped well and stored in cartons. I bake the cakes in uniform shapes so they can be packaged easily and stacked. Cakes generally should not be frosted before they are frozen. I turn the cakes, usually baked in small layer or loaf pans, out to cool. When cool, I wrap them in foil, slip them in a freezer bag, and put them in to freeze. Such unfrosted cakes will remain good for up to six months. Butter-type frostings are sometimes spread on the cakes, but the freezer life is cut way down. If you should decide to freeze frosted cakes, set in to freeze before wrapping to keep the frosting from sticking to the wrap.

Cake batters do not freeze successfully; neither do fillings, which become soggy, nor do seven-minute types of frostings, which become spongy.

Cookies: Most cookies can be frozen baked or unbaked. The higher the fat content and the lower the moisture in the dough, the better the product will keep. Generally, cookie dough will retain its quality for two or three months when frozen; baked cookies have a storage life of six to eight months.

Roll-type doughs may be shaped into logs and frozen in one piece —they can then be partially thawed and sliced for baking. Drop-type doughs that are dry and high in fat content can be dropped by spoon onto cookie sheets, then frozen raw to be baked later. Store in plastic bags and remove a few at a time for immediate use. Softer drop doughs should be baked before freezing. To serve baked cookies, thaw 5 to 10 minutes. Raw cookies may be put directly into a preheated oven.

Pies: All pies may be frozen either baked or unbaked. The crust seems flakier and the pie a little fresher when baked after freezing. Chess pie, which contains walnuts, or pecan pie should be baked first —rich fillings don't freeze as solid, and they often soak into an unbaked crust. Fruit, berry, or pumpkin pie will hold its quality when frozen for up to six months; others should be used within two to three months.

When thawing baked pies, let them set at room temperature for 2 to 4 hours in the wrapping, unless for some reason the pie might stick to the wrapping. Serve cold. Baked fruit pies may be thawed and then warmed for 30 minutes in a preheated oven at 300°F and served hot. When a pie has been baked until the filling is done and the crust lightly colored, then cooled and frozen, it can be put into a hot oven (375°F) and baked for 45 minutes, somewhat like partially cooked rolls. Raw pies that have been frozen should be placed in a preheated oven at 425°F, baked 20 to 25 minutes, then with the oven turned down to 350°F, baked another 50 to 60 minutes.

Index

314

Blueberry crisp, 135
Borscht, Ben's, 195–96
Boxty, 24
Boy's Song, A (Hogg), 85–86
Bradford, Viola May, 277–78
Brandy
    and cream cheese frosting, 104
    sauce, 212–13
Bread batter (sponge), 303
Bread flour, 292
Bread pudding
    caramel, 256
    honey raisin, 79–80
Breads
    barmbrack, 26
    brown, 194–95
    corn bread, upside-down sausage and onion,
        237–38
    cornmeal gems, 168
    federal loaf, 83–84
    flour for, 292
    freezing, 311–12
    golden egg, 102–3
    Mark's, with dill butter, 124–25
    oat, crusty, 25–26
    old-country, 183–84
    from a potato ball, 13–15
    raisin, stuffing, 100–101
    sorghum gingerbread, 158–59
    stuffing for veal leg roast, 57–58
    winter squash loaf, 159–60
    yeast, 302–4
    See also Biscuits; Buns; Rolls
Bride's cake with cream cheese and brandy
        frosting, 103–4
Brook Song, The (Riley), 88
Broth, chicken, 11–12
    gravy, 276–77
Brown bread, 194–95
Brown sugar, 299
Bumblebee, The (Riley), 114
Buns, citron, 41–42
Burnt-sugar cake with caramel marshmallow
        frosting, 150–51
Butter
    apple-, drops, 66–67
    as a baking ingredient, 297
    -crust pastry, 218
    dill, 125
    honey, glaze, 32, 167
    lemon, parsley and winter-growing chives,
        33–34
    parsley and lemon, 101
    plum, 170–71
Buttermilk
    biscuit dumplings, 269
    doughnuts, 160
Butternut cookies, 130–31
Butterscotch pie, 217

C

Cabbage
    carrot, and celery salad with sour cream
        dressing, 213–32
    colcannon, 255–56
    coleslaw (slaw)
        calico, 91
        great-aunt Mae's, 192–93

hot, 259
    with hot bacon dressing, 164
    German potato salad with, 97
    and meat with old-country bread, 183–84
    relish for stuffed and pickled bell peppers,
        145–46
    sauerkraut
        and apple salad, 45–46
        in a jar, 144–45
        roast pork and, with fried apples,
            259–60
Cady, Daniel L., 30, 36, 63, 230
Cake batter, two-egg cream, 140
Cakes
    angel food
        big fluffy, 60–61
        chocolate, 239–40
        two-egg, with lemon icing, 206
    bride's, with cream cheese and brandy
        sauce, 103–4
    burnt-sugar, with caramel marshmallow
        frosting, 150–51
    champion silver, with snow peak frosting,
        151
    chocolate
        angel food, 239–40
        French, with fluffy chocolate frosting,
            149–50
    Easter, 60–62
    feather, 16–17
    flour for, 292
    freezing, 312
    General Robert E. Lee, with lemon filling
        and lemon-orange frosting, 82–83
    gentleman's choice, served with whipped
        cream, 152
    ginger, 85
    happiness, 47
    hazelnut, with honey marshmallow frosting,
        71–72
    mahogany, with fudge frosting, 168–69
    mincemeat, old-fashioned, for, 205–6
    prune, 207
    raisin, with powdered-sugar glaze, 207–8
    raw-apple, 189
    red velvet, with ermine frosting, 284–85
    sand, 152
    shortcakes, creamed oyster, 19–20
    Simnel, with almond filling, 153
    snowy mountain, with snowy mountain
        frosting, 247–48
    sponge, egg-yolk, 61–62
    sunshine, 110–11
Cakewalk, 147–49
Calico slaw, 91
Candy (sweets)
    candied violets, 71
    hints for making, 288–91
    honey marshmallows, 93
    mock candied ginger, 211–12
    molasses, 278
    nun's sighs, 241–42
    old-fashioned sea-foam, 68–69
    peanut fudge, 278–79
    taffy apples, 200
Candy thermometer, 289
Caramel
    bread pudding, 256
    marshmallow frosting, 150–51

Caramelized sugar, 285
Carrot(s)
  and apple salad, 282–83
  cabbage, and celery salad with sour cream
      dressing, 231–32
  mock candied ginger, 211–12
  pie, 15–16
  salad with creamy dressing, 21
Cauliflower, scalloped, with cottage cheese,
     283–84
Celeriac (root celery)
  with cheese sauce, 262
  veal stew with dried morels and, 11–12
Celery, cabbage, and carrot salad with sour
     cream dressing, 231–32
Champion silver cake with snow peak
     frosting, 151
Cheese
  cottage, scalloped cauliflower with,
     283–84
  cream, and brandy sauce, 104
  sauce, 262
Chicken
  cock-a-leekie, 191–92
  with egg noodles, 89–91
  and feather-light dumplings, 31–32
  honey-coated, with morel mushroom
     seasoning, 51–52
  mulligatawny, 193–94
  smothered with mushroom gravy, 260–61
  Swiss-fried, 165
Chicken broth, 11–12
  gravy, 276–77
Chicken fat as a baking ingredient, 298
Chives, winter-growing, lemon, and parsley
     butter, 33–34
Chocolate
  cake
    angel food, 239–40
    French, with fluffy chocolate frosting,
      149–50
  custard ice cream, 129–30
  frosting, fluffy, 149–50
  glaze, 240
Choir practice, 239
Chowder, corn, 184–85
"Christ Arose" (Lowry), 53
Christmas baskets, 209–10
Christmas Carol, A (Guest), 242
Christmas Day, 243–45
Chutney, apple, 188–89
Cider
  spiced apples with, 110
  spicy mulled, 190
Citron buns, 41–42
Claudius, Matthias, 221
Clover blossom, red, tea, 74
Cloverleaf rolls, golden egg, 102–3
Cobbler, blackberry, with two-egg cream cake
     crust, 139–40
Cock-a-leekie, 191–92
Cocoa, fudge frosting with, 169
Colcannon, Fitzgerald's, 255–56
Coleslaw (slaw)
  calico, 91
  great-aunt Mae's, 192–93
  hot, 259
  with hot bacon dressing, 164
  mock, with cream dressing, 78

Cookies
  Ada Wilkin's hermits, 125–26
  angel kisses, 79
  apple-butter drops, 66–67
  bachelor buttons, 279–80
  best jumbles, 7
  butternut, 130–31
  dried-fig-filled, 67–68
  freezing, 312
  ginger crisps, 9
  Grandpa's, 208–9
  honey, 8
  mincemeat, old-fashioned, for, 205–6
  mincemeat drops, 8–9
  oatmeal
    apple crisp, 189–90
    Christmas, 213
    crispy, 144
  old folks', 84–85
  persimmon, 199–200
  walnut sticks, 53
Corn
  chowder, 184–85
  fritters, 117
  pudding, 177–78
  succotash, 254–55
Cornbread
  freezing, 311–12
  sausage and onion, upside-down,
     237–38
Corn flour, 294
Cornish pasties, 12–13
Cornmeal, 293, 294
  gems, 168
  mush (for stuffing), 225
Corn syrup, 300
  in candy making, use of, 288–89
Cottage cheese, scalloped cauliflower with,
     283–84
Country lass with a veil (dessert), 46–47
Country wedding, 94–95
County fair, 141–43
Cranberry apple pie, double-crust, 215
Cream (creamed)
  of asparagus soup, 19
  as a baking ingredient, 297
  dressing, 21, 78
  mayonnaise, 56–57
  oyster shortcakes, 19–20
  sauce, 283–84
  skin softener, 75
  strawberry, dressing (or frosting), 96–97
  See also Whipped cream
Cream cheese and brandy frosting, 104
Crisp pastry, 35
Cucumbers, dilled, in sour cream dressing,
     108
Curing spiced beef, 23
Custard
  chocolate, ice cream, 129–30
  floating island, 29–30
  pie, 27–28
    apple, 178
    rhubarb, 34–35
  soft, 235

D

Daddy's hot pepper sauce, 185–86
Dandelion wine, 105

Dark wheat flours, 293
Decoration Day (Memorial Day), 81–82
Deep-dish pies, 308
Denver biscuits, Mother's, 121–22
Desserts
    blackberry cobbler with two-egg cream
        cake crust, 139–40
    blueberry crisp, 135
    country lass with a veil, 46–47
    figs pickled in honey, 210–11
    floating island custard, 29–30
    Grandmother Sitha Jane's trifle, 234–35
    honey daffodil meringues, 21–22
    raspberry snow, 135–36
    rhubarb crunch, 72–73
    soft custard, 235
    See also Ice cream; Pies; Pudding
Dill (dilled)
    butter, 125
    cucumbers in sour cream dressing, 108
Double-acting baking powders, 296
Double-crust pie pastry, 139
Doughnuts
    buttermilk, 160
    freezing, 311–12
    Mama's snow party, 265–66
Dressing
    onion, for roasted suckling pig, 98–99
    pecan, 223
    pork sausage, 175–76
Dried beans
    baked, with German sausage, 109
    kidney, with ground beef and salt pork, 52–
        53
    lima, for succotash, 254–55
Dried fruit
    Ada Wilkin's hermits, 125–26
    dried-fig-filled cookies, 67–68
    fried pies with, 309
Drippings as baking ingredients, 298–99
Duchess potatoes, 234
Duck fat as a baking ingredient, 298
Duckling with raisin bread stuffing, 100–101
Dumplings
    buttermilk biscuit, 269
    feather-light, 31–32

E

Easter, 53–56
Easter cakes, 60–62
Easy-to-make mock candied ginger, 211–12
Effie's favorite chicken with homemade egg
        noodles, 89–91
Egg(s)
    as baking ingredients, 300–301
    golden egg bread or cloverleaf rolls,
        102–3
    meringues, 28–29
        honey daffodil, 21–22
    noodles, 90–91
    omelet, potato, 40–41
    pastry, 161
    pickled, 120–21
    Scotch, 233
    separating, 301
    two-egg cream cake batter, 140
    wash, 42
    See also Custard
Egg-yolk sponge cake, 61–62

Elk roast, braised, 245–46
Emma's everlasting yeast, 295–96
End-of-the-garden uncooked relish, 185
Ermine frosting, 284–85
Everday beef stew, 236–37

F

Fats as baking ingredients, 297–99
Feather cake, 16–17
Federal loaf, 83–84
Figs
    dried-, filling for cookies, 67–68
    pickled in honey, 210–11
Filled single-crust pie, 308
Filling
    almond, in Simnel cake, 153
    dried-fig, for cookies, 67–68
    lemon, for General Robert E. Lee cake,
        83
First Snowfall, The (Lowell), 264
Fish
    salmon, baked, 124
    trout, oven-baked, with parsley and lemon
        butter, 101
Fitzgerald's colcannon, 255–56
Fitzgerald's tea and milk, 256
Flag Goes By, The (Bennet), 119
Flaky pastry, 28
Flaky pie crust, 309–10
Floating island custard, 29–30
Floral oils, home-extracted, 75
Flour, 291–94
Flowers (edible), candied violets, 71
Fourth of July celebration, 119–20
Freezing baked goods, 311–13
    breads
        quick, 311–12
        yeast, 311
    cakes, 312
    cookies, 312
    pies, 312–13
French chocolate cake with a fluffy chocolate
        frosting, 149–50
Frenched pork tenderloin, 275
Fried pies, 309
Fritters, corn, 117
Frosting
    caramel marshmallow, 150–51
    chocolate, fluffy, 149–50
    cream cheese and brandy, 104
    ermine, 284–85
    fudge, 169
    honey marshmallow, 72
    lemon-orange, 83
    snow peak, 151
    snowy mountain, 248
    strawberry cream, 96–97
    See also Icing
Fruit
    dried
        Ada Wilkin's hermits, 125–26
        fig-filled cookies, 67–68
        fried pies with, 309
    fruit basket salad with strawberry cream
        dressing, 96–97
    See also names of fruit
Fudge
    frosting, 169
    peanut, 278–79

G

Game
  elk roast, braised, 245–46
  jugged hare, 44–45
  rabbit
    cutlets, 267–68
    pan-fried, 120
    stew, 254
  squirrel pot pie with buttermilk biscuit
    dumplings, 269
  venison
    cutlets stuffed with fresh pork dressing,
      175–76
    pot roast, 176–77
    shoulder with sausage, wheat and white
      bread, and corn meal stuffing, 224–25
General Robert E. Lee cake with lemon filling
  and lemon-orange frosting, 82–83
Gentleman's choice served with whipped
  cream, 152
German potato salad with cabbage, 97
German sausage, baked beans with, 109
Ginger
  cake, 85
  crisps, 9
  mock, candied, 211–12
  wine, Scottish, 285
Gingerbread, sorghum, 158–59
Gingersnap pie shell, 226
Glaze (glazed)
  chocolate, 240
  honey butter, 32, 167
  mustard-horseradish, 282
  onions, 25
  powdered-sugar, 208
Golden egg bread or cloverleaf rolls with fresh
  butter, 102–3
Gone-in-a-minute strawberry pudding, 92–93
Goose fat as a baking ingredient, 298
Grabbled potatoes, 92
Graham cracker crust, 310–11
Graham crust, 310
Grandma Boardman's floating island custard,
  29–30
Grandma White's brandy sauce, 212–13
Grandma's creamed oyster shortcakes, 19–
  20
Grandma's watermelon rind pickles, 146–47
Grandmother Sitha Jane's trifle, 234–35
Grandpa's cookies, 208–9
Granulated sugar, white, 299
Gravy
  chicken broth, 276–77
  mushroom, 261
  turkey, richly colored, 223–24
Great-aunt Mae's cabbage slaw, 192–93
Greens
  beet, beets with, 41
  wild, salad of, 38–39
Guest, Edgar A., 242, 249
Guinea chickens, roasted, 166–67

H

Halloween ghost party, 198
Ham, preboiled, 32
Happiness cake, 47
Hare, jugged, 44–45
harvest home venison pot roast, 176–77
Harvest Song (Orr and Latta), 162

Hat My Father Wore, The (McCarthy), 22
Hazelnut cake with honey marshmallow
  frosting, 71–72
Heavenly pies, 241
Herbal salt substitute, 74–75
Hogg, James, 86
Holiday celebrations
  April Fool's day, 42–44
  Arbor Day, 49–50
  Christmas, 243–45
  Decoration Day, 81–82
  Easter, 53–56
  Fourth of July, 119–20
  Halloween, 198
  May Day, 65–66
  Memorial Day, 81–82
  Mother's Day, 76–77
  St. Patrick's Day, 22–26
  Thanksgiving, 218–21
  Valentine's Day, 277–78
Holiday pudding with brandy sauce, 212–
  13
Home-churned ice cream, 128–29
Honey
  -apple
    gems, 192
    marmalade, 147
  butter glaze, 32, 167
  -coated chicken with morel mushroom
    dressing, 51–52
  cookies, 8
  daffodil meringues, 21–22
  figs pickled in, 210–11
  marshmallow frosting, 72
  marshmallows, 93
  pumpkin pie, 198–99
  raisin bread pudding, 79–80
  rose hip, 171
  as a sweetener for baking, 299–300
Horseradish
  mustard, glaze, 282
  sauce, fresh, 99
Hot pepper sauce, 185–86
Hot water pastry, 16
Hymb of Faith, A (Riley), 81

I

Ice cream
  chocolate, 129–30
  home-churned, 128–29
  peach, 130
  snow, 265
  vanilla (uncooked), 129
Icing, lemon, 206
Indian meal, 294
Irish spiced beef, 23–24

J

Jackson, Helen Hunt, 203
Jam, blackberry, 140–41
Jellied roast beef loaf, 232
Jerusalem artichokes, baked, with toasted
  sesame seeds, 33
Jugged hare, 44–45

K

Kidney beans (Sweet Wisconsin) with ground
  beef and salt pork, 52–53
Kitchen dance, 9–11

L

Lamb
  mutton, shepherd's sweet potato pie, 176
  rack of, with fresh mint sauce, 58
Lard as a baking ingredient, 298
Latta, E.R., 162
Laughlin's persimmon cookies, 199–200
Leavening agents, 294–97
Leeks, cock-a-leekie, 191–92
Lemon
  filling for General Robert E. Lee cake, 83
  icing, 206
  and mint sachet bags, 75
  -orange frosting, 83
  parsley, and winter chives butter, 33–34
  and parsley butter, 101
  sauce, 62
    whipped cream, 263
Lettuce, wilted, 116
Lima beans for succotash, 254–55
Liquids as baking ingredients, 302
Lowell, James Russell, 264
Lowry, Robert, 53

M

McCarthy, Daniel, 22
Machado, Shelly, 26
Mahogany cake with fudge frosting, 168–69
Mama's snow party doughnuts, 265–66
Maple syrup, 300
Margarine as a baking ingredient, 298
Mark's bread with dill butter, 124–25
Marmalade, honey-apple, 147
Marshmallow(s)
  caramel, frosting, 150–51
  honey, 93
    frosting, 72
May Day, 65–66
May in Vermont (Cady), 63
Mayonnaise, cream, 56–57
Meat
  cabbage and, with old-country bread, 183–84
  See also Beef; Game; Lamb; Pork; Veal
Meat loaf, jellied roast beef, 232
Meat pies, 308
  Cornish pasties, 12–13
Meat sauce, spicy, 233
Memorial Day (Decoration Day), 81–82
Meringues, 28–29
  honey daffodil, 21–22
Merkins's family apple and carrot salad, 282–83
Milk
  as a baking ingredient, 302
  See also Buttermilk
Mincemeat
  drops, 8–9
  old-fashioned, 205–6
  pies, 308
Mint
  and lemon sachet bags, 75
  sauce, 58
Mock coleslaw with cream dressing, 78
Mock ginger, candied, 211–12
Molasses
  candy, 278
  as a sweetener for baking, 300

Morel mushroom(s)
  dried, veal stew with celeriac and, 11–12
  seasoning, 51–52
Mother's butter-crust quince pie, 217–18
Mother's Day, 76–77
Mother's Denver biscuits, 121–22
Mother's favorite Easter cakes, 60–62
Mother's holiday pudding with Grandma White's brandy sauce, 212–13
Mother's mustard-and-horseradish-glazed pork shoulder roast, 281–82
Mother's old-fashioned winter succotash, 254–55
Mother's roast turkey with pecan dressing and richly colored turkey gravy, 222–24
Mother's rusk, 78–79
Mother's stuffed and pickled bell peppers, 145–46
Mother's uncooked vanilla ice cream, 129
Muffins, freezing, 311–12
Mulligatawny, 193–94
Mushroom(s)
  gravy, 261
  morel
    seasoning, 51–52
    veal stew with celeriac and, 11–12
Mustard and horseradish glaze, 282
Mutton, shepherd's sweet potato pie with, 176

N

Nectar, raspberry, ice-cold, 123–24
New potatoes, string beans, and bacon, 115
Noodles, egg, chicken with, 89–91
Nun's sighs, 241–42
Nuts
  butternut cookies, 130–31
  hazelnut cake with honey marshmallow frosting, 71–72
  pecan fudge, 278–79
  pecan dressing, 223
  walnut
    pudding with lemon whipped cream sauce, 263
    sticks, 53

O

Oat flour, 293–94
Oatmeal
  apple crisp, 189–90
  bread, crusty, 25–26
  cookies
    Christmas, 213
    crispy, 144
  topping for rhubarb crunch, 72–73
O'Daly family recipe for boxty, 24
Oil as a baking ingredient, 298
Oils, floral, home-extracted, 75
Old-country cabbage and meat with old-country bread, 183–84
Old-fashioned baked sweet potatoes, 246–47
Old-fashioned blackberry pie, 138–39
Old-fashioned carrot salad with creamy dressing, 21
Old-fashioned Duchess potatoes, 234
Old-fashioned mincemeat, 205–6
Old-fashioned pork pie, 275–77
Old-fashioned preboiled ham, 32
Old-fashioned Roses (Riley), 73–74

Old-fashioned sea-foam candy, 68–69
Old-fashioned social activities, *see* Social
    activities
Old folks' cookies, 84–85
Old Man's Nursery Rhyme (Riley), 266
Old October (Riley), 179
Old-time carrot pie, 15–16
Old-time light bread or rolls made from a
    potato ball, 13–15
Old-time rabbit cutlets, 267–68
Old Vermont Cellar Hole, An (Cady), 35–36
Old Winter on the Farm (Riley), 271
Old Years and New (Guest), 248–49
Omelet, potato, 40–41
Onion(s)
    corn bread with sausage and, upside-down,
        237–38
    dressing for roasted suckling pig, 98–99
    glazed, 25
    sausage-stuffed, 117–18
Orange, lemon-, frosting, 83
Orchard Lands of Long Ago, The (Riley), 187
Orr, John L., 162
Our Hired Girl (Riley), 134
Out to Old Aunt Mary's (Riley), xx
Oyster shortcakes, creamed, 19–20

P

Pan-fried rabbit, 120
Parsley
    lemon, and winter-growing chives butter,
        33–34
    and lemon butter, 101
Parsnip puffs, 59
Pasties, Cornish, 12–13
Pastry
    basic mixing patterns, 305–9
    butter-crust, 218
    crisp, 35
    crusts, techniques, and tips for, 304–11
    double-crust, 139
    egg, 161
    flaky, 28
    hot water, 16
    pork pie, 276
    tip-top, 216–17
Peach
    ice cream, 130
    pie with sour cream, 136
    preserves, sun-cooked, 172–73
Peanut fudge, 278–79
Pear pudding, 247
Pecan dressing, 223
Peppers
    bell
        apple chutney with, 188–89
        stuffed and pickled, 145–46
    hot pepper sauce, 185–86
Persimmon cookies, 199–200
Pickled (pickles)
    eggs, 120–21
    figs, in honey, 210–11
    quince, 171–72
    and stuffed bell peppers, 145–46
    watermelon rind, 146–47
Phosphate baking powder, 296
Pie crust
    basic pastry-mixing patterns, 305–9
    flaky, 309–10

graham, 310
graham cracker, 310–11
plain, 309
Pies
    apple custard, 178
    blackberry, 138–39
    butterscotch, 217
    carrot, 15–16
    cranberry apple double-crust, 215
    crusts, techniques, and tips for, 304–11
    custard, 27–28
    deep-dish, 308
    freezing, 312–13
    fried, 309
    heavenly, 241
    meat, 308
        Cornish pasties, 12–13
    mincemeat, old fashioned, 205–6, 308
    pork, 275–77
    pot pie, squirrel, with buttermilk biscuit
        dumplings, 269
    pumpkin
        chiffon, in a gingersnap pie shell, 225–26
        honey, 198–99
    quince, butter-crust, 217–18
    raisin, with tip-top pastry, 215–17
    rhubarb custard, 34–35
    sour cream peach, 136
    sweet potato, 160–61
        shepherd's, 176
    tart, 308
    turnovers, 308–9
Pie shell, gingersnap, 226
Pie social, 213–15
Plain and pulled candies, 288
Plain pie crust, 309
Plum butter, 170–71
Pomander balls, 258–59
Pork
    bacon
        salad dressing, hot, 164
        string beans, and new potatoes, 115
    ham, preboiled, 32
    pie, 275–77
    roast, and sauerkraut with fried apples,
        259–60
    salt, Sweet Wisconsin beans with ground
        beef and, 52–53
    sausage(s)
        dressing, 175–76
        fresh, 274–75
        German, baked beans with, 109
        and onion corn bread, upside-down, 247–
            48
        -stuffed onions, 117–18
        toad in a hole, 45
        wheat and white bread, and corn meal
            stuffing, 224–25
    shoulder roast, mustard-and-horseradish-
        glazed, 281–82
    suckling pig, roasted, with onion dressing
        and fresh horseradish sauce, 97–99
    tenderloin, Frenched, 275
Potato(es)
    biscuits, 167
    boxty, 24
    colcannon, 255–56
    Duchess, 234
    grabbled, 92

T

Table salt as a baking ingredient, 297
Taffy
  apples, 200
  tapioca cream, 238
Tales of the Airly Days, A (Riley), 252–53
Tapioca cream, taffy, 238
Tartarate baking powder, 296
Tarts, 308
Tea
  and milk, Fitzgerald's, 256
  red clover blossom, 74
Temperature of candy syrup, testing, 290–91
Thanksgiving, 218–21
There Is Ever a Song Somewhere (Riley), 131
There Was a Cherry Tree (Riley), 48
Thermometer, candy, 289
Thought for the Discouraged Farmer (Riley),
  106, 123
Tip-top pastry, 216–17
Toad in a hole, 45
Toasted squash or pumpkin seeds, 199
Tomato relish, 174–75
Trifle, 234–35
Trout, oven-baked, with parsley and lemon
  butter, 101
Turkey, roast, with pecan dressing and
  turkey gravy, 222–24
Turkey fat as a baking ingredient, 298
Turkey gravy, richly colored, 223–24
Turnips
  mock coleslaw with cream dressing, 78
  and potatoes, mashed, 270
Turnovers, 308–9
Two-egg angel cake with lemon icing, 206

U

Uncooked relish, end-of-the-garden, 185
Uncooked vanilla ice cream, 129
Upside-down sausage and onion corn bread,
  237–38

V

Vada's braised elk roast, 245–46
Valentine's Day, 277–78
Vanilla ice cream (uncooked), 129
Variety flours, 293
Veda's glazed onions, 25
Veal
  cutlets with fried apples, 39–40
  leg roast, stuffed, with sour cream sauce,
    57–58
  stew with celeriac and dried morels, 11–12
Vegetables, *see* names of vegetables
Vegetable shortening as a baking ingredient,
  298

Venison
  cutlets stuffed with fresh pork dressing,
    175–76
  pot roast, 176–77
  shoulder with sausage, wheat and white
    bread, and corn meal stuffing, 224–25
Vera's pear pudding with cream or whipped
  cream, 247
Vera's pickled eggs, 120–21
Vinaigrette sauce, 38–39
Viola's raisin pie with tip-top pastry, 215–
  17
Violets, candied, 71

W

Walnut
  pudding with lemon whipped cream sauce,
    263
  sticks, 53
Water as a baking ingredient, 302
Watermelon rind pickles, 146–47
Wedding in the country, 94–95
Wedding punch, 104
We Plough the Fields (Claudius), 221
Wheat flours, dark, 293
Wheat germ, 293
When the Frost Is on the Punkin (Riley),
  196–97
When the Green Gits Back in the Trees
  (Riley), 3
Whipped candies, 288
Whipped cream
  for big, fluffy angel food cake, 61
  lemon sauce, 263
White flour, presifted, 292–93
White granulated sugar, 299
Whittier, John Greenleaf, 155
Wild blackberry jam, 140–41
Wild greens for salad, 38–39
Wild plum butter, 170–71
Wild rabbit stew, 254
Wilted lettuce, 116
Wine
  dandelion, 105
  ginger, Scottish, 285
Winter-growing chives, lemon and parsley
  butter, 33–34
Winter-parsnip puffs, 59
Winter squash loaf, 159–60

Y

Yeast, 294–96
  everlasting, Emma's 295–96
Yeast breads, 302–4
  freezing, 311
Yeast starter, potato ball, 13–14

ABOUT THE AUTHOR

JANE WATSON HOPPING lives, farms, and cooks
in Medford, Oregon. She and her husband,
Raymond, also run a smokehouse business where
they smoke and cure fish, meats, and wild game of
all sorts. Mrs. Hopping has taught her "pioneer"
skills to thousands of children and has appeared at
fairs and on local television. She is now working
on her next book.